NO MERCY, NO JUSTICE

NO MERCY, NO JUSTICE

The Dominant Narrative of America
versus
the Counter-Narrative of Jesus' Parables

Brooks Harrington
FOREWORD BY *John C. Holbert*

CASCADE *Books* • Eugene, Oregon

NO MERCY, NO JUSTICE
The Dominant Narrative of America versus the Counter-Narrative of Jesus'
Parables

Cascade Books
An Imprint of Wipf and Stock Publishers
199 W. 8th Ave., Suite 3
Eugene, OR 97401

www.wipfandstock.com

PAPERBACK ISBN: 978-1-5326-4582-2
HARDCOVER ISBN: 978-1-5326-4583-9
EBOOK ISBN: 978-1-5326-4584-6

Cataloguing-in-Publication data:

Names: Harrington, Brooks, author. | Holbert, John C., foreword.

Title: No mercy, no justice : the dominant narrative of America versus the
counter-narrative of Jesus' Parables / by Brooks Harrington ; foreword by John
C. Holbert.

Description: Eugene, OR : Cascade Books, 2019.

Identifiers: ISBN 978-1-5326-4582-2 (paperback) | ISBN 978-1-5326-4583-9 (hard-
cover) | ISBN 978-1-5326-4584-6 (ebook)

Subjects: LCSH: 1. Religion and justice. | 2. Mercy. | 3. Jesus Christ—Parables.

Classification: BL65.J87 H29 2019 (print) | BL65.J87 H29 (ebook)

Manufactured in the U.S.A.   DECEMBER 27, 2018

For my father John,
who has taught me by his words and actions to be a person upon
whom people in trouble can rely.

For Maxine,
my love, conscience, and partner through everything for more than
forty years.

For our daughter Elizabeth and our son-in-law Gregg,
our daughter Katherine and our son-in-law Spencer,
our son Clay and our daughter-in-law Ashley,
and our grandchildren Lucas, Sarah, Livingston, and Harrison
—that they may walk God's way of justice and mercy.

For my coworkers in the vineyard of the Methodist Justice Ministry:
Juliana, Norma, Linda, Jodie, Yajaera, Nicole, and Sarah.

Table of Contents

Foreword

"*No Mercy, No Justice*" is a very powerful book and not for the faint of heart.

Brooks Harrington is a unique Christian person. He was, and is, an attorney, having tried numerous cases, many of which had to do with abuse and domestic violence often against children. And he is an ordained clergyperson, now serving as the director of a justice ministry connected to First United Methodist Church in Ft. Worth, Texas. Let me say, by means of full disclosure, Brooks was a student of mine at Perkins School of Theology in a class of introductory preaching. He was a truly outstanding student and preacher then, topping his graduating class. But what was startling about him was his enormous commitment to the ideas he has expressed in this book, namely, the need to address with full honesty the deep and complex relationships between justice and mercy in the life of Christian faith. He speaks again and again of his work in the courtroom and on the streets among the homeless and abused of his city, probing for ways to address those two central issues in Christianity. He writes of the "dominant culture," the one we live in where justice is sought and applied often devoid of mercy. But also he addresses those Christians who would expect only mercy and never God's justice against their refusals to show mercy to all. In rich biblical analyses, from the prophets of Israel and especially from the potent parables of Jesus, he shows how justice without mercy may be calloused and cruel, while mercy without justice may be empty and simplistic.

I admit readily that the book was a real workout to read, not because the prose was not limpid and clear, but because I felt convicted again and again by my own complicity in the dominant narrative, and my own unwillingness to tender mercy to all and not to receive the justice from God that I should expect for my failings. I found the final chapter's retelling of Mark 4–5 a beautiful summation of the book's central claims. That chapter alone is worth the book's price, but it will not have its full impact until the rest has been read.

When Brooks Harrington came to see me just before his graduation from seminary, he announced that he was going back into the work of the law. I was surprised, for he had been serving as a pastor (details of which you will read in his book), and I imagined he would continue to do that. But he went on to say that the study of theology had taught him how to use his great skills as legal advocate in new and richer ways. And he is doing just that now. I thank the God who called him to that work, and I thank God and Brooks for this book that challenges and provokes.

John C. Holbert
Professor *Emeritus* of Homiletics
Perkins School of Theology
Southern Methodist University

Preface

IN THE STORIES TOLD about people, unless otherwise noted I have changed their names and a few identifying features to respect their privacy. The changed names are initially placed in quotation marks. The events retold in the stories are all true.

Introduction

TORAH, THE PROPHETS, AND the Gospels tell us that Jesus did not come just to open heaven for believers. Jesus did not come to be worshiped. Jesus did not come to sacrifice himself for us so that we needn't sacrifice ourselves for anyone. Jesus did not come to give and suffer for us so that we needn't give and suffer for anyone. Jesus did not come to found a church that would perpetuate itself by accumulating property and by keeping members comfortable and assured of God's love just the way we already are and just the way we already live. Jesus came to give birth and blueprint to a people who would together with Jesus' living spirit transform a world terribly broken. Jesus was sent by our Father to form and inspire a people who would build a community of justice and mercy that would challenge a world dominated by unjust and merciless competition for things, shallow pleasures, and the honor and power that comes with their accumulation. Jesus' life and teachings are the perfect incarnations of God's will for such a community. Faith and belief alone are not critical for the people of God. Love, manifested in our justice and our mercy, is critical.

Despite God's eternal will revealed in Torah, the prophets, and the Gospels, the world remains terribly out of whack. Millions of children, women, and men continue to suffer terribly from its injustice and mercilessness.

The community that Jesus came to form, and particularly the North American church, is failing in its God given mission. It seems most intent upon making "churchians," not Christians. Much of this is due to our own human nature. Our minds and souls are the battlegrounds between our urges to fear, fight and dominate, and our capacities for justice, mercy, and sacrifice for the common good. A cause of our failure is that we are seduced and overcome by a merciless and unjust account of

1

how to live that is utterly counter to the way of God and Jesus. This account has become the relentless and pervasive dominant narrative of our America—the story of the only way to live to obtain meaning, honor, and satisfaction. The American church has been seduced by this account, and has aided and abetted our individual seduction. This dominant narrative is in utter conflict with the counter-narrative of Jesus set forth in his parables, particularly in their accounts of justice and mercy. The world being created by the counter-narrative of Jesus is a challenge and a judgment of the world created by this dominant narrative.

CHAPTER 1

Unjust and Merciless

ANYONE WHO DOESN'T RECOGNIZE that life is unjust and merciless is a fool. When I deny that life is unfair and merciless because I have received much more than my share of life's blessings, I am among the greatest of fools. That I might be personally so blessed does not make life itself any less unjust or merciless.

Life is unjust because of the random and merciless way that blessings and curses are meted out. Life is no less unjust and merciless because some are randomly born into plenty and hope and the promise of rescue from every crisis, while others are born into deprivation and despair and resignation. Some receive, as accidents of their births, intelligence and physical capacities valued in their cultures. Others are born with less valued intelligence and lesser physical capacities relative to their culture's ideals. Those who are blessed by their accidents of birth often turn from the call to empathy and assistance by blaming the less blessed and the unblessed for their plights. The abundantly blessed tell ourselves that the life that benefits us so much is not merciless and unjust because the less blessed and unblessed are responsible for their own deprivations. So we, the abundantly blessed, aided and abetted by the loudest voices in our culture, are practically indifferent to the suffering of the poor and their children.

I am afraid that I was a complete fool until one night in a ghetto in Washington, DC, when I hope I started being a little less of a fool. Joe Quantrille (his actual name) and I were out on the street at about 2 in the morning during the winter of 1980 or 1981, looking for a potential witness in a homicide case. Joe was a legendary homicide detective with the DC police department. I was an Assistant United States Attorney for the District of Columbia, assigned to the Career Criminal Unit. Because DC is a hybrid jurisdiction, the United States Attorney's Office for the District of Columbia prosecutes violent, local street crimes as well as federal criminal code violations. A homeless man had been bludgeoned to death, his body found at the bottom of a dark, outside stairwell leading to the basement door of a downtown DC church. The word on the street among the homeless was that the murder had been committed by another homeless man. This suspect was on parole for a series of armed robberies. That is why the Career Criminal Unit to which I was assigned was involved in this investigation. The robberies for which the suspect had previously been convicted, served time, and then paroled were all against homeless men, and all involved the kind of cruel beating inflicted upon our current victim. My unit focused upon people on parole for violent crimes. Our goal was to put together "perfect" prosecutions, so that repeat violent offenders would finally be brought to justice and sentenced to prison for the rest of their lives, ending their danger to the community. Joe and I were looking for a homeless man named Willie who had only one ear and who had reportedly told his friends that he had seen the beginning of the murder before he ran away. We were hitting all the homeless shelters and outside in DC in the early morning dark, when we could look over and question the men we found there with less risk the potential witness would run from us.

This investigation was my first education into the lives of the homeless. We had been asking homeless men we found if they knew where Willie, a man with only one ear, might be sleeping. We were told about homeless men with only one leg, or only one foot, or only one hand, or only one eye. But nothing about a man with only one ear. We didn't know whether these men were telling us the truth or just didn't want to be involved. I was with Joe at a night homeless shelter while men were coming out of a shower. I remember being shocked by the wounds they carried on their bodies.

We were getting out of the police car to visit a homeless camp in a park, when a call came over the police radio for the closest police units to respond to a reported shooting scene with possible fatalities and the gunman still on the scene. The location was within a few blocks of our location, so Joe responded with me in the passenger seat. Ours was the first police car to arrive at the scene. It was a brownstone, three-story house on Capitol Hill. Joe ordered me to remain behind in the police car while he dived into the house with his weapon drawn, not knowing exactly what he was going to find. There was no way I was waiting in the car.

What I visualize to this day about that night was how very dark it was outside the house, but how every light inside was burning, with so many black faces peering out of every window at us. The house was once a grand, single-family home from the days when that neighborhood was prosperous. The neighborhood had changed. This shooting and our response was happening in 1980 before the gentrification of that neighborhood, before the poor had been pushed out into Maryland. An enterprising slumlord had turned the house into a kind of apartment building, with a family unit of a man and a woman and some number of children living in each of the rooms.

When we entered the front door, we saw a staircase leading from the entry way to the second floor and the bottom of another staircase leading from the second to the third floor. A living room was to our left with a curtain between the entry way and that room. A man had pulled open the corner of the curtain, and was looking at us, with a child of maybe four holding onto his leg. We asked where the shooting was in the house, and how many men with guns were there. The man just pointed up the stairs and pulled the curtain shut.

Joe went up the stairs with his handgun drawn, with me right behind him. On the second floor, we saw a series of bedroom doors, all cracked opened with people peering out. From every room we could hear the sound of children crying and screaming. And we could smell the residue of gun smoke. Joe started going into the bedrooms, yelling "PO—lice!" slamming the doors open and leaping into the room, his handgun sweeping from side to side to cover the entire room. This caused the children in those rooms to scream harder. Angry men were cursing and yelling for him to get out. A woman said there was only one gunman and pointed to the bedroom at the end of the hall.

By then uniformed officers had responded. About six police including Quantrille were lined against the hallway walls, their pistols in hand. A sergeant wanted to get a SWAT team in but Joe ignored him, speaking firmly but calmly through the door, asking the gunman to give up and no one else would get hurt.

Abruptly, a beautiful, naked ten year old girl opened the door and stepped back. She was trembling as if she was cold, but the room seemed sweltering to me. In the room there was a man lying on his back on the bedroom floor with the top of his head blown off, a shotgun lying across his legs. The top of his skull was stuck in pieces to the wall behind him, blood and holes plastered around it. There was a woman lying on a bed moaning and bleeding, a shotgun wound to her stomach, the blanket and mattress under her soaked with blood. And there was a three-year-old boy in the corner, wearing nothing but a T-shirt, gasping and crying so hard he couldn't catch his breath to make a sound, tears rolling down his face and snot pouring out of his nose.

There had been too much poverty, too much anger, too much alcohol, too many drugs. After an argument, the man had shot the mother, and then, facing the enormity of what he had done, put the muzzle of the shotgun in his mouth and pulled the trigger, all with the two children in the small bedroom.

I followed behind as two uniformed officers went through the rest of the bedrooms to make certain no one else had been shot and to find any witnesses. We eventually made our way back to the first floor. I stumbled into the kitchen at the end of the first-floor hall, and was shocked out of my wits to see a growing puddle of red, red blood on the floor. Next to the puddle on the linoleum floor was a bare mattress covered with a thin blanket. And under the blanket were two toddlers. At first, I panicked that one or both of them had been shot. Then I realized that the bedroom where the shootings had taken place was just above the kitchen. When the man shot himself in the head, his heart kept pumping for a time and much of his blood poured out onto the bedroom floor above the kitchen, leaking through the floor of the bedroom and through the ceiling and onto the floor of the kitchen below. As I looked up, I saw the blood leaking through the kitchen ceiling. The two toddlers, who were unharmed physically, were fast asleep. Had they heard so much gunfire in their short lives that they could just roll over?

Detective Quantrille and I followed the woman's ambulance to the Washington Hospital Center Trauma Unit, waiting to see if she could be revived enough to give her account of what happened. But she had already lost too much blood and died about an hour later.

What would happen to the ten-year-old girl and the three-year-old boy? What would happen to the toddlers asleep on the mattress in the kitchen?

The victim had died, but so had the perpetrator. Justice had been done by the perpetrator's own hand. But what of those child victims? Who would take care of them now? What of the emotional wounds they would bear for the rest of their lives?

Not our problem. Criminal case closed. Next case.

Through some of my thirty-five-plus years since that night, I have dreamed of those children. Strangely, I didn't dream or think about them at all for years after that night. Then they fought their way into my dreams. I have dreamed in particular of the three-year-old boy, always crying against that wall in that bedroom, unable to make a sound. And in some versions of this dream, that three year old takes me by the hand and leads me downstairs to the two, still sleeping toddlers on the mattress in the kitchen next to the blood. He doesn't say anything, and I still don't know what he wants me to do. Or I tell myself I don't know.

I don't know what became of these four children, but I can make an experienced guess. Maybe one of them turned out to be Superman or Wonder Woman and got out of that neighborhood without a criminal record, with his or her hope and possibilities tenaciously intact. But waiting for each of these three little boys and one little girl were lives of hopelessness and anger, drugs and violent crime, unemployment, illness, and multiple pregnancies with different unmarried partners. It is overwhelmingly likely that random, angry violence continued to be a routine in their "neighborhood." And the only response of the criminal-justice and predominant social systems was to assign a person like me, a prosecutor waiting at the end of the justice conveyor belt, insisting that they should be put in jail until they grew too old and tired to be angry and violent anymore.

During my year on the street investigating violent crimes in inner-city DC, the parts of the District where the tourists didn't go, the only hopeful and empowering voice I heard was the proclamation of Jesus' way by the African-American churches. I didn't know it at the time, but the experience in that house that night and the year in the ghettoes were my first steps toward this other Way. I hope that I am still walking toward it.

But why didn't I worry about those children at the time, when I could have gone back and found out their names and perhaps could have done something to help them? Maybe because the only version of justice and mercy I was hearing was the dominant system's. Under that system, those children were somebody else's problem until they committed felonies and got onto the conveyor belt to prison. Under that system, they certainly weren't due anything from me.

According to that system's notion of justice, what was "due" as a matter of justice to the homeless people in this story? Weren't they just the losers in the societal contest? Hadn't they just failed to compete

well? Didn't they just choose homelessness, choose to lose, and fail to do
enough to win?

What had been due, before the shooting, to the man who shot the
woman and then killed himself? What was due to these children before
and after the shootings? Again, I am asking what was due them as a matter of justice—of duty and obligation. Was it anything that could have
kept any of them out of their plight in the first place? Or saved them from
it? Within the justice or the mercy of the dominant system?

Hell, no. Because bound up with the justice of *what* is due is the
question, *from whom* is it due? If I am influenced by the dominant narrative, I don't want anything to be due from me to a poor child in the ghetto
as a matter of justice and obligation. I want my occasional acts of mercy
to be voluntary and free, based upon my whim and impulse, whatever
the needs of poor children. But under this narrative, those children I
encountered that night had been trapped in a plight of poverty, violence,
and hopelessness.

There are millions of children in this country still in that plight.
Thousands are in your city, even if you live in a medium-sized one. This
isn't just a story about what happened decades ago in Washington, DC.
According to our secular notions of justice, from whom is anything "due"
to children caught in this trap of poverty, violence, and hopelessness by
the accident of their births? Maybe, subject to the political winds and
whims, a little food support and some Medicaid, a little TANF and a little
WIC, but nothing that would change their situation and outcomes. Nothing that would even up the playing field a bit. They only have a mythically
"equal" opportunity to compete in a heartless, free-market economy with
the comfortable, nurtured, groomed, protected, encouraged, and highly-
educated children of the middle and upper classes as their competitors.
Shouldn't they be able to pull themselves up by the bootstraps on the
boots they don't have, using the cultural language and mannerisms they
have never been taught, to make their way out of the graves into which
they were randomly born?

That is no opportunity at all. That so-called opportunity is not even
an illusion; it's a lie. The honest answer to what the justice of the dominant
system would grant these children as their "due" and would make a difference in their plight, is nothing. Nothing at all is due them. And likely
these particular four children were so wounded by their childhoods that
they grew up to be adults who people with the resources to be merciful
would not consider "deserving" of mercy.

What mercy was due them within the dominant, secular system? Mercy that would really help, would really have made a difference? Doubtless you recognize a trick question. Because within the dominant system, mercy is never "due" to anyone from anyone, no matter their plight. Justice and mercy in this system are separate. Very little justice and no mercy are actually due.

But what about the justice and mercy due them within God's covenantal community under Jesus' counter-way? Why are we comfortable Christians so complacent about the plight of these children? Why do we professing Christians choose the dominant secular system's versions of justice and mercy, and not the counter-justice and counter-mercy of God and Jesus? Why do we aspiring Christians avoid seeing the lives of these children and the adults they grow up to be? And why do I adopt a terminology that makes Jesus' and God's way a "counter" narrative, and the dominant, secular narrative the baseline? God's Way should be the baseline, the standard against which all other ways are judged and compared. It is a testament to the effective dominance of the dominant, secular way that I use these sets of terms.

CHAPTER 2

The Justice and Mercy of God?

WHAT I EXPERIENCED THAT night, and many other days and nights in DC, led me on a path to ordination, inner-city ministry, and then a combination of law practice and ministry.

Fast forward more than three and a half decades from that night in 1981 in DC. I am still a practicing lawyer, but I am also an ordained minister in the United Methodist Church. A group of aspiring Christians who work and volunteer with the homeless in our city of Fort Worth, Texas, host a breakfast for our unsheltered brothers and sisters in the richly-appointed gathering room of our wealthy downtown church. We cook or buy the food and drink ourselves, welcome between 80 to 110 of our brothers and sisters at 7:15 a.m. on Sundays, offer a hopefully encouraging and empowering devotional based upon the teaching of Jesus and his love for the poor, serve the food, celebrate and share communion with them, feed them and eat with them. After the breakfast we invite our unsheltered brothers and sisters to join in our "own" chapel worship service that we call "DiscipleChurch," and in a discussion group after the service that is very much like a Wesleyan class meeting from the eighteenth century. There is no space between the "e" and the "C" in "DiscipleChurch" because we believe that when discipleship and the church are separated, we are no longer the church. The weekly emphasis in our services is to try to discern and act out the will of God and to be true to God's nature, particularly through service to and inclusion of our homeless and impoverished friends. We have received much, much more from them than they have ever received from us.

For almost ten years it was part of my calling to preach at Disciple-Church. One Sunday I preached from one of my favorite passages from the prophets—Micah 6:8.

He has told you, O mortal, what is good; and what does the
LORD require of you, but to do justice, and to love mercy, and
to walk humbly with your God.

At our discussion group after the service, our good friend Bill Lanford
challenged me and everyone there to hear this passage anew. "How can
God expect us to *do* justice while *loving* mercy? Aren't those contradic-
tory? How are we to give people what they have coming as a matter of
justice, while granting them what they don't have coming as a matter
of mercy? Or is it the age-old dualism of making a distinction between
how we ought to act and how we should feel? Doing hard but just things
to people while wishing in our hearts that we could be merciful instead?
And . . . just when does God ever succeed in doing both justice and mercy
at once?" I recall thinking, "Wouldn't it be more like Jesus to 'do' mercy
rather than justice? But don't we live in a world in which we desperately
need both, yet a world in which we are required to choose one or the
other?"

This issue of how to reconcile justice and mercy, of how to be just and
merciful at once, of when and how to be just to one and when and how to
be merciful to another, has been one I have been wrestling with through
careers as an attorney and as an ordained United Methodist minister. The
struggle is now focused in these two callings in my present ministry. In
one career, I served as a prosecutor of violent crimes including rape and
murder, and then Deputy Chief of Felony Trial as an Assistant United
States Attorney in Washington, DC. Then I was a lawyer in private practice dedicated to winning civil lawsuits, protecting and vindicating my
clients and acquiring wealth and comfort for myself and my family. In
the other career, I was the pastor of an inner-city church in a neighborhood struggling with gang violence, drug addiction, teenage pregnancy,
under-employment, poverty, hopelessness and all the rest I had seen in
DC during my time there as a prosecutor. And for the last thirteen years
and counting, I have been called to joint roles as lawyer and as clergy
through a ministry founded at my church called the Methodist Justice
Ministry. Through the Methodist Justice Ministry, two other attorneys,
two legal assistants, and I provide free legal representation to obtain legal
protections for indigent victims of family violence and child abuse and
to provide financial and in-kind assistance, social work, free professional
counseling, and pastoral support, advice, encouragement and friendship
to enable woman and children to find new lives free of violence and fear.

Through my careers, I have known hundreds of economically poor, suffering children and women desperately in need of justice *and* mercy, victims of crime and of what they have experienced of an unjust and merciless economic and political system worshiped idolatrously by its primary beneficiaries. I have also known hundreds of lost and violent men who were and are also desperately in need of justice and mercy. And I have known thousands of comfortable churchgoers who have no desire to know or see either the victims or the abusers, no desire to be merciful themselves to the victims, and who want only harsh justice for the abusers meted out by someone's dirty hands. I have come to know that it is not enough for me, as an aspiring Christian, to be merciful to the women and children victims, but solely a just punisher of the abusers and merely an indignant judge of the indifferent and comfortable churchgoer.

I have been to murder scenes and autopsies of murder victims. I have served and even been a leader within a criminal-justice system that coldly condemns, mercilessly warehouses, and is relentlessly unforgiving of young men who have never had a just chance to avoid drugs, violence, and nihilism. I have been, and still am, a witness to the physical and emotional wounds of abused woman and children. Daily, I see women, children, and men treated unjustly and mercilessly because of accidents of their birth: their own genetic capabilities and physical limitations; their race and ethnicity; their countries of birth; the values, capabilities, and failures of their parents and of the neighborhoods they did not themselves choose. I see poor women, children, and men treated mercilessly and unjustly by a seemingly efficient but heartless economic system whose main beneficiaries and advocates have no concern for the terrible human costs of that system. I know the plight of women and men treated like mere costs of doing business by an economic system through which they cannot provide basic necessities for their children even though they work more than full-time. Daily, I see women cruelly and relentlessly abused in every way—physically, emotionally, and spiritually—by "intimate" but abusive partners, until the women believe the lies the abusers tell them about themselves, believing in their souls that they are due no mercy from anyone, that their plight is merely what they were due because of their so-called inadequacies and failures.

Have I been called only to be merciful to the victims and just to the merciless? The answer is yes under the dominant system. The answer is no under the counter-Way of Jesus.

The way our dominant secular, economic, and social system understands and pursues justice and mercy is neither just nor merciful. So the
way that the people of God are called to understand and pursue God's
mercy and justice has become a critical and personal issue for me in every way. In prayer and hope, I have turned to the way God understands
and pursues justice and mercy, as attested by Scripture and particularly
by the life and teachings of Jesus. The starting point for an aspiring Christian's understanding and pursuit is an understanding of *God's* justice and
mercy and of how *God* pursues these.

> Thus says the LORD: "Do not let the wise boast in their wisdom,
> do not let the mighty boast in their might; do not let the wealthy
> boast in their wealth; but let those who boast boast in this, that
> they understand and know me, that I am the LORD; I act with
> mercy, justice and righteousness in the earth, for in these things
> I delight," says the LORD. (Jer 9:23–24)

God acts with justice *and* mercy . . . and in the earth. But how?

One set of related answers to this question, based upon the evidence,
can be to deny that God has ever acted for justice and mercy "in the
earth." God is either ineffective or distant and uninvolved, or effectively
non-existent. Or justice and mercy are not important to God "in the
earth" or anywhere, only right belief and praise. Or perhaps God's justice
and mercy will only be acted out by God when each of us dies, or when
the final and collective Last Judgment arrives. Under this last answer,
God acts justly and mercifully "in the earth" only by keeping meticulous
score of our justices and injustices, of our mercies and our mercilessness
"in the earth," to be totaled up and acted upon "in the end."

Another set of answers includes that God acts mercifully to some
and justly to others, but not mercifully and justly to both and everyone at
once. Or God alternates justice and mercy, deciding when and to whom
to be merciful or just based upon our deserving as judged by God. For
instance, God is merciful to the victims of injustice and just to those who
are merciless. Or God chooses who will be the beneficiaries of divine
mercy capriciously or mysteriously. Based upon the assumption that God
is always a mover behind all that befalls, the seeming randomness of life
is strong evidence for this caprice or mystery. But a problem in this set of
answers is that we humans, along with all of creation, desperately need
a God who is just and merciful in ways that we can comprehend a little
and try to follow and even imitate. Our dominant culture chooses to be

merciful to some and just to others, and this is part of why so many of us are in our present plight. We need a God who will lead us to a better Way, to a better conception of justice and mercy and to a less dualistic way of seeing. We need a creation with a beating heart and a caring mind at its center, a heart and mind that want to rescue and redeem the victim *and* victimizer. We need the God that Jesus called *Abba* when it comes to justice, mercy, and everything else.

Another answer—the one I am searching for in this book—is that God's justice and mercy are simultaneously part of God's very nature, that dualistic and conflicting versions of justice and mercy are not God's, and that God is just and merciful at once and to all. What I am searching for is an understanding that God's mercy is an aspect of God's justice, and that God's justice is an aspect of God's mercy.

How should God's people act out God's justice and God's mercy "in the earth?" Our options follow how we answer the question about how God is acting out mercy and justice "in the earth." If our answer is that God does not act with justice and mercy in the earth, since the unjust and the merciless prosper while the just and the merciful are held back, there is arguably no calling for God's people to act with justice and mercy in the earth. And this is the way most of us live most of the time.

If our answer is that God is merciful to some and not merciful to others based upon what we deserve, so may the people of God act the same way. And this is the way most of us live some of the time.

But if our answer is that God is always just and merciful to all, are we not called to discern the nature of a justice and a mercy that can be enacted simultaneously and seek to (however imperfectly) act both out at once?

One of the oldest descriptions of God in the Hebrew Scripture is found in Exodus 34:5–7 in the remarkable story of God's passing before and revealing God's self to Moses:

> The LORD descended in the cloud and stood with [Moses] there, and proclaimed the name "The LORD." The LORD passed before him and proclaimed:
>
>> The LORD, the LORD,
>> a God merciful and gracious,
>> Slow to anger
>> and abounding in steadfast kindness and faithfulness,
>> keeping kindness for the thousandth generation,
>> forgiving iniquity and transgression and sin,
>> *yet* [my emphasis] by no means clearing the guilty . . .

So in one of the earliest descriptions of God—God's self-description—God is described as merciful, giving what is not due, and as just, giving what is due.

In the Old Testament, God is described as "merciful" through derivatives of the Hebrew word *chesed*, also translated as "kindness," and through derivatives of the Hebrew *racham*, which is derived from the word for a woman's womb. And God is described as "just" with derivatives of the Hebrew *tsadeq* and *mishpat*. That Hebrew word *tsadeq*, like the Greek word *dikaios*, is variously translated as just and righteous.

> Gracious is the LORD and just. Our God is merciful. (Ps 116:5)

> Great is your mercy, O LORD; give me life according to your justice." (Ps 119:156)

> The LORD is just in all his ways, and merciful in all his doings. (Ps 145:17)

> Therefore the LORD waits to be gracious to you; therefore he will show mercy to you. For the LORD is a God of justice; blessed are all those who wait for him. (Isa 30:18)

Following these basic affirmations that God is just *and* merciful, the basic affirmation of the Torah is that a child of God must obey Torah to be just, and a critical part of that just obedience to Torah is mercifulness.

In Deut 10:17–20, the LORD gives Moses another self-description:

> For the LORD your God is God of gods and Lord of lords, the great God, mighty and awesome, who is not partial and takes no bribe, who executes justice for the orphan and the widow, and who loves the alien, providing them with food and clothing. You also shall love the alien, for you were aliens in the land of Egypt.

God's justice is fused with God's mercy to the vulnerable. So the people of God are likewise called to be just by being merciful to the vulnerable. "You shall not deprive a resident alien or an orphan of justice" (Deut 24:17). "Cursed be anyone who deprives the alien, the orphan and the widow of justice . . . All the people shall say 'Amen'" (Deut 27:19). Torah made mercy to the vulnerable a matter of the obligation of justice, not a matter of charity. (For further instance: Exod 22:25, 23:6, 23:11; Lev 19:9–10, 13, 33–34; 23:22, 25:1–55; and Deut 15:11, 24:12–15.)

The Hebrew prophets urge God's people to be just and merciful as well, in accordance with the justice and mercy of God, as in Micah 6:8:

"He has told you, O mortal, what is good; and what does the Lord require of you but to do justice, and to love mercy, and to walk humbly with your God?" In addition:

> [I]f you truly act justly with one another, if you do not oppress the alien, the orphan and the widow . . . then I will dwell with you in this place, in the land that I gave of old to your ancestors forever and ever. (Jer 7:5–7)

> I will take you [Israel] for my wife forever; I will take you for my wife in justice and judgment, in kindness and in mercy. (Hos 2:19)

> The word of the LORD came to Zechariah, saying: Thus says the LORD of hosts: Render true justice, show kindness and mercy to one another; do not oppress the widow, the orphan, the alien or the poor. (Zech 7:8–9)

> Therefore, O King, atone for your sins with justice, and your iniquities with mercy . . . (Dan 4:27)

We see in the teachings of Jesus this view of the complementary, supportive, and intertwined natures of God's justice and mercy.

In the Beatitudes recorded by Matthew, Jesus teaches that those who hunger and thirst for justice are blessed (Matt 5:6), and in the very next breath that those who are merciful are likewise blessed (Matt 5:7). How could these have been in conflict in Jesus' mind and heart?

And in Matt 23:23, Jesus says: "Woe to you, scribes and Pharisees, hypocrites! For you tithe mint, dill, and cummin, and have neglected the weightier matters of the law: justice and mercy and faith. It is these you ought to have practiced without neglecting the others."

In my reading, Torah, the prophets, and Jesus testify that God is just and merciful always to everyone, and that the people of God are called to be the same.

CHAPTER 3

The Dominant Narrative of America

IF GOD IS INDEED committed to justice and mercy, if justice and mercy are inseparable aspects of God's Truth and Way, we Christians often show by the way we live our lives and spend our resources that we (God's so-called people) are not so committed.

Part of our failure is due to our fallible humanity. How hard it is for us to discern what is just and what is merciful in any given situation. How hard it is to overcome our fear and competitiveness with empathy and generosity, particularly when so many voices in our American culture are profiting from fear and advocating predatory competitiveness.

But very much of our failure to be just and merciful as God wills us to be is attributable to the power of the dominant, secular narrative of our time and place. This narrative has successfully shaped our characters and directed our behaviors. Even we aspiring Christians have accepted this dominant, secular view of justice and mercy provided by the culture, not God's justice and mercy revealed in Torah, the prophets, and particularly in the life and teachings of Jesus. This dominant narrative includes a version of justice and mercy that serves and supports the rest of the narrative.

Walter Brueggemann writes in the first chapter of his wonderful book *The Practice of Prophetic Imagination: Preaching an Emancipating Word*:

> [P]rophetic proclamation is the staging and performance of a contest between two narrative accounts of the world and an effort to show that the YHWH account of reality is more adequate and finally more reliable that the dominant narrative that is cast among us as though it were true and beyond critique.[1]

1. Walter Brueggemann, *The Practice of Prophetic Imagination: Preaching an Emancipating Word* (Minneapolis: Fortress, 2012), 3. Subsequent references will be made parenthetically.

Professor Brueggemann writes that there has been a "long vigorous contestation between two narratives and two consequent construals of reality" (*Practice*, 3). These two narratives are always the dominant narrative of the secular powers of any time and the counter-narrative of God. Brueggemann writes:

> The present form of that contestation, I propose, is the felt and often denied tension between the gospel narrative that specializes in social transformation, justice and compassion, and the dominant narrative of our culture that I have elsewhere termed "military consumerism." (*Practice*, 3)

Brueggemann further describes the contemporary American dominant narrative:

> The dominant narrative—one I have characterized as "therapeutic, technological, consumerist militarism"—is committed to the notion of *self-invention* in the pursuit of *self-sufficiency*. Between a beginning in self-invention and a culmination in self-sufficiency, that narrative enjoins to *competitive productivity*, motivated by pervasive anxiety about having enough, or being enough, or being in control. Thus it is an acting out, in quotidian ways, of the modern sense of an autonomous self that eventuates in a rat race that readily culminates in violence if and when that self is impinged upon in inconvenient ways. (*Practice*, 4)

He adds: "[T]he dominant narrative is seldom lined out, rarely seen in its coherence, and hardly ever critiqued in its elemental claims" (*Practice*, 4).

Here, I attempt to "line out," "see in its coherence," and "critique" that dominant narrative of America—particularly as it provides versions of justice and mercy and their relationship, and particularly as that narrative impacts the economically poor.

The dominant narrative of a culture, as I understand Professor Brueggemann to be saying, is the culture's dominating story of life's meanings, values, marks, and measures of success and failure, approved and disapproved manners of behavior, and paths to honor and happiness. The narrative includes the culture's boundaries for insiders and outsiders. The dominant narrative is always seeking to become ever more dominating. It always serves the insiders at the expense of the outsiders, bolstering and maintaining the insiders' positions and privileges. Such a dominant narrative may not be totally successful in intimidating and silencing every other counter-narrative in a given culture. Most people in a given culture do in fact live by more than one narrative. But the dominant narrative of our American culture seeks to dominate by condemning and belittling every other version of reality with its own standards about behavior, success, meaning and happiness. Our American dominant narrative is pervasive and relentless. Its proponents actively suppress any counter-narrative. The members of the dominant group associate economically and socially only with themselves. So any counter-narrative seems to these opinion makers and trendsetters to be odd and even ridiculous.

To me, it is useful to think about a dominant narrative as a song that plays everywhere and all the time to everyone. It is so loud, relentless, and pervasive that every other song sounds discordant and grating, and finally is not heard at all.

The narrative that seeks to be dominating, pervasive, and silencing of all other narratives in this American culture proclaims that success, honor, meaning, and happiness come solely from the maximum, continuing acquisition and consumption of expensive things and transient pleasures. The more expensive and ostentatious the things, the more honor and happiness to the consumer. The more transient and intense the pleasure, the more success and satisfaction to the consumer. We are conditioned to go from acquisition to acquisition, from pleasure to pleasure without ceasing.

Yet after we acquire the things and experience the pleasure, they prove not to fulfill the dominant narrative's promise. We are left still empty. And we cannot enjoy the moment. We are like children on Christmas morning who open present after present but enjoy none of them. When all the presents are unwrapped and scattered around the floor, we just want to unwrap more. So we move on in search of more stuff and more pleasure, hoping that these will finally fulfill the empty promise.

We are told by this narrative that in order for our lives to be happy and meaningful, we must have the most fashionable and trendy clothes, the most advanced and current electronics, the biggest house, the most expensive vehicle with the most bells and whistles, the memberships in the most exclusive clubs, the most expensive and self-indulgent vacations, the cruises in which we gorge ourselves on food and the trips to glitzy casinos where it is always time to drink and gamble, the most lavish "dining experiences," the most delicious and unhealthy foods, the beer or whiskey or wine of the insider, the beautiful, "most interesting" people, and the most casual sexual hook-ups with whomever we want for the evening and don't know very well and don't want to. Character, discipline, sacrifice, self-denial count for almost nothing.

We do not live in a community at all, screams the dominant narrative at every moment. We live in a competition, what the ancient Greeks called an *agón* (the root of our English word "agony"), a zero-sum game of winners and losers. Within this *agón,* other people must lose for my family and me to win in our quest for the honor and happiness that comes with stuff and pleasure. Our only relationship with non-family members is as fellow competitors for the success, honor, meaning and happiness that come from defeating the "other" in this pervasive competition. We have no neighbors to love as we love ourselves.

A critical and necessary aspect of the dominant narrative is that the individual must be unfettered in his or her pursuit of these things and pleasures. Whatever enhances the individual's pursuit is good, and whatever inhibits it is bad. The only needed justification for my acquisition of the thing or the pleasure is that I want it now, and that incessant want is created by the dominant narrative. Any consideration of whether that acquisition is good for me or for the community is discredited.

An effect of this narrow focus on satisfying the individual appetite, on the wants and urges of the individual as the norms for every activity and institution, is that individual fear is validated and empowered. In fact, we are encouraged to make our individual fears sovereign. Just as our want for some new stuff is sufficient justification for acquiring it, the dominant narrative teaches that our subjective fear of someone or some group is sufficient to exclude them. If someone of some other group makes me afraid—the poor, the homeless, the alien, the felon, the "other" ethnicity or race, the "other" religion or nationality—that fear alone is adequate justification for me to demand that they be excluded. Just as the dominant narrative values no inhibition of the individual's appetite for things and pleasure, the narrative does not tolerate any such inhibition of the individual's fear. No imperatives of understanding and inclusion have any weight. Our political, social, and even religious lives are not arenas for morality. These are only arenas of competition among wants, urges, and fears. The louder, better organized groups of individuals with shared urges and fears decide who is included and who excluded. Social conscience does not enter in. There are no "better angels of our nature." We are only our bellies and our guts, according to this dominant narrative.

We should expect a certain amount of self-obsessed, other-destructive, and self-destructive behavior in any society, even those whose narratives teach that meaning and happiness come from sacrifice, attention to the common good, and care for the vulnerable and weak. But when self-obsessed, other-destructive, and self-destructive behavior becomes the standard, as it has in America, when such narcissistic behavior is celebrated, it is necessary to ask what about the society's particular narrative is inspiring this behavior. It is the height of hypocrisy for the proponents and main beneficiaries of our dominant narrative to blame its victims for its natural and necessary effects.

Within the culture of the dominant narrative, a problem or challenge suffered by an insider must be fixed or eliminated, and quickly, or we will be due to feel outraged at the injustice. If we consider something out of whack for ourselves or our family members, based upon our wants and fears, it must be put back in whack immediately and exactly how we want it. We insiders feel that we are due immediate elimination of whatever challenges us having what we want instantly. Our dominant narrative teaches this relentlessly. The narrative teaches us that *we* should not be kept on hold when we call our doctors for medication that will cure us immediately of all of our symptoms. The narrative teaches us that *our* child should be cured immediately of any illness. It teaches that *our* child should never be wait-listed instead of being admitted immediately to the preschool or private school or college of our choice. We should never be required to pay more taxes than we want or be denied some claimed deduction by someone we derisively call a "bureaucrat." We should never suffer delay in a loan being approved. No one should be driving slower than we are in the left highway lane, nor should anyone be tailgating us when we are driving in that lane. A plumber should respond immediately to our call about a leak in a water line in our wall. No one should ever tell us that we should not buy that gas-guzzling, club cab, pick-up truck, or that luxury Cadillac SUV, because of the effect upon the environment or the needs of the poor.

But within the culture of economically poor Anglo-Americans, African-Americans, and Hispanic-Americans, unwanted problems and even serious crises are often just to be endured because they will not be fixed. For the economically poor, the world is permanently out of whack. At first so many members of these communities feel that they are due better, but after a time they become resigned that they will not receive better.

The doctor's office does not call back because they are on Medicaid or, as more and more will be, without any insurance at all. When they or their children become seriously ill, they have to wait all night in an emergency room of the county hospital to be seen at all. What would be the point of complaining? Their children aren't wait-listed for admission to the preschool or private college of their choice; they aren't listed at all. They don't make enough in income to pay taxes. The only loan they can hope to be granted is a predatory title or payday loan, and the predators don't make the working poor wait for those. The poor can't afford a plumber. The outsider poor and their children see how differently the comfortable insiders and their children are treated. At first they are angry; as they get older they are resigned.

In reality, people in any group in our culture are conflicted by competing narratives. The dominant narrative has not yet succeeded in totally silencing narratives that foster community and personal sacrifice and discipline, though I fear that it is closer than it has ever been.

So many economically poor but spiritually rich individuals I have been blessed to know live within a narrative in which endurance, hard work, intimate relationships of love, and friendships based upon mutual support and sacrifice provide the greatest success, meaning, and happiness in life. I have witnessed loving sacrifices freely made by the economic poor—people with low incomes who are willing and even eager to take at-risk or abused children into their homes, thus making themselves even poorer—that I have never seen among us comfortable who have been so conditioned by the dominant narrative.

I know very many comfortable, aspiring Christians in America who are moved by the word of God and the teachings of Jesus to want to live lives of generosity, sacrifice, and mercy. They yearn at times to experience the greater joy of using their abundance to serve Jesus through mercy to those in need. Their hearts are moved by the teachings of Jesus:

[J]ust as you did it to the least of these . . . you did it to me . . . [J]ust as you did not do it to one of the least of these, you did not do it to me. (Matt 25:40, 45)

Where your treasure is, there your heart is. (Matt 6:21)

No one can serve two masters. For a slave will either hate one and love the other, or be devoted to one and despise the other. You cannot serve God and wealth. (Matt 6:24)

Do not worry about your life, what you will eat or what you will drink, or about your body, what you will wear. Is not life more than food, and the body more than clothing? (Matt 6:25)

But the dominant narrative is so relentless, pervasive, and penetrating, and they are surrounded by so many peers whose focus is on the accumulation and personal enjoyment of more and more stuff and pleasure. At times they feel conflict within their own hearts and minds between the pervasive dominant narrative and the counter-word of Jesus. But regardless of the experience of spiritual conflict, the end result is that so many still spend a staggering amount of money on themselves and their families and a relative pittance on the poor, even though it may be a larger pittance than most all of their social and economic peers. I believe that the church has failed them by not insistently presenting them with the clear choice of God's counter-narrative that teaches that so much deeper, wider, and higher joy and satisfaction come from sacrificial generosity and mercy than from the self-obsessed acquisition of more stuff and more pleasure.

The American church itself lives by both of these conflicted narratives. Most churches have ministries to serve the poor, the outcast, and the vulnerable, true to the counter-narrative of the Christ. But these ministries are often moved away from the main church building so that the insider-members will not be made afraid by contact with the poor. And these same churches spend a relative pittance upon these ministries and relative fortunes upon the comfort of their members, the luxury of the church building, the quality of the organ and the music program, and the pleasure and intensity of the Sunday morning worship service. This all reflects the priority of stuff and pleasures of the dominant narrative. Too often, the church business officers, the property or foundation trustees, and the security staff have vetoed the church's proposed ministries to the poor and outcast. Many churches have locks and security guards to keep the poor, the outcast, and the vulnerable from even entering the main church property. And so many churches have clergy who are torn between discipleship within the counter-word of Jesus, and discipleship to the dominant narrative by maximizing their own salaries and material comforts. They well understand in their minds and souls that the church is to be the home of the living, counter-narrative of God. But the need to pay the increasing expenses on the growing church property and the desire to move up the clergy ladder based upon worship attendance and financial contribution lead so many to deny that there is tension between the dominant narrative and the counter-narrative of God.

The dominant narrative victimizes the "privileged" insiders by leading them to shallow, unsatisfying lives. It victimizes the church and the clergy by subverting its call to proclaim clearly and insistently the counter-narrative of God as the only source of meaning, value and happiness. Most of all, the dominant narrative victimizes the poor and those born on the outside. This victimization is necessary for the dominant narrative to survive. It is the foundation and assumption of this particular American dominant narrative.

I need to be very careful here. The suffering of the outsider caused by the dominant narrative is experienced by every race and ethnic group. The experiences and exposures I describe are not limited to or even concentrated in any racial or ethnic group. The people whose sufferings I have seen come from all those born on the outside.

The dominant narrative is communicated to the poor through the same pervasive advertising and media to which we are all exposed. Consider a young teenaged girl, a child of a poor, single mother, who is inundated like the rest of us by a narrative that insists that honor and happiness can come only from acquisition of stuff and pleasures. She is surrounded by adults who have been unable to escape their poor neighborhoods to enter into the insiders' world despite years of hard work at uncertain and low-paying jobs. She is surrounded by angry, exhausted, disillusioned, cynical adults and peers who tell her that she will never be accepted by the insiders, never be able to acquire the means to the necessary stuff and pleasures and never be a somebody by the narrative's standards. Character for its own sake, hard work at tough jobs, steadfast endurance of life's vagaries and inequities, sacrifice for family, friends and community—these are not valued within the dominant narrative. In fact, these qualities are belittled. She sees adults who have worked hard all of their lives and still haven't been able to acquire the things and the pleasures that the narrative says are necessary for honor, meaning, and happiness. Their hard work has been rewarded with little more than minimum wage and the disdain of the insiders. Adults of character and sacrifice and hard work are not the heroes of the dominant narrative. People who obtain all the stuff they desire and access pleasure after pleasure with as little work as possible are the heroes of the culture created by the dominant narrative. She sees the children of the insiders who have their paths greased. And she sees on social media, the internet, television and motion pictures that the greatest, most immediate pleasure in life is sex. What does she have to trade for stuff and pleasure?

In our Justice Ministry, we encounter daily young women who have turned to being valued by young men as sexual objects and who have turned to the immediate pleasure of uninhibited sexual gratification that is so glorified by the dominant narrative. In my experience, so many of these poor, young women—again of every race and ethnicity—feel that their sexuality is the only way to be somebody, to be noticed, to be wanted and valued and honored and loved, to obtain stuff and pleasure. So many of these poor young women are without any realistic hope that they ever will be able to better their material situations by delaying gratification. So they turn to the pleasure of casual sexual hook-ups now. To living with a series of men without waiting and testing whether their current man has any commitment to a true, lasting relationship or to parenting the child whom they helped conceive. To ornate tattoos as a source of individuality and distinction. To the escape of drug use. To running the streets while someone else cares for their children. To running up debt from predatory lenders so they can have the stuff they want now and feel the pleasure they think they need now. Particularly when confronted with the impact their choices have on their children, so many of these women have deep regrets, and the conflict in their hearts can be overwhelming. Part of each of them wants to be a good, nurturing, dependable mother. Part of them has heard the counter-narrative of love and sacrifice. But the dominant narrative of stuff and pleasure drowns it out, just as it does for the comfortable.

We have also encountered through the Ministry so many poor, young men who have experienced the same feelings and urges I describe for the young women. They have given up hope of distinguishing themselves, of being somebody, under the rules of the *agón* of the dominant narrative. Or they seek to be somebody under those rules through acquisition of stuff and intense but shallow pleasures of sex and drugs and the thrill of violence. They seek to prove their value by sexual conquests and then to avoid paying child support for the children they have fathered. They seek to prove their worth by violence against their peers and by drugs and crime, by a shallow masculinity that interprets physical intimidation of women and men as value and honor, and by the acquisition of gaudy cars and clothes with money they haven't made in honest employment. Yet I have seen these same young men display real shame and regret at their failure to support and parent their children. And I have had personal conversations with them at the courthouse about the bitterness and pain of being abandoned by their own fathers and about their own desire not to do the same to their own children.

The dominant narrative provides no meaning or satisfaction to anyone.

CHAPTER 4

The Counter-Narrative of God

THE WORD OF GOD is always a narrative that is starkly counter to any used by dominant insiders to solidify their positons at the expense of the outsiders. As Dr. Brueggemann wrote in chapter 1 of his *The Practice of Prophetic Imagination: Preaching an Emancipating Word*, the people of YHWH are called to "a contestation between narratives." We are called to live into a counter-reality with counter-standards of meaning, honor, and satisfaction, counter-manners of behavior, and counter-goals, divisions, and boundaries. This has been true throughout the history of the counter-word of God.

For example, in the Moses story, the dominant narrative of Egypt was that the Pharaoh was himself the most powerful of gods, the current scion of an eternal, divine dynasty, due to be obeyed and served slavishly, so appropriately deaf to the cries of his suffering Israelite slaves. Pharaoh and all the Egyptians "set taskmasters over them to oppress them with forced labor" (Exod 1:11). "The Egyptians became ruthless in imposing tasks on the Israelites, and made their lives bitter with hard service in mortar and brick and in every kind of field labor. They were ruthless in all the tasks they imposed upon them" (Exod 1:13–14). The dominant narrative of the time was that the Hebrews were due to be enslaved at the Pharaoh's divine pleasure, Pharaoh was due to be served by the Hebrew slaves, their first-born sons were due to be killed, and these slaves were due to be required to make bricks without straw. Moses delivered a counter-narrative that YHWH, not Pharaoh, was the true, only, all-powerful God, and that YHWH, very unlike Pharaoh, heard and heeded the cries of the Hebrew slaves (Exod 2:23–24). The counter-narrative was that YHWH, not Pharaoh, was due to be worshipped and obeyed, and that YHWH, unlike Pharaoh, willed that the vulnerable be protected not exploited and willed liberation not slavery. Part of the counter-narrative was that the Hebrew slaves, not the Egyptian elite, were due divine favor—because of their suffering. So YHWH intervened for them justly and mercifully. The plagues were the great demonstration that YHWH, not Pharaoh, was God. Through an overwhelmingly superior display of power, YHWH brought the people of YHWH out of slavery to the Sinai wilderness, where they were given Torah, a way of being together in community that protected the vulnerable and the poor who had been oppressed by the dominant narrative of Pharaoh. Thus were they given the blueprint for a covenantal community. In that counter-narrative to the dominant narratives of all the Pharaohs of all time, YHWH gave humankind a vision of a community in which the people who were usually oppressed and exploited were protected by covenant:

> If you lend money to my people, to the poor among you, you shall not deal with them as a creditor; you shall not exact interest from them. (Exod 22:25)

> You shall not pervert the justice due to your poor in their lawsuits. (Exod 23:6)

> For six years you shall sow your field and gather in its yield; but the seventh year you shall let it rest and lie fallow, so that the poor of your people may eat; and what they leave the wild animals may eat. You shall do the same with your vineyard, and with your olive orchard. (Exod 23:11)

> You shall not strip your vineyard bare, or gather the fallen grapes of your vineyard; you shall leave them for the poor and the alien: I am the LORD your God. (Lev 19:10)

> When you reap the harvest of your land, you shall not reap to the very edges of your field, or gather the gleanings of your harvest; you shall leave them for the poor and for the alien: I am the LORD your God. (Lev 23:22)

> If any of your kin fall into difficulty and become dependent on you, you shall support them; they shall live with you as though resident aliens. Do not take interest in advance or otherwise make a profit from them, but fear your God; let them live with you. You shall not lend them your money at interest taken in advance, or provide them food at a profit. I am the Lord your God, who brought you out of the land of Egypt, to give you the land of Canaan, to be your God. If any who are dependent on

you become so impoverished that they sell themselves to you, you shall not make them serve as slaves. They shall remain with you as hired or bound laborers. They shall serve with you until the year of the jubilee. Then they and their children with them shall be free from your authority; they shall go back to their own family and return to their ancestral property. For they are my servants, whom I brought out of the land of Egypt; they shall not be sold as slaves are sold. You shall not rule over them with harshness, but shall fear your God. (Lev 25:35–43)

If there is among you anyone in need, a member of your community in any of your towns within the land that the LORD your God is giving you, do not be hard-hearted or tight-fisted towards your needy neighbor. You should rather open your hand, willingly lending enough to meet the need, whatever it may be. Be careful that you do not entertain a mean thought, thinking, "The seventh year, the year of remission, is near," and therefore view your needy neighbor with hostility and give nothing; your neighbor might cry to the LORD against you, and you would incur guilt. Give liberally and be ungrudging when you do so, for on this account the LORD your God will bless you in all your work and in all that you undertake. Since there will never cease to be some in need on the earth, I therefore command you, "Open your hand to the poor and needy neighbor in your land." (Deut 15:7–11)

If the person is poor, you shall not sleep in the garment given you as the pledge. You shall give the pledge back by sunset, so that your neighbor may sleep in the cloak and bless you; and it will be to your credit before the LORD your God. (Deut 24:12–14)

You shall not withhold the wages of poor and needy laborers, whether other Israelites or aliens who reside in your land in one of your towns. You shall pay them their wages daily before sunset, because they are poor and their livelihood depends on them; otherwise they might cry to the Lord against you, and you would incur guilt. (Deut 24:15)

You shall not deprive a resident alien or an orphan of justice; you shall not take a widow's garment in pledge. Remember that you were a slave in Egypt and the Lord your God redeemed you from there; therefore I command you to do this. When you reap your harvest in your field and forget a sheaf in the field, you shall not go back to get it; it shall be left for the alien, the orphan, and the widow, so that the Lord your God may bless you in all your undertakings. When you beat your olive trees, do not strip what is left; it shall be for the alien, the orphan, and the widow. When you gather the grapes of your vineyard, do not glean what is left; it shall be for the alien, the orphan, and the widow. Remember that you were a slave in the land of Egypt; therefore I am commanding you to do this. (Deut 24:17–22)

During Elijah's time, the dominant narrative was that God's favor was with the royal family of Ahab and Jezebel, and that they were therefore due to be obeyed and served. Part of that dominant narrative fostered the worship of gods in addition to YHWH. Elijah's powerful counter-narrative was expressed:

So Ahab sent to all the Israelites, and assembled the prophets at Mount Carmel. Elijah then came near to all the people, and said, "How long will you go limping with two different opinions? If the LORD is God, follow him; but if Baal, then follow him." The people did not answer him a word . . . (1 Kgs 18:20–21)

At the time of the offering of the oblation, the prophet Elijah came near and said, "O LORD, God of Abraham, Isaac, and Israel, let it be known this day that you are God in Israel, that I am your servant, and that I have done all these things at your bidding. Answer me, O LORD, answer me, so that this people may know that you, O LORD, are God, and that you have turned their hearts back." Then the fire of LORD fell and consumed the burnt-offering, the wood, the stones, and the dust, and even licked up the water that was in the trench. When all the people saw it, they fell on their faces and said, "LORD indeed is God; LORD indeed is God." Elijah said to them, "Seize the prophets of Baal; do not let one of them escape." Then they seized them; and Elijah brought them down to the Wadi Kishon, and killed them there. (1 Kgs 18:36–40)

During the prophet Amos's time, the dominant narrative of the royal and priestly families of Israel was that they were due God's favor, and that the poor were not. This self-serving narrative was advanced to justify the insiders' use of their power, wealth, and position to exploit the poor and to maintain their wealth and power. Amos brought a counter-narrative, one that proclaimed that God's protection was for the poor, and that the exploiters of the poor were due God's judgment and punishment:

Thus says the LORD:
For three transgressions of Israel,
　　and for four, I will not revoke the punishment;
because they sell the righteous for silver,
　　and the needy for a pair of sandals—
they who trample the head of the poor into the dust of the earth,
　　and push the afflicted out of the way;
father and son go in to the same girl,
　　so that my holy name is profaned;
they lay themselves down beside every altar
　　on garments taken in pledge;
and in the house of their God they drink
　　wine bought with fines they imposed. (Amos 2:6–8)

Hear this word, you cows of Bashan
　　who are on Mount Samaria,
who oppress the poor, who crush the needy,
　　who say to their husbands, "Bring something to drink!"
The LORD God has sworn by his holiness:
　　The time is surely coming upon you,
when they shall take you away with hooks,
　　even the last of you with fishhooks. (Amos 4:1–2)

Whereas Amos spoke for the LORD to the insiders of the Northern Kingdom of Israel in the eight century BCE, Micah spoke to the privileged of the Southern Kingdom of Judah late in that same century. The dominant narrative of Judah was much the same as that of Israel. The landed wealthy and the royalty claimed blessing and sanction from the LORD to oppress the rural poor. They claimed that because they were blessed and beloved of God, they were invulnerable. Micah's counter-narrative was:

And I said:
Listen, you heads of Jacob
　　and rulers of the house of Israel!
Should you not know justice?—
　　you who hate the good and love the evil, who tear the skin off my people,

and the flesh off their bones;
>   who eat the flesh of my people,
flay their skin off them,
>   break their bones in pieces,
and chop them up like meat in a kettle,
>   like flesh in a cauldron. (Mic 3:1–3)

Hear this, you rulers of the house of Jacob
>   and chiefs of the house of Israel,
who abhor justice and pervert all equity,
>   who build Zion with blood and Jerusalem with wrong!
Its rulers give judgment for a bribe,
>   its priests teach for a price,
its prophets give oracles for money;
>   yet they lean upon the Lord and say,
"Surely the Lord is with us! No harm shall come upon us."
>   Therefore because of you Zion shall be plowed as a field;
Jerusalem shall become a heap of ruins,
>   and the mountain of the house a wooded height. (Mic 3:9–12)

Isaiah proclaimed God's counter-narrative to Judah in the late eighth century that was much like the one proclaimed by Micah. Again, the dominant narrative of the powerful of Judah was that the LORD's favor rested upon Jerusalem and particularly upon its royal and priestly elites, because of their correct temple sacrifices. Part of that dominant narrative was that the wealth and power of those elites proved that they were favored by the LORD. Isaiah's counter-narrative was that the LORD's favor and protection depended upon Torah faithfulness, particularly upon protection of the weakest members of the community:

Hear the word of the LORD,
>   you rulers of Sodom!
Listen to the teaching (*torah*) of our God,
>   you people of Gomorrah!
What to me is the multitude of your sacrifices?
>   says the LORD;
I have had enough of burnt offerings of rams
>   and the fat of fed beasts;

I do not delight in the blood of bulls,
    or of lambs, or of goats.
When you come to appear before me,
    who asked this from your hand?
    Trample my courts no more;
bringing offerings is futile;
    incense is an abomination to me.
New moon and sabbath and calling of convocation—
    I cannot endure solemn assemblies with iniquity.
Your new moons and your appointed festivals
    my soul hates;
they have become a burden to me,
    I am weary of bearing them.
When you stretch out your hands,
    I will hide my eyes from you;
even though you make many prayers,
    I will not listen;
    your hands are full of blood.
Wash yourselves; make yourselves clean;
    remove the evil of your doings
    from before my eyes;
cease to do evil,
    learn to do good;
seek justice,
    rescue the oppressed,
defend the orphan,
    plead for the widow. (Isa 1:10–17)

How the faithful city
    has become a whore!
    She that was full of justice,
Righteousness lodged in her—
    but now murderers!
Your silver has become dross,
    your wine is mixed with water.
Your princes are rebels
    and companions of thieves.

Everyone loves a bribe
    and runs after gifts.
They do not defend the orphan,
    and the widow's cause does not come before them. (Isa 1:21–23)

The LORD rises to argue his case;
    he stands to judge the peoples.
The LORD enters into judgment
    with the elders and princes of his people:
It is you who have devoured the vineyard;
    the spoil of the poor is in your houses.
What do you mean by crushing my people,
    by grinding the face of the poor? says the Lord God of hosts.

The LORD said:
Because the daughters of Zion are haughty
    and walk with outstretched necks,
    glancing wantonly with their eyes,
mincing along as they go,
    tinkling with their feet;
the Lord will afflict with scabs
    the heads of the daughters of Zion,
    and the LORD will lay bare their secret parts. (Isa 3:13–17)

For the vineyard of the LORD of hosts
    is the house of Israel,
and the people of Judah
    are his pleasant planting;
he expected justice,
    but saw bloodshed;
righteousness,
    but heard a cry!
Ah, you who join house to house,
    who add field to field,
until there is room for no one but you,
    and you are left to live alone
    in the midst of the land!
The LORD of hosts has sworn in my hearing:

Surely many houses shall be desolate,
  large and beautiful houses, without inhabitant.
For ten acres of vineyard shall yield but one bath,
  and a homer of seed shall yield a mere ephah.
Ah, you who rise early in the morning
  in pursuit of strong drink,
who linger in the evening
  to be inflamed by wine,
whose feasts consist of lyre and harp,
  tambourine and flute and wine,
but who do not regard the deeds of the LORD,
  or see the work of his hands!
Therefore my people go into exile without knowledge;
  their nobles are dying of hunger,
  and their multitude is parched with thirst. (Isa 5:7–13)

During the prophet Jeremiah's time, the dominant narrative of Judah was still that God's favor rested on the temple establishment. The LORD's glory was present in the temple. Israel was therefore due God's protection from any alien invader. Israel was impervious to any threat, regardless of whether the people observed Torah, because the LORD dwelled with them in the temple. The dominant narrative proclaimed that living as a child of God centered upon faithfully carrying out the temple ritual and obeying the dominant narrative of the priestly insiders. Jeremiah brought a counter-narrative:

The word that came to Jeremiah from the LORD: Stand in the gate of the LORD's house, and proclaim there this word, and say, Hear the word of the LORD, all you people of Judah, you that enter these gates to worship the LORD. Thus says the LORD of hosts, the God of Israel: Amend your ways and your doings, and let me dwell with you in this place. Do not trust in these deceptive words: "This is the temple of the LORD, the temple of the LORD, the temple of the LORD."

For if you truly amend your ways and your doings, if you truly act justly one with another, if you do not oppress the alien, the orphan, and the widow, or shed innocent blood in this place, and if you do not go after other gods to your own hurt, then I will dwell with you in this place, in the land that I gave of old to your ancestors forever and ever.

Here you are, trusting in deceptive words to no avail. Will you steal, murder, commit adultery, swear falsely, make offerings to Baal, and go after other gods that you have not known, and then come and stand before me in this house, which is called by my name, and say, "We are safe!"—only to go on doing all these abominations? Has this house, which is called by my name, become a den of robbers in your sight? You know, I too am watching, says the LORD. (Jer 7:1–11)

In Jesus' time, a dominant narrative was that those who scrupulously followed Torah in every particular—especially the dietary, Sabbath, holiness, and purity provisions—were due favored health, position, and influence. Those who did not obey Torah in every particular, even if their failures were because of poverty and lack of the means to obey, were due an inferior, outcast position, poverty, and suffering. Jesus' counter-narrative can be heard in his teachings:

The sabbath was made for humankind, and not humankind for the sabbath. (Mark 2:27)

"Then do you fail to understand? Do you not see that whatever goes into a person from outside cannot defile, since it enters, not the heart but the stomach, and goes out into the sewer?" (Thus he declared all foods clean.) And he said, "It is what comes out of a person that defiles. For it is from within, from the human heart, that evil intentions come: fornication, theft, murder, adultery, avarice, wickedness, deceit, licentiousness, envy, slander, pride, folly. All these evil things come from within, and they defile a person." (Mark 7:18–23)

His counter-narrative can be witnessed vividly in his association with those the dominant narrative considered to be unclean.

When the Pharisees saw this, they said to his disciples, "Why does your teacher eat with tax-collectors and sinners?" (Matt 9:11)

And there can no more radical counter-narrative than Jesus' sermon on the plain from Luke 6:

Blessed are you who are poor,
    for yours is the kingdom of God.
Blessed are you who hunger now,
    for you will be satisfied.

Blessed are you who weep now,

for you will laugh.

Blessed are you when people hate you, when they exclude you and insult you and reject your name as evil, because of the Son of Man.

Rejoice in that day and leap for joy, because great is your reward in heaven. For that is how their ancestors treated the prophets.

But woe to you who are rich,

for you have already received your comfort.

Woe to you who are well fed now,

for you will go hungry.

Woe to you who are laughing now,

for you will mourn and weep.

Woe to you when all speak well of you, for that is how their ancestors treated the false prophets.

(Luke 6:20–26)

In Paul's time, the dominant narrative proclaimed that the foundation of the power of the Roman Empire was the divinity of the Emperor. Temples raised to the "divine Augustus" proclaimed in stone in every provincial capital that Caesar was the "Son of God," and that he and his successors were "Lord," "Savior," and the bringers of "Peace" through military pacification. The dominant narrative proclaimed that it was therefore the will of God that Rome rule its vast empire with military might and tax its subject peoples. Paul bore God's counter-narrative that the Jesus crucified by Roman justice was resurrected by the only, true God and was the only, true "Son of God," the only, true "Lord" and the only true "Savior." God's counter-narrative proclaimed by Paul was that true power was found in weakness and sacrifice, and not in conquest and fear, and that true peace would come from love and not force of arms.

We would make a mistake if we believed that America has never been plagued by dominant narratives that have proven to be false. Narratives that seemed once so true and dominant in the history of America have been and are supplanted by narratives more approximating the counter-narrative of God. A once-dominant narrative relentlessly proclaimed that white males were willed by God to own black men, women, and children, steal their labor and oppress them as they wished without legal protections. A successor dominant narrative kept black men, women, and children in poverty and third-class citizenship through Jim Crow laws, disenfranchisement, intimidation, and lynching. Another narrative taught that women should not be allowed to vote, own property, or take employment outside the home because they were intellectually, physically, and emotionally inferior to men. Another once-dominant narrative justified the slaughter of the First Nations and the theft of their lands because they were less than human. A narrative that struggles still to dominate preaches that America is God's favored nation and that God wills whatever advances the power and position of America. Another narrative remaining all too dominant proclaims that the earth and its fruits are all here for humans to use up, and that the human species is due to spread over the entirety of creation in ways that despoil the earth and drive other species to extinction. Idolatrous dominant narratives did not exist only in biblical times. All dominant narratives proclaim that they express divine and eternal truth. God eventually proves them all to be false. Our own dominant narrative of the worship of things and pleasures presents itself as valid for all times and places, and as the manifestation of God's will for us and everyone. Yet it is no truer than the previous dominant narratives.

CHAPTER 5

Justice and Mercy under the
Dominant Narrative of America

WHAT ARE JUSTICE AND mercy? What makes an act "just" and what makes it "merciful"?

Generally, "justice" is rendering what is "due." For instance, the *Oxford English Dictionary* defines the "just" person as one who is disposed to "give everyone his or her due." The *Catechism of the Roman Catholic Church* states: "Justice is the moral virtue that consists in the constant and firm will *to give their due to . . . the neighbor.*"[1] And, "Society ensures social justice by providing the conditions that allow . . . individuals *to obtain their due.*"[2]

We also see this language describing justice as rendering what is "due" in passages of Scripture.

> You shall not pervert the justice due to the poor in their lawsuits. (Exod 23:6)

> Do not withhold good from those to whom it is due, when it is in your power to do so. (Prov 3:27)

> Ascribe to the Lord the glory due his name . . . (1 Chr 16:29)

> I will give to the LORD the thanks due to his righteousness,
>   and sing praise to the name of the LORD, the Most High. (Ps 7:17)

---

1. The *Catechism of the Roman Catholic Church* (New York: Doubleday, 1994), par. 1807, emphasis added.

2. Ibid., par. 1943, emphasis added.

> Do not drag me away with the wicked,
> > with those who are workers of evil
> who speak peace with their neighbors,
> > while mischief is in their hearts.
> Repay them according to their work,
> > and according to the evil of their deeds;
> repay them according to the work of their hands;
> > render them their due reward. (Ps 28:3–4)

> Who would not fear you, O King of the Nations?
> > For that is your due;
> among all the wise ones of the nations
> > and in all their kingdoms
> > there is no one like you. (Jer 10:7)

> Pay to all what is due to them—taxes to whom taxes are due,
> revenue to whom revenue is due, respect to whom respect is
> due, honor to whom honor is due. (Rom 13:7)

All this is in the language of justice. When we see justice as rendering or receiving "what is due," justice becomes the central issue of all of life.

What is due, as a matter of justice, from me to a member of my family? To my spouse, my mother or father, my child, or my sibling? What is due, as a matter of justice, from me to my friend? To my co-worker? To my supervisor and to my employer? To my employee? To a fellow driver just in front of me in the passing lane on a highway? To a stranger on a plane with me? To a stranger lying injured and unconscious on the side of the road I am traveling? What is due from me, in any given situation, as a citizen and member of a community to other citizens and members? What are all these due from me? These are justice questions.

Is anything due from me to a poor child trapped in poverty through no fault of his own and by an accident of birth, abused by his father, neglected by his drug-addicted mother, ill, and hungry? Is anything at all due from me to that child, as a matter of justice, when I can argue that I am not at fault for that child's being trapped in poverty and abuse? As understood, this is a justice issue, not merely a mercy issue.

The other side of these questions is: What is due to me in all the same settings and within the same relationships or encounters? From a member of my family, my spouse, my parent, my child, or my sibling?

What is due to me in a given situation from my friend, my co-worker, my supervisor, my employer? What is due to me from strangers I encounter when I am in need? What would be due to me as a matter of justice if I were the one lying on the side of the road, injured and unconscious?

Taking it further, is anything due from me to the creation? What is due the earth from our species? Anything at all? Is everything we are able to take from the sea, the sky, the earth, the rivers, and the ocean due to me and my species? As a matter of justice, is nothing due from us to the creation? Or is creation due for us to be protective stewards?

What is due to me from life? Nothing or everything I want? And if I do not receive from life ninety or more years of comfortable, protected, pain-free living, would I be justified in feeling that I am a victim of injustice, and that I have been cheated of my rights? Our basic outlooks on life are determined by what we feel is due and not due to us from life.

But what is life due from me?

What is due from me to God, and what is due to me from God?

Perhaps the most overlooked question is, what am I due from myself? What pangs of my conscience or urges from my appetites and fears should I observe, indulge, or deny? What permissions am I due to be given from myself? What limitations and self-imposed disciplines am I due to have imposed upon me by myself? What times of quiet and meditation, or of hedonistic pursuits? What endurance of hardships or flight from burdens? What sacrifices and what selfishness? What living for others and what living for myself? What impulsiveness and what prudence am I due to be granted by myself? What formation of character and what giving in to temptation? Am I due from myself to choose to be merciful or just? Or am I due from myself only to seek my own wealth and pleasure? Have you known individuals who have been unjust to themselves? Have you never been unjust to yourself by failing to render to yourself what was due? All these issues about justice to myself beg the questions of who and what I am and therefore what that "I" is due from me. Am I just my appetite for food, sex, and pleasure? Or am I primarily my mercy and justice?

From beginning to end, Holy Scripture is mainly about three justice issues. What is God due from me? What is the other person due from me? What am I due from myself?

Consider then the general definition of "mercy." Our English word "mercy" is taken from the Old French *merci*, which meant pity. According to the *Merriam-Webster Dictionary*, "mercy" means "kind or forgiving treatment of an offender," "lenient treatment to someone who does not deserve it," "help given to someone in a desperate situation," or "an act of divine compassion." The overall sense is that mercy is distinguished from justice, because justice is due and therefore obligatory, but mercy is free, gracious, and therefore not due or obligatory.

The version of justice of the dominant narrative, given its vision of society as a zero-sum contest among individuals for things and pleasure, is that a person is only due whatever he or she can win within the competition and is not due what he or she does not win. Under this dominant narrative, all that anyone is due as a matter of justice is a place in the *agón*. All anyone is due as a matter of justice is the opportunity to acquire whatever she wants according to some minimum rules, without any obligation or even urge to share with others, or to consider the consequence to the community of the acquiring. The dominant narrative teaches us to say: "I earned it. It's my private property to do with as I please. The smarter and more successful I am, the more I am due to obtain and use for my own benefit and the less that others are due from me. These things and pleasures are my just deserts for being so smart, hard-working and successful." The poor and suffering are simply those who have justly lost the competition. Under this version of justice, my economic victory and their economic defeat are both just, because everyone always receives exactly what is "due" from the contest.

So within the dominant narrative, according to its most vocal apologists and beneficiaries, justice and mercy are in inevitable and unavoidable conflict. One effect is to minimize the influence and value of mercy. Justice is required; mercy is merely optional. When it comes to economic and social justice, you can't be just and merciful at the same time. Justice, ensuring that people receive no more or less than what they are due, is a matter of right and obligation. Mercy is merely charity—a rare, occasional, optional, and discouraged bestowing of a mite of our excess.

The dominant narrative teaches that you can't run a society, and certainly not a business, on mercy. You cannot make mercy obligatory and enforceable. You can only run a society, a business, or a judicial or economic system on justice, with standards of who is due what from whom that are narrowly construed. Under this narrative, what is due will always favor those in the positions of power and privilege, and disfavor those in need on the fringes. Failing to be merciful, or even being aggressively merciless, is not unjust. It is just "business." It's not "personal."

To be too merciful—to give people too much too often of what they are not due—undermines the justice and integrity of the competition. More than occasional mercy would make people less self-reliant, would undermine their work ethic, and would reduce the productivity and efficiency of this system. The dominant narrative teaches that rendering only what people are due is critical to achieving excellence. Softening this dominant view of justice that people are due whatever they can win, but not due what they do not win, would undermine the system. Within this narrative, human beings are only motivated to work hard by selfishness and greed for things and personal pleasure, not by the common good or by the needs of the suffering and vulnerable. If you change the system so that people are provided what they have not killed for themselves, "these" people will not be motivated to work hard. You will be rewarding failure, which is definitely not just.

But in truth the starting lines of the competition for stuff and pleasure are segregated, with one set of competitors up front and with many, many more competitors starting miles behind or not even allowed onto the same track in the same stadium. The reality of our society is that the same goal is not possible for all competitors, even as the narrative says that only those who reach that one goal will be successful and happy. The children of the outsiders don't get to run for the same finish line as the children of the insiders, and they can't start from the same starting blocks. The dominant narrative conditions us to believe that this is just, as if this injustice and mercilessness to the children of the outsiders is all that is due them.

Within the world created by the dominant narrative, we are not to live as if our fellow citizens were neighbors. We on the inside live as if our society is a *Gran Prix*, a race among elite competitors for the grand prize of ostentatious wealth, shallow pleasures, and honor based upon acquisition of that wealth and pleasure. The rest, and definitely the clients of the Methodist Justice Ministry, live out the *Hunger Games*, not only for food and necessities, but for the stuff, shallow pleasures, and so-called honor that will not satisfy. As the prophet wrote: "Why do you spend your money for that which is not bread, and your labor for that which does not satisfy?" (Isa 55:2).

Somehow, claims the narrative, if I focus only on my rights and prerogatives, my appetites, urges, desires and so-called needs, an invisible hand will ensure that the entire system and everyone in it will benefit. So I receive from the narrative not just license but also encouragement to be

greedy, merciless, and heedless of the effects of my greed and mercilessness on others and the community.

Within the world created by the dominant narrative, the winners of
the *agón* associate only with other winners. The winners separate themselves into their own neighborhoods and segregate their children into
their own schools. The winners socialize and network only with other
winners. This is their just reward from winning the competition. So many
comfortable Americans have no contact at all with an economically poor
person, except perhaps their maids, yard men, waitresses, and the fore-
man of the roofing crew. These are merely the losers in the *agón*. They
have no faces. They are just human machines, who exist to serve the insiders in some way. They are due nothing outside of low pay, which is all
that they can win for themselves in the contest. They are the "others" to be
feared and avoided. The winners have no personal understanding of the
struggle and growing hopelessness of the lives of the economically poor,
and particularly of their poor children.

The churches have fallen short by not challenging this duality, this
so-called conflict between justice and mercy, prioritizing justice over
mercy, choosing mercy only for us and ours while demanding a strict
and hard justice for everyone else. The church, called to be the loudest
voice for mercy in human creation and the source and home of God's
counter-narrative, has let the culture convince us that we are only called
to be merciful to the "deserving" poor, which is to say the poor in whom
we can see ourselves. This makes mercy all the more sporadic and ineffective. Too often, it is all about making the giver feel good and barely
about helping all those in need of mercy. There is still no more segregated
time and place in America than Sundays at church, particularly by economic class. Many churches have hired security personnel to keep poor
people from asking their members for help as the members are walking
from their Cadillacs and Mercedes to their church sanctuary to worship
Jesus of Nazareth.

The protectors of the dominant narrative—those who benefit the
most from its power and pervasiveness—must shout down any alterna-
tive narrative. Any criticism of the dominant narrative's mercilessness is
condemned as un-American. This is just one of the ways that the dominant narrative seeks to silence any counter-narrative.

As to the power of this narrative, how many of your family and
friends have never acted mercifully to anyone other than members of
their immediate family or very close friends? I am not speaking about

occasional charitable contributions. I am speaking about sacrificial mercy acted out from an individual's heart to another individual. How many people do you know, love, and admire who go years without personally helping someone in need who isn't a member of their immediate family or close social circle? This has not always been the way in this country. Neighbors helped one another, sacrificed for one another, helped get one another through hard times. My experience in the last thirteen years working in the Methodist Justice Ministry, going into our clients' homes and witnessing their regular, sacrificial generosity, is that the economically poor commonly help others outside their immediate family. It's the comfortable—the winners of the *agón*—who generally do not. This is the effect of the dominant narrative.

The great lie of the dominant narrative is that anyone within our system can by hard work acquire the things and pleasures necessary for success, honor, and satisfaction. I have known hundreds and hundreds of men and women who work themselves to physical and emotional exhaustion at multiple jobs that don't pay enough to support a family, to save, or to get out of debt. They have to turn to predatory pay-day and title lenders to make it through any crisis, and the burden of those debts then bury them deeper into the grave of poverty. The place they start on the material ladder has nothing to do with their merit and everything to do with accidents of birth. The place they are stuck on that ladder has nothing to do with a lack of hard work. I know children of the rich and accomplished who just can't seem to find hoe handles to fit their hands. But they inherit their parents' positions on the ladder. I know personally hundreds of young people from poor families who have no help, no soft landing spot, absolutely no room for mistake, and so no grace. I know hundreds of young people from rich families—inheritors of the winners of the *agón*—whose every transgression is excused, covered up, and forgotten. Surely there are the amazing exceptions—the young person from a terrible home circumstance who has extraordinary gifts and finds mentors and sponsors along the way to enable them to "rise above their raising." These special, admirable individuals are used by the dominant narrative to serve as justification for a merciless system.

But the claim that anyone can make his or her way out of poverty today with hard work is a terrible lie. I can tell you anecdotally that people in America in low-paying jobs will never get out of poverty, no matter how hard they work. There is no direct connection between wealth and great character, and no direct connection between poverty and poor character.

The poor are oppressed by the world created by this dominant narrative. They are told over and over by this pervasive narrative that to be valuable and happy everyone must have all the stuff and pleasure they want, whenever they want it. Any shortcomings in their lives, any lack of meaning and joy, and any dissatisfaction and yearning, can only be overcome and filled with more and more stuff and shallow pleasures. The poor are as much the children of this world as the rich. So low-income people run up huge consumer debt to obtain the stuff and pleasure. Drug and alcohol addiction and obesity are epidemic among the economically poor, because alcohol, drugs, and cheap, delicious and unhealthy food have become the only stuff and shallow pleasures that are available to them and that can anesthetize them from their sense of failure.

The dominant narrative's version of justice and mercy does not satisfy our souls or foster the community we desperately need. This version is in deep conflict with God's answer to our needs for satisfaction and community. This version is deeply in conflict with the justice and mercy of the world being created by God's counter-narrative. Within our dominant narrative, the tension between justice and mercy is not even felt. Justice is always required, while mercy is always optional and rare. Within the dominant narrative, Micah 6:8 becomes Money 6:8: "Do justice, by giving everyone no more or less than what they are due according to your closed rules, and act mercifully only rarely and only when it makes you feel good about yourself."

The dominant narrative doesn't work for anyone. It doesn't work for the poor, who are kept in poverty and hopelessness, who are unhappy and defeated because they cannot realize the immediate gratification of obtaining the stuff and shallow pleasures that the all-pervasive and relentless dominant narrative tells them are the only sources of value and meaning. It doesn't work for the middle classes, who are able to obtain more stuff and shallow pleasures than the poor but only by piling up back-breaking debt, and who continue to experience dissatisfaction because these alleged sources of meaning and value are not satisfying to anyone's soul. And it doesn't even work for the wealthy because the only thing worse than failing to obtain that for which you yearn but which will not satisfy you, is actually obtaining it and experiencing the yearning and dissatisfaction anyway. And it certainly doesn't work for the community.

The dominant narrative appeals to and is the product of the worst aspects of our beings—fear, suspicion, greed, the will to dominate, and the resulting mercilessness. As we shall see, the counter-narrative of God and Jesus appeals to and is the product of the image of God within each of us—humility, self-discipline, empathy, generosity, a yearning for true community, and the resulting mercifulness.

CHAPTER 6

The Toll of the Dominant Narrative

To APPRECIATE THE TOLL upon the poor of the dominant narrative's version of justice and mercy, I offer real stories of the plight of the poor. The dominant narrative has created a separate world for the comfortable. Within the world created by the dominant narrative, the life of a comfortable person is generally marked by a succession of quickly satisfied desires, while the life of a poor person is generally the experience of frustrated and denied needs and wants. To paraphrase the opening of Leo Tolstoy's *Anna Karenina*: "The lives of the comfortable are all alike. The lives of the poor are each unique in their own suffering and hopelessness." The comfortable generally do not know the poor as persons, so the poor are judged and stereotyped in ignorance. The comfortable do not know their stories and do not care to know. I recount here the stories of some economically poor individuals I have known so that the comfortable Christians who read this book will at least hear their stories and struggles, and feel their humanity.

**

When I was an Assistant United States Attorney for the District of Columbia, I obtained a jury conviction of a man for raping a defenseless, intellectually impaired, physically handicapped thirteen-year-old who was sleeping in her upstairs bedroom while her mother was hosting a party of friends downstairs. The man went upstairs to use the bathroom, saw the helpless girl asleep in her bed, and raped her. I hated that man. I truly hated him.

I had just started my Felony I assignment, one of eight Assistant United States Attorneys in DC prosecuting nothing but first-degree murders and rape cases. (Felony II cases were all the rest of the felonies, from murder in the second degree to simple drug possession and theft.) A Felony I assignment was the goal of almost every prosecutor in that office. I had succeeded. With that attainment and experience behind me, I was on my way to an eventual position in a large and prestigious DC law firm, to an apex position in the system created by the dominant narrative.

But then there was "Karen," I will call her. One of my very first Felony I cases. The main challenges in this prosecution were to qualify Karen as mentally competent to testify and then to persuade and enable her to do so. There was no witness to this crime besides Karen. The assailant had used a condom, and so there was no semen to find and test. There were signs of trauma, but this man had not been caught in the act, and Karen was scared and didn't report what happened until late the next morning. There was a party downstairs in her mother's home and every man there had gone upstairs to use the bathroom. Karen really needed to testify for me to obtain a conviction. She knew the assailant after many encounters and her identification of him by name and photo was likely to be sufficient for conviction, *if* she was able to testify before a judge and jury.

Karen was not merely thirteen and intellectually impaired. She suffered from club foot, dwarfism, a deformed hip, and hydrocephalus. She had an almost bare skull, with a few wisps of hair growing out the top of her forehead, and a normal sized trunk for her age. But she had shriveled little legs and no use of one hand. She couldn't walk or even crawl. And she possessed the biggest, toothiest, face crinkling smile that makes tears well up in my eyes even now, thinking about her as I am typing this.

Karen had a devoted mother and three loving siblings. The mother could not afford in-home nursing assistance for Karen, so had to quit her low-paying job to care for her. The family's only income, as I recall it now, was from Social Security disability for Karen, food stamps and rent assistance. Maybe Aid to Families with Dependent Children was still in place back then. Regardless, that family was barely getting by, going from financial crisis to financial crisis. But there was an abundance of love in that home.

Karen had to testify or this man might get away scot-free to do it again. Both Karen and her assailant were due the justice of his being convicted and sentenced to jail for as long a sentence as I could obtain for him.

The court appointed defense attorney did his duty and challenged Karen's competence to testify. Competence for a witness in this setting means the capacity to know truth from fantasy. Competence means the ability to recall facts accurately, to understand questions about an event and to answer them honestly and fully in open court. Because the defense counsel asked for an evaluation of her competence and an evaluation of her capacities to appreciate reality, Karen was evaluated by a court-appointed forensic psychologist. The results shocked us. The psychologist opined that Karen was without a functional I.Q. and that she was not competent to testify in court.

I went to see this expert, and asked her to show me the tests and the results that were the bases of her opinion. One test and conclusion stands out in my memory. On a drawing of a farmyard, Karen could not identify or name pictures of a cow, a horse, a donkey, a duck, a chicken, a bee, or a butterfly. She could identify and name a robin.

Confined to her mother's inner-city apartment, Karen had never seen a cow, a horse, a donkey, a duck, a chicken, a bee, or a butterfly. She had seen these on television, but no drawings of them. She had seen a robin in a nest outside her upstairs bedroom window. So she could identify and name the bird.

And she was painfully shy and intimidated by the testing process. She had never met the psychologist before. And the expert was white. Karen had only seen a few white people face to face in her life. Her mother said I was the first white man who had ever been in their home. The first time we met at her home, Karen sat in a wheel chair and I sat in a kitchen chair in front of her. And while I was making eyes at her and getting her to laugh, she kept reaching out and scraping my hand with the fingernails on her good hand. It wasn't until her mother told me later that I understood that Karen was checking to see if I was wearing white make-up. (Tears again.)

So we found another psychologist, this one from Children's Hospital with a long history with Karen, to test the defense expert's conclusion. The threshold decision on competence would be made by the judge, not the jury. And the trial judge was Chief Judge Carl Moultrie (actual name), one of the finest judges and human beings I have ever appeared before in my forty-one plus years of trial-law practice. Chief Judge Moultrie was a judge with great street sense as well as great law sense. I felt confident we would leap the hurdle because I knew that Karen was much brighter than she had tested and because the Chief Judge would be able to see this. And our other psychologist found that Karen was able to discern truth from fantasy, able to recount a history and understand and answer questions and competent to testify.

But that left the challenge of getting Karen to tell her terrible, embarrassing story, complete with the legally required anatomical details, in front of Chief Judge Moultrie and then in a courtroom full of absolute strangers, by far the largest group of people she had ever spoken before. If she was too shy or scared to testify, she was indeed incompetent. This was to be a functional test. I would be very limited in how much I could ask her leading questions. But if she could not tell her story, there would be no evidence before the jury, and Chief Judge Moultrie would have to dismiss the case.

So I went repeatedly to Karen's mother's house so Karen would know and trust me. Looking back on it, it was a privilege to be welcomed so warmly and trustingly into that home.

Karen did well in the initial hearing before Chief Judge Moultrie, and he ruled that the jury could hear her account. And when the trial came, and after the jury had been picked, after our psychologist had testified, and Karen's mother had told the jury all about Karen and her disabilities and her courage and her hidden but actual intelligence, and after the circumstantial evidence had been offered, I wheeled Karen into the center of that circular courtroom, her tiny body swallowed by the chair, looking nervously from side to side until she saw the man who raped her. As I am typing this, I have tried 136 cases to jury verdict in my career, and I remember it as the most dramatic moment in my entire courtroom career. The Chief Judge let me sit in a chair right in front of Karen in the middle of the circular court well, so she was essentially telling her new, good friend the story, including the legally necessary anatomy. When I asked her if she could identify the man who did this to her, she pointed right at him, and called him by name. To lessen the inherent prejudice of the in-court identification process when a victim or witness points at the only person sitting at the defendant's table next to the defense attorney, the Chief Judge had positioned the defendant in a seat in the gallery among other African-American men. Karen had no hesitation in identifying him.

Some of the jurors were crying so hard after her testimony that Chief Judge recessed us for the day, before defense counsel cross examined Karen. And there were two male jurors who looked as if they wanted to come out of that jury box and jump the defendant. So we got them out of there for the evening.

The next morning, the defense attorney came to me early before trial resumed, and said that his client had a change of heart overnight. He wanted to plead guilty to save Karen the anguish and stress of the cross-examination.

The defense counsel was, of course, looking for a plea deal, to reduce the maximum possible sentence. (There was no death penalty in DC at that time.) I said no to a plea deal. The defendant would have to plead guilty to the lead charge in the indictment. And I would be asking for the maximum sentence whether he pleaded out or not. I would have been shocked if the Chief Judge gave him less than the max under these facts. It wasn't too late for a deal. There never was going to be a deal in this case.

Hate doesn't make deals.

So the defendant pleaded guilty to the indictment, received a maximum sentence, and was sent to Lorton Penitentiary, the DC prison in Virginia.

Next case. I never went back to see Karen. I am ashamed of that now. She thought I was her friend.

About a year later, after I had been promoted to Deputy Chief of the Felony Trial section and was working with the Chief and my good friend Steve Gordon (actual name), a different defense counsel for the assailant came to see me. It had taken a year, but word had finally gotten out among the Lorton inmates of what the defendant had done to little Karen. Counsel suspected not Karen's mother, but Karen's uncle for bringing that word. There were convicted murderers, armed robbers and drug dealers within that prison population, but they would not tolerate for long a man who would rape such a defenseless young girl. The defendant was, as this lawyer told me, a "corpse with the temporary use of his arms and legs." And he wasn't going to die easy or pretty. The lawyer pleaded with me that no one, not even this man, deserves to die like that. Oh yeah?" I thought. "You didn't hear the evidence and see Karen." Defense counsel had asked the warden at Lorton to get his client transferred. He begged that I add my voice to the request that the man be moved to safety to another federal prison facility far away where no one knew him. As the person who obtained his conviction and as Deputy Chief of Felony Trial, he thought that a request from me that the man be moved would add to the weight of the request. I'd be saving a life, he said. How often do any of us have a chance to do that? I'd be cutting a life short not to do this. Cutting off the possibility that the man might change.

At first I refused without hesitation. I still hated the rapist. The longer this very good defense attorney spoke, the angrier I felt. Because I knew he was right. I gave the excuse that I couldn't be intervening in every case of a prisoner in danger in Lorton. The prison officials have to run that place. The violence in that place was a deterrent against people committing crime. I was sure (I wasn't) that he was overstating the risk to this particular defendant, I said.

But in my heart, his murder by a fellow inmate would feel like justice truly and finally rendered, what this horror of a human was merely "due." I thought he was "due" whatever he got at the hands of his inmates. That was that. Justice had been delayed, but wasn't going to be denied much longer.

I went home that evening. I couldn't sleep. I was thrashing around the bed so much that my wife Maxine asked me what was wrong. She wouldn't let it go. I finally told her. She recalled Karen's case very well, of course. We had lived that together. My wife listened and finally told me that she was afraid that if the defendant was killed, I would come to regret not having acted to prevent it. No, she agreed, he was definitely due much worse than he had received. But not even our justice system provided for the death penalty, much less a suffering death. And my failure to do what I could would be doing an injustice to myself, something that I was not due. I was better than that, she said. And she had noticed that the job was turning me meaner than I had to be. It alarmed her. Do it for me, she said. Not for him.

So, mainly for myself and my wife, I made the call. I recommended that he be moved. And he was. I have no idea how much weight my request carried. But I made the request.

Despite my hatred, I felt better after I had done that. In retrospect, it may have been the effect of the gospel I had heard from those African-American churches.

Under the dominant narrative's version of justice, I should have let him die. He certainly wasn't "due" the mercy he wanted—to be moved and saved, at least for a time. He was due worse than he had received. But I wasn't due making myself a killer.

I don't know where the defendant is now. This was about thirty-five years ago. He may have died in prison. It's likely that the parole board denied parole every time he came up, or he became institutionalized and didn't want out.

If he survived prison, he is probably out on the street. What kind of a life can he be living? Did what family he had reject him? How has he been able to support himself? Is he living with a sense of regret, of anger at himself, of shame? Is he a registered sex offender, so probably homeless and unsheltered, unable to find a place to live? Or is he like so many of us, finding some way to blame someone or something else for the grave he jumped into? A man with a felony conviction for child rape is in a grave he can't escape.

Who knows how it all turned out? God knows. Karen had a much reduced life expectancy and so may have died some time ago. If so, she is finally well and joyful. But who knows how the defendant and I will turn out.

I don't want to overstate this. All I did was make a phone call, and I don't know what effect it actually had. But maybe I'll receive mercy someday for my act. After all, "Blessed are the merciful, for they shall obtain mercy" (Matt 5:7).

Under God's mercy, the defendant will receive mercy, too. Under our dominant narrative's version of mercy, he'd have already died a bloody death.

But this raises another facet of justice, of what is due from someone to someone else. Sometimes we are both the "someone" and the "someone else." Sometimes, we are the someone from whom the justice is due and the someone else to whom it is due. What was I due from myself in that situation? What was I due from the angry, hating me? To persist in doing nothing, and letting him die, in the name of secular justice? To allow myself to act out of my angry, hating, shadow self? Or was I due to allow myself to be merciful?

Once we start asking what we are due from ourselves, once we begin to look at our lives that way, the questions go on and on.

"Blessed are the merciful, for they shall obtain mercy." Maybe at least a part of what Jesus meant by that was that the greatest mercy we can receive is to be merciful.

In some ways, I was as merciful to myself as I was to the defendant.

Under the dominant narrative, what was Karen due after the case was closed and "justice" was done? What was due her from members of the community, with so many resources in the world to help her and her mother? Not a damned thing. But what was Karen due from the people formed by the counter-narrative of Jesus? She was due all the mercy we could give and all the mercy we could receive ourselves by being merciful to her. Respect, friendship, attention, presence, love, material help, laughter, and tears.

**

As an Assistant United States Attorney and eventually Deputy Chief of Felony Trial, in the name of "justice," I was instrumental in sending hundreds of young, impoverished, violent men to prison for the rest of their youths and into their middle age. I personally tried eight first-degree murder cases to jury verdict. The one case I recall best is the one where a merciless injustice was done at my hands. In that case, I obtained the wrongful conviction of a stone-cold innocent man for first-degree murder and rape, only to have him totally exonerated of the crimes by incontrovertible DNA evidence after he had served twenty-eight years in prison. I was convinced at the time I tried the case that I was righteously meting out justice to the defendant and protecting the community from a predator. I was convinced then that if he were not convicted, he would walk out of the courtroom and murder and rape again. I was tragically wrong. In fact, I was inflicting a merciless injustice. In retrospect, I didn't "do justice" or "love mercy" in that case. My failure has haunted me since I found out what I did. It has been no consolation to either me or my innocent defendant that I was "just doing my best with the evidence that I was told I had." Without my conviction that the defendant was guilty, without my talent, and without my commitment to winning the competition of the trial, this merciless injustice would never have happened. Such, I fear, is not so atypical of the human justice system.

Briefly stated, the facts of the case are these. In 1981, a female student at a local university was working late at a business in a building close to Rock Creek. She left work close to midnight and tried to walk home to her apartment. She never made it. A search party from her work went out the next morning and found her body in thick brush on the banks of Rock Creek, maybe a hundred yards from the building. She had been raped and shot in the head. The district and particularly students at the university were in an uproar, of course. I think it was fair to say that the police were under intense pressure to identify the murderer and lock him up.

The facts of this investigation and prosecution have been widely publicized after the exoneration. They have been the subject of a civil suit brought after the exoneration by some of the most effective and dedicated lawyers I have ever encountered. My original prosecution consisted of three parts, like legs on a three-legged stool. One leg of this stool was public testimony from a paid informant that the defendant confessed the crime to him. A second leg was the opinion of an FBI hair examiner that foreign pubic hairs recovered from the body of the victim and pubic hairs taken from the defendant were "microscopically indistinguishable." In fact, at trial this expert testified that he had performed thousands of comparisons of hair from the body of a victim and from the body of a suspect, but had only encountered one occasion in which two different people had microscopically indistinguishable hair. The third leg was proof that the actual defendant had tried to rob a young woman of similar appearance to the murder victim at the same general location only nineteen days before the murder, a crime that started as purse snatching and terminated in what we argued was a sexual approach before drivers on a nearby parkway jumped to the young woman's rescue.

We didn't have a fourth leg. DNA comparison didn't exist in 1982 when I tried the case.

The defendant was very well defended by able counsel, but the jury still found him guilty. I had not been assigned to try the case until long after the investigation and indictment. I thought the case was a loser, largely because a deal was made with the informant to pay him reward money and dismiss felonies in exchange for his public testimony at jury trial. It was the only time I knew of a deal made with an informant for public testimony before a jury. Most of the time, informants were used only as a basis for obtaining an arrest or search warrant. Their identities remained secret, and they certainly did not testify at a public trial. Being known as a snitch is hazardous to health. I thought the deal unfortunate because I hated vouching for the credibility of such a witness before a jury. If he had good testimony about the defendant's confession to a crime, why demand a reward for it? Tell the truth and protect the innocent. But not many witnesses to street murders and rapes are deacons of the local Baptist church. I was convinced that the defendant committed the crime and would kill again if I didn't take him down, so I swallowed my qualms about using the informant's testimony and went after a conviction.

In retrospect, maybe I should have pushed my supervisors harder about not using the snitch. But if I didn't present that testimony, any conviction would probably not have been upheld on appeal. The judge might not even have let the jury deliberate without the informant's testimony.

Regardless, all of the prosecutors who handled the case through the grand jury investigation were convinced the defendant did the crime, and we were afraid of the consequence to the community if he was acquitted. I was convinced the defendant committed the crime. The so-called microscopic match between the defendant's pubic hair and the hair recovered from the rape and murder victim's body corroborated the snitch's claim that the defendant confessed the crime to him.

There are two terrible mistakes that the criminal-justice system can make. One is that an innocent man is convicted. The second is that a guilty man is acquitted. In retrospect, given that I now know the defendant was stone-cold innocent, I am afraid that I was too concerned about the second type of mistake.

Almost three decades later, when I was the legal director of the Methodist Justice Ministry, I received a call from my old office, informing me that DNA evidence had exonerated the defendant. The snitch must have lied. But that still left the hair match about which the FBI hair examiner had been so positive and aggressive at trial. Then I was told that the "science" of hair comparison, and the significance of so-called "microscopically indistinguishable" hair comparisons, had been discredited after the conviction but before the exoneration.

Comparisons of DNA from the developing national collection bank had revealed that the rapist and murderer of the victim was actually a man who worked as a janitor in the business where the young murder victim had been working before she tried to walk home.

An innocent man had served twenty-eight years in prison for a crime he did not commit. Twenty-eight years without seeing or holding a baby, or hearing a child laugh, or touching a woman, or petting a dog, or walking through a flowered field, or sitting at a café and watching lovers walk by, or drinking a beer. Twenty-eight years in fear, stoking his own anger and resentment.

We have all read about the numbers of exonerations produced by DNA, after innocent people spent years in prison for crimes they did not commit. We have all read about prosecutor's offices resisting exonerations, dragging their feet. And I fear there is a lack of concern and compassion by many of our fellow citizens for prison conditions, and for the plight of people on parole, and even for people wrongly convicted. "So what if we convict an innocent person occasionally. I'm sure that person committed crimes for which he was never charged." Why are we so sure? Because they are black or brown or poor? And why do we think it is so occasional? Because the system benefits and protects us, and we want to believe in it? Because we are empathy-impaired by the dominant narrative?

This is another impact of the distorted version of justice and mercy of our dominant narrative. Within that narrative, other people are only competitors. They are fungible and disposable. Within that narrative, we need not be concerned if we lose whole groups of people to crime, hopelessness, and violence, and even to conviction for crimes they did not actually commit. They are not due anything from us, certainly not mercy. If they cannot acquire what they need, that is their problem, not ours, and it is only just. Mercy is only occasional and optional, and for them, non-existent. Mercy for "them," those dangerous people in those suspect groups, is not "due" and is to be avoided. Who has ever been elected criminal district attorney by promising to be just *and* merciful to victims and defendants alike?

I don't know much about the family background of my wrongfully convicted defendant. (I know his name very well, I assure you. I am just not using it here to avoid causing him any more pain than I already have.) I know that he had been recently discharged from the military before he was arrested and charged with the murder. But what I am sure of is that he was homeless at the time the murder was committed by someone else. His homelessness made him vulnerable to this claim by the informant. It exposed him to many dangers—of violence, of illness and exposure, of a reduced life expectancy, of betrayal, of arrest for vagrancy or trespassing, of lack of privacy, and of prejudice against the homeless. The informant reported that the defendant was drunk in a group of homeless men at a traffic circle in DC when he allegedly confessed to the crime. Because the defendant was homeless, he had no safe, private place to drink. So he was an easy mark for the informant. If he hadn't been homeless, he wouldn't have been falsely accused of this. The defendant already had a criminal record before he was arrested and charged with the murder, and that record made it impossible for him to get into public housing or get a decent paying job so he could get off the street. He was trapped in homelessness.

Ironically, when I found out that he had been proven innocent, I had already received an advanced education into the plight of homeless people. The mayor of my city had appointed me chairperson of the homelessness commission here. The commission researched and drafted a ten-year plan to eliminate chronic homelessness in the city. I had spent time on the street and in the shelters, getting to know homeless folk and their lives. They were no longer "them" to me, to be feared, suspected, and shunned like stray dogs. "They" had become "him" and "her," Romero and Claude and Mary Beth and Maria. I learned some things. The majority of the homeless are employed. They just don't make enough to get into their own apartment. Maybe half have criminal records, which, like my innocent defendant, disqualifies them from public housing. This culture never forgets and forgives when it comes to a felony, no matter how long ago it was committed, no matter how young the person was when they made the mistake. And maybe half are homeless because of disability or disease, or addictions that could be treated if they had resources. Many people I met on the street, in the homeless shelters and in the homeless camps, had been one illness or one accident away from losing their job and being evicted. When that accident or illness came, they became homeless. When their particular disaster occurred, they had no place to go but to a homeless shelter or camp. And the longer they stayed homeless, the less likely they would ever be able to get free of it.

One of the worst prejudices in the United States is the pre-judging that whatever homeless person you encounter is lazy, a liar, a thief, and a danger. So every homeless person is to be shunned, and barriers are to be built to keep them out. One of the worst consequences of homelessness is that people will not look you in the face. The churches are among the worst at giving in to prejudice and fear about the homeless being in the same facilities where their members are. Churches that provide a ministry to the homeless will typically build or use another facility a distance away from the main church building, and hire security to keep all homeless persons out of the main church. What justice and mercy are they following? God's or the dominant narrative's?

I received the greatest of mercies from my innocent defendant, one I definitely was not "due" as a matter of justice. When I was told he was innocent, I was advised to say nothing publicly because a lawsuit was in the offing against the District and the investigating police officers. I was asked to say nothing that would embarrass my old prosecutor's office. Candor and apology were to be avoided within the dominant narrative. Certainly, I should not admit making any mistake myself. Dozens of people, no doubt out of kindness to me, told me that I had nothing to regret or apologize for. There had been no DNA back then. I was "just doing my job with the evidence I had."

It didn't feel that way to me. I was an aspiring Christian and an ordained minister of the United Methodist Church. So I wrote my innocent defendant a letter of apology and regret. I sent it to him through the attorney who had obtained his exoneration. I wrote that no words from me would be adequate given what he had suffered, but that I felt that not writing my regret and apology to him would be even worse than whatever I could say. I apologized that I had been so convinced he was guilty when he was wholly innocent. I told him that I thought at the time that I was doing my best, but that my best had proved to be a terrible failure. I asked him to forgive me but wrote that I would understand if he did not. I never expected to hear back from him. But he wrote back quickly, saying that he had forgiven me and now considered me his friend. What an amazing man!

I felt that I was due his hatred and contempt as a matter of justice. And I felt that I was surely not due the mercy of his forgiveness. But he treated me as if I was due his forgiveness and his friendship. He astonished me. How different his justice and mercy were from the justice and mercy of the dominant narrative. This extraordinary man forgave me for my part in putting him in prison for twenty-eight years for a crime he did not commit. Under the dominant narrative, I was not due this absolute, undeserved gift of forgiveness. Under the dominant narrative, he and I are merely competitors. We have no other relationship. So he could have tried to sue me as he did the investigating police officers. Why should he have let me off the hook? Why should he have cared if it would not have been just for me to be held civilly liable? A great injustice had been done to him, so perhaps it would have been a kind of "eye for an eye." Under any narrative, my innocent defendant was not due his conviction and imprisonment. And yet he showed the greatest mercy to me that I ever received. In forgiving me, he treated me like a friend and even a brother. And he rendered unto himself the justice of being merciful.

**

Later in my private practice of law, I played a very small part as a plaintiff's attorney in a bad-faith suit against an insurance company. A jury found that this company deceived its customers about legally mandated health-insurance coverage, leading to a child's permanent loss of the use of two of her limbs because legally mandated coverage for needed expensive surgery and therapy was denied by the company. At the time, health-insurance companies generally included a provision in their group health-insurance coverage policies that had the effect of excluding coverage for a birth defect of an already covered family's newborn. Their contractual coverage of the newborn would not start until the second day of an infant's life, and would not cover "pre-existing conditions," meaning conditions with which the child was born. Since, by definition, a "birth" defect is present at birth, and since the coverage didn't start until the child had turned two day's old, a birth defect was a "pre-existing condition" that went uncovered. Any care that was needed to treat that birth condition was not covered by the policy.

Imagine being a working person with health-insurance coverage through your work. Imagine being pregnant and being assured that your insurance covered the costs of your prenatal care, your labor and your delivery, and any complications you suffer. Imagine being assured that your coverage would pay for care for your newborn, just as it pays for medical care for any member of your family. The blessed day comes, and your child is born. But you learn immediately that this child has a serious birth defect and is in critical need of immediate treatment. Your little girl was born without fully formed joints in two of her limbs. Unless she started immediately with expensive surgery and then therapy, to cut and loosen the connective tissue and create joints halfway down her limbs, your little girl would never be able to use those limbs normally.

But then you are informed that your group health-insurance policy does not cover treatment for this condition because it is a birth defect, a condition pre-existing the start of the child's coverage on day two of her life. The needed treatment will costs hundreds of thousands of dollars, but you don't have the money and don't have the credit rating or collateral assets to get it. You make a little too much income to qualify for any government assistance but not nearly enough income to pay for the care yourself or secure the loan. The small window of time in which your little girl's condition can be treated effectively passes. Now her condition is permanent. Your beautiful little girl, and she is beautiful, now has sticks for limbs.

The insurance company saved millions and millions of dollars by this standard one-day delay in beginning coverage for newborns, using this standard exclusion of coverage for "pre-existing" birth defects. Families lost those same millions. Some borrowed to pay for the needed treatment and went into bankruptcy when they couldn't pay off their debts. More often, the child just failed to receive the needed treatment. The human toll to the families hit by this was enormous.

But you could only expect an insurance company to be just, to decide who was due what from the company, according to the dominant narrative. It was only just for them to follow strictly the language of their policies that had been bargained for in the marketplace. This was just business to those responsible for maximizing profits. It wasn't personal.

Why was there a bad-faith suit? Because the legislature in the state where all this occurred had passed a law before this little girl's birth, forbidding health-insurance companies from writing policies that included provisions delaying coverage of a newborn for one day and then calling birth defects excluded, pre-existing conditions. The statute declared that any such provisions were unenforceable in policies already in effect.

The family, of course, didn't know about this statute. Amazingly, neither did the adjusters and their supervisors of the health-insurance company who denied the family's claim for payment of the costs to treat their little girl's condition. Evidence at trial showed that the upper executives of the company had kept their own people in the dark about the change. So their own adjusters kept denying covered claims, thus saving the company and its stockholders lots of dollars. The evidence elicited at trial showed that the company executives in the regional headquarters had made "an administrative decision" to wait until a knowledgeable claimant confronted them with the new law forbidding the denial of coverage. They would only honor a claim when their noses were rubbed in the new law by an extraordinarily well-informed consumer.

In order to recover punitive damages, we had to prove "bad faith" in the conduct of the company and its denial of the coverage mandated by stature. "Bad faith" required more than proof of a contract violation. To paraphrase, "bad faith" required proof that the conduct was outrageous and shocking. I still recall parts of the defense argument to the trial judge, asking the judge to keep the jury from even considering the case. The defense attorney argued that this wasn't outrageous or shocking conduct. This family had not paid the increased premiums to pay their share of the increased coverage of these birth defects. The family had received all that was due them, all that was just, based upon the premiums they had actually paid. Indeed, it wasn't just for them to enjoy the benefits of any coverage if they hadn't paid for it. Their premium amounts had been determined as if birth defects were not covered. The company couldn't financially comply with the new statutes and stay solvent. The company disobeyed the new law temporarily and had corrected its mistake when it had been caught. This family had all the legal remedies they could justly ask for—reimbursement of their actual, out-of-pocket expenses to treat the condition—without punitive damages. It wasn't the company's fault that this family failed in its duty to obtain that treatment or that the parents were uninformed consumers. The claims adjusters were guilty of no more ignorance of the new law than the parents were. Wasn't it up to the family to call it to the attention of the adjuster? What the company had made was merely a business mistake that violated one small law of the state insurance code. At most, it was merely an illegal business decision; it wasn't an unjust or outrageous one.

Underlying that argument, and the conduct of this company, was the same version of justice, of what is due to whom from whom, of the dominant narrative. It was up to that poor family to win the *agón* with the insurance company, to "get" the coverage, to kill the coverage so they could eat it. Since the family had failed to force the company to provide it, they didn't win the competition. So they weren't due the coverage. It was an argument remarkable for its candor.

For the company executives, what they claimed was "due" to this family was completely divorced from mercy, from the human toll of what they were claiming. To them, this suffering family, with this little girl, weren't neighbors, weren't members of the same community. They were competitors trying to win some of the company's money. I feel certain that many of these executives were nominal Christians. Some, at the least, likely attended church on Easter and Christmas. Many may have worshipped faithfully, tithed, and considered themselves devout "Bible believers." But I cannot discern how their beliefs and the teachings of Torah and the prophets and Jesus impacted the cold, detached, unjust, and merciless way they treated this and so many families.

A large part of it was the dominant narrative and its version of justice and mercy. Good people entered the corporate board room, the belly of the dominant narrative, and removed their faith like it was a dirty shirt. They were probably kind and supportive to one another, caring and considerate of the secretaries and administrators who worked for them, gentle to their spouses and children and elderly parents. But professionally, they were predators. And the feeling they surely had deep in their souls where the image of God dwelled, that what they were doing was unjust and merciless and just plain wrong, was killed by the dominant narrative. But I still wonder, while they were carrying out this scheme to save the company money and maintain profits for the shareholders, did they ever picture, did they ever worry about, the suffering families whose anguish this scheme was increasing?

One of the great enemies in this story is role ethics. A role ethic is a set of standards and behaviors that is justified only by the role the actor is playing. For instance, it is wrong to tie a helpless person to a gurney, bind his arms and legs, stick needles in him, open a curtain to allow people who hate him and want him dead to watch him die, and then inject poison into his veins until his heart stops. But it supposedly is not wrong, according to role ethics, if you are an executioner. Then, you are just doing your job. For further instance, it is wrong to invite an injured person to describe her injury in a way that is not anatomically possible, so that the injured person will lose a lawsuit and suffer loss of benefits. But, according to role ethics, it is supposedly not wrong to do this if you are an attorney "representing your client zealously but within the bounds of the law." And according to role ethics, it is evidently not wrong for a vice president of an insurance company (and I know plenty of honorable vice presidents who would not have engaged in this conduct) to carry out a scheme to withhold information about coverage of birth defects from suffering families until they discover it for themselves. It's just business. The role ethics we follow grows from the dominant narrative and its version of justice and mercy.

We are under pressure by the dominant narrative to divide our lives into silos. In this silo, the business silo, we operate under the dominant narrative that teaches that what is due to people is only what they can take from us, with mercy as a non-player. In this other silo, the silo of our relations with family and friends, our family and friends are due love and nurture and generosity from us. In this other silo, the solo of our occasional encounters with the poor and the outcast . . . well, we try to avoid that silo. And in this other silo is the church and Scripture. Maybe we hear a great sermon and respond by contributing a bit of our surplus to a mission to Kenya. Maybe we actually aspire for a moment to be poor in spirit, meek, merciful, pure in heart, just, peacemaking. Maybe we even resolve for just a moment to serve God and not wealth. But then we get home, and even on the drive home, we enter again into the many silos of the dominant narrative, and we are drowned by advertising for the stuff we must have to be valuable and happy people, and we get to the workplace and find that the meek inherit the dirt, not the earth.

The judge and the jury saw through the arguments and defenses of the company. The family and that precious little child were awarded damages. To me, the jury essentially found the company guilty for obeying the teachings of the dominant narrative. Within the world created by the dominant narrative, that little girl was due only what she could take from that company. The rules of the corporate competition dictated that the executives in that company maximize the profits and minimize the loses. That rule of corporate competition, produced by the dominant narrative, trumped the statute. Honoring that family's claim would have been a loss.

Justice? Did that beautiful little girl receive what she was due? Well, from whom? And when? I'm certain that that little girl, grown now into a woman, would trade all that money for the ability to be able to play with her own children like a normal mom.

As this suit was ongoing, insurance companies were lobbying Congress to eliminate such bad-faith lawsuits against health-insurance companies in state courts, to force claimants into arbitration and to free insurance companies from the justice meted out by outraged jurors. In other words, they sought to change the rules of the game this one company hadn't followed in this case anyway.

**

After one semester in seminary, I was appointed to a dying United Methodist church in one of the poorest neighborhoods of my city.

Two of the first people I met there I'll call "Lupe" and "Sonia." Lupe was an eight year old girl. Her mother was in prison on a long sentence for drugs. I don't think Lupe knew who her father was, but I may recall that incorrectly. In any event, he wasn't in her life and he didn't contribute anything for her. Lupe was raised by her maternal grandfather. I'll call him "Bert." They lived about a quarter mile from my church, on the other side of a busy four-lane street lined with bars and pay-day loan shops and immigration *abogados* and *notarios*. Bert and Lupe lived on a dead-end road that wasn't paved, that wasn't even graveled, and that became impassable when it rained. Not many city councilpersons ever drove down that street. The house that Lupe and her "Grandad" lived in had holes where many of the window frames should have been. There was junk scattered in the front and back yards. Rats lived in the junk. There wasn't much distinction between the inside and the outside of the house, in terms of clutter or temperature, although it was a little dryer inside when it rained. Bert sometimes couldn't afford the utility bills, so the house was too often without electricity and running water.

I had seen bad living conditions when I was on the street in DC; I had never seen anything like this.

Bert loved Lupe, and he was all she felt she had. Her mother had been in her life only in spurts, just long enough to get high and get busted again. The only woman really in her life was her aunt "Sonia," who had her own issues and who could also be in and out.

Bert was a drunk. I am not calling him anything he didn't call himself. Bert was disabled by alcohol. When I drove by his house early some mornings, he usually already had an open beer in his hand. He was overweight and wheezing, and I worried he had an illness he would transmit to Lupe. The total of his income was from food stamps for Lupe, a little bit of social security disability, and the sale of junk. He didn't have many expenses. He certainly didn't spend much on rent.

Maybe the worst aspect of Lupe's living conditions was her sleeping "accommodations." She slept in the living room downstairs on the couch. There were bedrooms upstairs, but the stairway had collapsed. Lupe had no sheets. She had only a sleeping bag. She had a pillow with no pillowcase. Every time I brought Bert sheets and pillowcases for Lupe, they walked away. I suspected that he sold them. Or they were stolen by his houseguests.

I first met Lupe at the elementary school close to my little church. We had started an after-school boys club and an after-school girls club run by some beautiful (in every sense) young women who had been on the staff of my old law firm to tutor, mentor, and encourage the boys and girls, and to try to discourage them from joining their older brother's street gangs or to give into the pressures of drugs and crime and sex. I got to know the principal and the faculty of the school well. I was in the school a lot. The principal introduced me to Lupe and asked for my help. He said he had nowhere else to turn.

The problem he asked me to help with was Lupe's chronic head lice. The school's understandable rule was that a child discovered with head lice was sent right home and not allowed to return to class until inspection by the school nurse proved the lice were all gone. Head lice are very friendly creatures. They like to make the acquaintance of every child they can.

But the school couldn't just send a child walking home alone, particularly a child-like Lupe who would have to cross alone a very busy,

four-lane, city street. And Bert didn't have a phone. His truck was chronically broken down. Plus, the school was uphill from his house, and he
had a serious breathing issue. So Lupe would be quarantined all alone in
a lice room at the school until it was time to go home. Then she would be
told not to return until Bert had eliminated the lice with a lice shampoo
and by picking out all of the lice nits one by one from her hair.

The other children made fun of Lupe mercilessly. Her clothes were
always dirty and rumpled, her hair was matted and unwashed, her socks
never matched. She was short and overweight. And she had lice. They
shunned her company, even on the playground. Yet Lupe was so sweet
and desperate for friendship and affection. It was heartbreaking.

I talked to Bert about the lice. He immediately got angry. He couldn't
afford "the goddamn shampoo." He didn't have the time or the eyesight
or the lighting (or the sobriety) to pick all the nits out. He was sure that
Lupe wasn't getting the lice from his house. It must be from the other kids
at that school.

"Well, Bert, if you aren't using the shampoo and picking out the nits
one by one, what are you doing?"

He said he was spraying WD-40 on her pillow.

I'm not making up a syllable of this.

I obtained a signed paper from Bert allowing me to take Lupe from
the school to my church to shampoo her hair and pick out the nits.
Whenever she had lice, the school was to call me about it, not Bert. We
purchased a supply of lice-killing shampoo, some tweezers and a bright
flashlight. A woman church member would always come to the church to
help when I called. It was a weekly battle. Lupe was so grateful.

Yet there were greater concerns about Lupe's living situation. Bert's
residence was something of a gathering place for men of like lifestyle.
They were all drunk most of the time I went by. One consolation was that
there didn't seem to me to be any hard-drug use. Some of these men were
not old. Lupe was very vulnerable. And she was guileless.

One woman of the church took Lupe under her wing. Her name was
"Virginia." If it had been up to Virginia, she would have adopted Lupe.
Lupe was spending many nights at Virginia's home, which was modest
but very clean and a palace compared to Bert's place. It was a palace of
welcome and love by any standard. Lupe was begging Bert to let her stay
overnight with Virginia more and more. And Virginia was trying to teach
Lupe how to be a young lady, including what to avoid and when to make
an outcry.

Bert became suspicious. He forbade Virginia from having any more contact with Lupe. Virginia was putting ideas in her head. She was making Lupe dissatisfied with Bert's home. Bert surely loved his granddaughter Lupe. But he couldn't survive without the food stamps he received for her. Bert declared that Lupe could no longer stay the night with Virginia.

Virginia came to me at the church in tears, telling me what Bert had decreed. In a few moments I wish I could relive, I stormed down to Bert's house, confronted him, told him angrily that he should be grateful for Virginia's involvement and demanded that he take back his ban. He started cursing at me. I accused him of being afraid of losing Lupe's food stamps. I reminded him that I had asked him and asked him to improve her sleeping situation and to get the drunks out of his house. And then I said the forbidden phrase: "If you don't let Virginia help you with Lupe, I'm calling CPS on you."

That was the end. Bert cut off all contact between Lupe and me, Virginia and anyone at the church. The school was ordered not to allow us to speak to her. I called CPS. He moved Lupe to another house almost overnight.

I actually never saw Lupe again.

And her aunt Sonia?

Sonia was Lupe's mother's sister.

I first heard about Sonia when her two children, one about thirteen and one about six, showed up at the church one night. I can still picture them standing in the outside doorway of my office. We had a church full of children there, providing food and tutoring. Sonia's two children were standing together, holding hands. They looked embarrassed and anxious.

The thirteen year old girl said they had heard about the church from Lupe. And she started crying. Her mother Sonia had run away. She was on drugs again. She had been gone for days, and she and her brother had run out of things to eat. Could I help?

I offered to buy them some food and to take them where they needed to go. They had walked a long way from their rented house to the church.

"Thank you for the food," they said. "But we really hope that you will help us bring her home."

They thought they knew where she was.

I surely hadn't been taught how to look for a lost drug addict in law school or in seminary. But I had in the U.S. Attorney's Office.

It was about 8:30 at night. The children got into my car, the girl in the front passenger seat and the boy in the back. The girl directed me to a house only four blocks away from my church. It was a single story, clapboard residence with a tall, wrought-iron fence around it, the only fence like that in the neighborhood. The gate was chained with a padlock. The girl and boy started to get out.

"Wait. Tell me first what we are doing here."

The girl said that the house was owned by an old man who manufactured and sold methamphetamine there. And he exchanged meth for sex with women like their mother. They had found their mom there in the past. The children told me this in a matter-of-fact manner. Of course they knew about such things. What thirteen- and six-year-old children do not?

"You think we can just walk through that gate? It looks locked to me."

"He'll let me in," said the girl.

"Why?"

"Because he wants to f*** me." She was thirteen years old.

"That's why you brought me along, to protect you?"

"No, we brought you along because you're a lawyer."

"What good is that?"

"You can threaten to have him locked up if he doesn't let her go?"

I passed over her mistake about what my kind of lawyer can do.

"Why do you think she is in there?"

"We were here before, and he wouldn't tell us whether she was or wasn't. He's never refused to tell us before. So we think she is there. Or she has been."

"You've been through this with your mom and this old man before?"

"Yes."

All three of us walked to the gate, and the girl leaned on the buzzer. Eventually, we could see a light in a window where a curtain parted. Then the front door opened in, behind a barred outer door.

"Who's that with you?" called an old man's voice.

"My lawyer," called the girl.

"Sir, I am just the pastor of the Methodist church a few blocks from here. These children came to me because they are worried that their mother is in your house. She hasn't been home for a while. Can you tell them whether she is in there?"

"So you ain't a lawyer?"

"I am a lawyer. But I am here as a pastor to help these children."

"Long way from a f***ing courthouse, ain't you? Long way from your church, too."

"Will you let us through this gate so we can talk without yelling?"

"This ought to be good," he said. "Preacher, you got a lot to learn about this neighborhood."

He let us through. He retreated to the porch and stood in the open door to his house. There was no porch light, and I could barely see him in the dark of the doorway.

"Is she here or not?" asked the girl?

"No."

"Has she been here in the last few days?"

"What's that matter?"

The four of us were standing at the door, when the little boy burst by the man and ran into the house crying, "Momma, Momma, are you here?" The old man started to run in after him, cursing. He turned around and said to me, "If you come in here, I'll shoot you."

The old man came back, dragging the boy by the hair. The boy was kicking at him. "She's not in here," the boy said.

"Has she been here in the last few days?" I asked him again. "Do you know where she might be?"

"Get off my property right now or I'll be the one calling the police."

"No you won't," I said. "You aren't going to invite the police anywhere near your property. I can smell what you are cooking in there from this door."

"Git," he said. "You come back here, and you'll get a face full of buckshot," and slammed the door.

A few years later, that old man threatened a clerk with a billy club at a convenience store near the man's house. The clerk shot him dead. No charges were brought against the clerk. The police and the entire neighborhood thought the old man needed killing.

After we left the old man's house that night, the girl asked me to drive them to a dilapidated motel on a main thoroughfare not far away. By now it was about ten at night.

"There's a man there who mom sometimes does coke with," she said.

"How do you know this?"

"She's my momma. I know." She was thirteen years old.

The exterior of the motel was made of scarred, peeling white stucco. There was an office in the middle of the entrance to the parking lot. Behind that in a horseshoe shape were six shacks with two rooms in each of them. The girl directed me to turn off my lights and to drive behind the office shack and stop. Then she got out of my car and crept up beside one of the shacks, peering in a side window. She came running back to the car.

"She's in there! She's lying on the bed. I don't see no one else in there."

The little boy jumped out of the back seat. He ran up to the door to the motel room and began pounding on it. "Momma, Momma! Open up! It's me! Come home, momma! Please come home! Please!"

This went on for some minutes with no response. A light came on in the motel office and the rooms all around. The girl went back to the side window and tried to pull open the screen and window and crawl in. Just then, the motel room door jerked open.

"I'm coming, dammit. You don't have to wake the dead."

It seemed like we just had.

During the years to come, I really got to know Sonia. Bert was her father. She had a brother and a sister, both of whom were in prison for drugs. Sonia was the oldest sibling. Her mother was diagnosed with breast cancer when Sonia was eleven. Bert was already an alcoholic, and the mother was the only steady wage earner in the family. And she bought Bert his beer. When the mother died when Sonia was twelve, the family went hungry and went through multiple evictions. Bert was grieving, still drinking, already lung sick, and still useless. When Sonia was thirteen, she turned to prostitution to support the family. She had barely started menstruating. At first, she was dating high school guys who paid for sex at the end of the date. Then it was picking up drunks in bars and taking them to a flophouse motel next door. Then she found a pimp who brought johns to her at that motel. That way she didn't have to talk to them and pretend to seduce them. Sonia got pregnant when she was fifteen with the daughter who knocked on my door. Sonia knows that her daughter's father was a john. She just doesn't know which one or what his name might be. No names were ever shared.

Sonia found solace, anesthesia really, in harder and harder drugs. She was subject to bouts of depression, which just shows she had a good grasp of the reality of her situation. Oddly, she avoided a significant criminal record. The main reason that she had stayed out of prison was that she was never on probation. All her convictions were for prostitution, for which she had to do only a few days in county jail. If she had ever been placed on probation, she would have been drug tested regularly, and her use would have been detected and punished.

Sonia was a complicated, compelling person. Mean and vulnerable, hard to the world and tender to her children when she was straight and sober, grateful and sullen, all at the same time. She would resolve to make a better life, and actually live a better life for long periods. But a life that started where hers had could only get so much "better." Then she would sink back into doubt and self-contempt, and sabotage herself and her children with her. Like she was doing the night I met her at that flea-bag motel. "Heaven on Earth," that motel was named. Maybe if you are high enough.

Sonia was actually very bright. She was uneducated but not at all stupid. When you couldn't keep up with what she was saying, she could turn belittling. She could be loyal and even forgiving. But she better not catch you pitying her, or looking down your nose at her, or assuming that you thought you knew when she was about to sabotage herself again, or she would cloud up and storm on you, and then she actually would leave.

And what she really did not want you to do was to ask her to consider how unlucky she had been and what a bad hand life had dealt her. "I've had enough cards, she would say. My cards just look bad to some people because I was the one playing them. What if I had been ugly or fat and no one wanted to screw me for money? Then my whole family would'a been out on the street." She was convinced that everybody had made as many mistakes as she had, just different kinds of mistakes. It was one of her ways of defending herself from feeling defective. God, I liked her.

The rest of this story is tragically predictable. After the rescue at Heaven on Earth, she agreed to enter a twenty-eight day rehab program provided by the county. I still can picture the two of us standing outside the entrance on the second floor, holding hands and praying. Then she went in for her fourth inpatient rehab stay. I felt like I'd finally gotten something accomplished in my ministry. It was still pretty much about me in the early days. Probably still is. I hope it still isn't.

After Sonia cleaned up, I found her a job as a file clerk in a small company. The owner was a good friend of mine and a Christian and wanted to help. We bought her some clothes at Target so she could fit in. We found her an apartment with a rent she could afford, helped with the security deposit and procured some nice used furniture. Her daughter was so very happy and appreciative. Her son was having real issues in his new school, fighting almost every day. How could it have been otherwise? His teacher was understanding, but the principal wouldn't tolerate it. The son was suspended indefinitely. Sonia then had to come up with more money for child care or let the boy stay home alone. She didn't even tell me about the problem at first. She seemed to me to be doing well, so I had moved on to trying to help other people.

Her daughter, who was then fifteen, called me one Sunday morning between worship services at my church. Her mom had run away again. It felt as if the devil were laughing at me. But things have been going so well, I said. So what, she asked, weary beyond her years.

I went on a search for Sonia all day and night that Sunday, hitting all of her former drug haunts. I flushed her out of one. She got away from me, because she was willing to drive a lot more dangerously than I was. She drove as if she were terrified of my catching her. As if I were the problem rather than the drugs. As if this was something I thought she had done to *me*, ruining one of *my* success stories. And she didn't want to be one of my stories any longer. Maybe she understood me better than I did. I left a note on a drug-house door, convinced she was hiding inside, a note that lectured her for giving into the demons of her past. Like I knew.

The next night, I found out that her fifteen-year-old daughter was pregnant. The devil was laughing some more. So it felt. And I don't really believe in the devil. But whether or not the devil exists doesn't depend upon whether I believe it. What I do believe is that believing in the devil just takes God and us off the hook for the broken way things are.

I wondered if Sonia would try to come back to work at the insurance company. I wanted to make some lame excuse to the employer, in case she would try. He told me that she had stormed out of the job on the day she ran away from her children. I think I remember that he told me that she broke something out of anger. Then she stomped out. I asked if he knew what brought that on. He confessed that he was telling Sonia's immediate supervisor about her background, about what she had been through, her past prostitution and drug use, how hard her life had been. He was telling her supervisor so he would be understanding and gentle with her. But some other employee overhead what was intended to be a private conversation. This employee told one person and then it spread the way things like that will. Sonia heard some whispering behind her back. How could she stay there? It made her feel small and strange and broken. She wouldn't be pitied. She wouldn't be judged. My friend was very remorseful this had happened. But he couldn't let her come back.

After that, I decided that I had made things worse by being so aggressive, that I had to wait for her to approach me for help. After months passed, I went looking for her again. I found the house where she and the children were staying. The daughter came to the door and apologized but said that Sonia didn't want to talk to me or see me ever again. If I didn't leave, Sonia would call the police.

The daughter looked really pregnant.

I did hear from Sonia, but years and years later. She telephoned me from another state. She told me that her daughter was trying to have her civilly committed. I told her that I wasn't licensed to practice law in that state and couldn't help. I wondered if she had indeed sunk deeply into mental illness. I was surprised to hear that she was still alive. I asked more about her. I asked about Lupe. But when I told Sonia I couldn't help her fight the civil commitment, she hung up. When I called her back at the number on my cell phone call register, she wouldn't answer. She still won't.

**

The dominant narrative is all about getting certain things accomplished, certain things acquired. Activities have to be useful. You have to kill something to be able to eat it or you are wasting your time. People aren't due anything if they aren't getting things acquired that they want acquired. Under this narrative, it's a terrible waste of energy and focus to try to salvage someone who has disappointed again and again, no matter their reasons. They are just competitors or tools, you know. Or they are opponents or means to your end. People are not due mercy within this narrative, and a tiny part of the reason for this is that mercy is so damned inefficient and unproductive.

What was Lupe due? Not from government. What was she due from life? What was she due from the Christians who just walked on by her as she lay by the side of the road, having been beaten by life. Under the dominant narrative, nothing was due to her that she couldn't get on her own. Certainly not mercy. She was just one of the millions of children in this country who are trapped in poverty and hopelessness, who are effectively abandoned by parents who were effectively abandoned themselves. Parents who continue to abandon themselves. These children are considered to be "due" nothing from us except maybe a free public education, food stamps, and Medicaid. And most of us don't feel Lupe was due anything from us personally. Virginia tried, and Lupe's life defeated Virginia as well. I tried.

Maybe all we accomplished was to make Lupe feel, for a little while, that she was worth loving, that she was due protection. But in retrospect, I think that I was too intent upon fixing Sonia's and Lupe's lives. I was too hopeful that their lives could be fixed. I was too much about my accomplishing this.

I don't want to forget Lupe. I don't want to forget Sonia. I don't want to forget Sonia's children. What chance did any of them have to heal from their wounds? Summon up your empathy for a little girl who could depend upon the presence in her life of only one person, her granddad, who was utterly undependable in every other way. And for Sonia's children, who never knew whether their mother was coming home at the end of the day or whether she would sink back into the escape of drugs.

I can't condemn Sonia, even as the dominant narrative tells me to condemn, dismiss, and forget her. I can't blame her for any aspect of her plight. Yes, she repeatedly buried herself in the same grave. But she was born deep in it. Yes, she got out just a little but crawled right back in, and got out and crawled back in, and so on. And she pulled her children in with her. Down deep as she could get into her own heart and soul, she just didn't believe that she was due being anywhere else except that grave. Within the dominant narrative, she was due nothing. To try to be merciful to her was a waste of scarce resources and time. The same as with Lupe and Sonia's children.

But, as with Lupe, maybe just for a time Sonia realized how much I thought of her, that to me she was an infinitely valuable human being, that I loved her, and that she was and is due love. Under the counter-narrative of Jesus, the fruit that this may or may not bear is not up to me. It's up to God and Sonia. But under the counter-narrative of Jesus, loving and feeling loved are in themselves the greatest of fruits and the greatest of mercies. No mercy is ever wasted.

✳✳

Raul Gutierrez (his actual name) is the brother I never had. He was a fellow student in seminary. After a year, he joined me as co-pastor of the inner-city church. Raul was born in a house with a dirt floor in Zacatecas, Mexico. He came to the U.S. as a boy with his father, an evangelical preacher. Raul became a U.S. citizen and graduated from college and then seminary here. He is, of course, bilingual. I was a lawyer and minister with some connections to the inner circles and the money downtown. We were like the separate ends of a bridge. Working with him in that hard neighborhood was the best time in ministry I ever expect to have. Raul is Christian to the marrow. He had such love and understanding for our neighbors. He didn't have to try. Love and understanding just bubbled and poured out of him. To Raul, justice is like breathing in, and mercy is like breathing out.

As I have written, our little church was close to an elementary school. Raul and I would meet at the church early in the morning to talk and plan. Then we would drive together to our seminary in the next city. One morning when winter was just hitting, we drove out of the church and beside the school playground. We saw dozens of children playing before school without winter coats and shoes in a biting, cold wind.

"What if?" we started. What if we could raise the money to buy new winter coats and shoes for the children whose families just couldn't afford them, for the children who would otherwise go without? By the time we returned to the church from classes that afternoon, we had talked out the plan. It would take maybe 150 coats and about the same number of pairs of shoes. We could approach a huge outlet to see if we could get them at cost. As a non-profit and a church, we wouldn't have to pay sales tax. We could rely upon the teachers at the school to identify for us which children would actually go without coats and winter shoes and to provide to us with their sizes. Then we would have a list of names and sizes for each class. We would buy the total number of coats and shoes needed in each size. We would put the child's name on each coat and pair of shoes. We would bag the coats and shoes for each class. The teachers would hand them out. This would strengthen the relationship between the teacher and the child. We could involve our church members in the buying and the sorting. All planned out.

We just didn't have the money.

Again, I am not making up a syllable of this.

We walked into the church when we got back from seminary. Our boys and girls clubs were about to begin, and we had English as a Second Language and tutoring classes in the church building that night. Raul and I were the only church employees, so no one else was in the church when we entered. We had an old telephone answering machine, the type with a cassette. The message light was blinking. I hit the button to listen.

The voice message was of a remarkable man of the highest character with whom I had gone to high school. I'll call him "Morris." I don't think

I had talked to him for years. Morris was very successful in business. He was also extremely and sacrificially supportive of programs that would help children from economically poor families get out of their graves. He was director of the charitable foundation founded by a local professional athlete. Through the foundation, the athlete and Morris made charitable contributions to programs that helped poor children in need. There had been an article in the local newspaper recently about what we were trying to do at the church for poor children in our neighborhood. Morris's voice on the recorder said that the foundation was making an unsolicited $15,000 contribution to the church for our children's programs. This call came the very same day the idea of the coats and shoes had first occurred to Raul and me. The. Very. Same. Day.

The donation paid for the coats and shoes. In the mind of that neighborhood, our church became the place you came for help. We would regularly see families driving by in their torn-up cars and trucks, pointing at the church. See. That's the church. Those are the people. Once an eight year old I hadn't met before came to see me at the church. Someone had told him that he was surely going to hell because he had vandalized a car. I told him he was not. Then I asked him why he was asking me. "Because everyone says you know Jesus."

This out-of-the-blue, God-is-good donation of the $15,000 is a wonderful, heartwarming example of the mercy of exceptional people like Morris and the athlete within the dominant narrative I am so critical of here. Many would say it was a vindication of the system and rebuttal of my criticisms.

And there are so many effective charitable foundations funded and directed by the leading beneficiaries and advocates of the dominant narrative. Foundations started with a family's wealth, and beacons of hope within the general mercilessness of the dominant narrative. My Methodist Justice Ministry receives contributions from three of these foundations now.

But there is just not enough of this generous mercy, *which takes nothing away* from the generosity of the people who are so merciful. Are there not still millions of children trapped in poor neighborhoods? I am not writing here about governmental programs to deal with the issues of inequality and poverty, drugs and violence, and the breakdown of the family. Too many people who are in favor of such governmental programs fail to be generous with their own personal assets and abilities. Here, I am asking why, out of the billions of dollars in aggregate fortune of all the

Christians in America, so little is shared by them with the poor and the suffering, why so little mercy is bestowed by them when compared to their total resources?

The reason is not just our sinfulness.

The reason is the dominant narrative that resonates with our sinfulness and that Christians have allowed to trump Jesus' teachings about justice and mercy. One of the main messages of the gospel is, "Be not afraid." We are all made so afraid within the world of the dominant narrative that we won't have enough, no matter how much we have, that we are driven to obtain more and more to keep our fears from coming true. Certain news media are dedicated to convincing the most privileged, protected people in history that we are victims, that we are vulnerable, that we have to hang on to everything we can acquire as protection from "them" and that "they" are trying to take what is ours. Politicians who appeal to our fears are rarely defeated. Many news media and businesses find that fear is a growth industry. Yet Jesus says, "Be not anxious." Who are we going to believe, Jesus or the forces selling fear by this dominant narrative?

Without taking anything at all from the generosity of this donation, we need to ask why those children needed the donations of the coats and shoes. It was because their hardworking parents weren't paid high enough wages at their full-time jobs to be able to provide for their children's basic needs. It was because the dominant narrative claims to value hard work and claims that hard work is the main criteria by which we determine what is due to people, but doesn't value hard work enough to pay a living wage to hard workers. Why don't we? We don't because we have been sold the fear that "we" won't have enough, or as much as we want, if "they" have enough for basic necessities. Why does this constitute justice within the dominant narrative? Because within this *agón*, a person is due whatever they can get and not due what they cannot. So it was a matter of justice, says the system in the way it actually operates, that these children needed the mercy of these good men. This mercy was needed, but not due, because justice said that they were due no more than they had.

There is much more dignity when a child, woman, or man receives what is due them, as opposed to what is not due but donated. And one of the greatest dignities comes when parents can provide for their children through their own respected, hard work at fair-paying jobs.

**

We had a plague of gang violence in the neighborhood of the church. Rival gangs of males in their teens and early twenties. The gangs named themselves with three letters. *Barrio* in Spanish translates to neighborhood in English. And because *barrio* in Spanish is pronounced as if it were *varrio*, the first letter of the gang name was always a "V." So the gangs running our neighborhood were called "VDH" and "VRI" and "VMS," with lots of gang tags on walls.

There was a time when a new member's initiation into a gang would require him to drive the neighborhood with his vehicle headlights on bright and then to shoot at any car whose driver blinked their lights back at him. Then gang members started driving up to a rival gang member's home in the dead of night to shoot it up. One night a woman who had come to our church for food was killed as she lay sleeping in her bed, more than twenty bullets pouring through her house, one bullet hitting her in the head. Her son was a member of a rival gang. In retaliation for her murder, another home was shot up.

Members of our church led a demonstration march through the rival neighborhoods, trying to en-*courage* people to join in the protest and speak out against this random violence. Children were afraid to go to sleep in their own beds, but adults were still afraid to speak out for fear of retaliation. And people were afraid to tell the police who they knew was doing the shooting.

We worked with the local police gang unit to try to get people who knew the gunmen to confide in the police. Because the church had been providing free food, clothing, and financial assistance and even free legal advice to many families of the gang members, we were able to sit down separately with the leaders of each gang to appeal to them to stop putting innocent people in their cross-fire.

Then came the most extraordinary evening I have ever witnessed take place in any church. I had a good friend who was an attorney and a professional mediator. His tactic in lawsuit mediations was to talk and talk until the eyes of the parties rolled back in their heads and they would make concessions to get him to stop talking. I'm only kidding about that a little. But he was also a legendary, golden glove, heavy-weight boxer. Partly because he was the attraction, one winter's night about twenty members of both rival gangs met in my church's fellowship hall and hammered out some rules of engagement.

It was the most extraordinary night.

One of the ways that we persuaded the young men to attend was to promise them that the police would not be there. Some of these men had warrants out for their arrest, and some had not yet been identified by the police as gang members. But within thirty minutes of the young men's arrivals, through separate entrances, the police gang squad burst through the door. My lawyer, mediator, ex-golden gloves champion friend walked calmly up to the officers and asked, "You got a warrant?" "No," one of the police said. So I said to them, "You aren't welcome here tonight. I promised these young men you wouldn't be here. Don't turn me into a liar." And the officers left, muttering. They went outside and started writing down the license numbers of the vehicles the young men had come in. I went outside. "Please don't do that. Not tonight." They left.

During the meeting, we saw a lot of posturing, what the gangs called mad dogging, among the members. Lots of insults and history and threats of revenge. Lots of cursing and insults in street Spanish that my friend and I didn't understand. The gang members were sitting in folding chairs next to opposite walls. One young man would say something inflammatory. Everyone at the opposite wall would jump up and threaten to walk out, and then everyone on the original side would jump up and make for the door. And my friend and I would get in between them, and block and plead and coax and push them back to their chairs. And then my friend would start taking and talking, and their eyeballs would roll back in their heads.

But they listened. What they heard is what they already knew and the reason they came. Their mothers, their sisters, and brothers were afraid in their beds. They all wanted the shootings into darkened houses in the dead of night to stop.

So the gangs reached an agreement. From then on, if any gang member wanted to shoot a rival gang member? He would have to call him out, meet him face to face, and shoot it out in a place where no one else could be hurt. Anything else would be cowardly. Families and family neighborhoods were no-fire zones. No more collateral damage.

Consider. In a church of Jesus of Nazareth, the Prince of Peace, we worked out an agreement not that the violence would stop and that these men would see one another as brothers with so much in common, but only that there would be no more shooting of innocents.

One of the strangest events of the night happened at the end of the meeting when everyone was leaving. The young man who was the most feared of all of the young men there had said nothing throughout the meeting. But then he spoke up as we were having one gang leave completely before the other. "Anybody messes with this church or hurts the priest or his friend answers to me personally," he announced to everyone there. "No one is going to hurt them," a leader of the other gang answered. Priest? Who was that? Then it hit me. The priest was me. They came from Roman Catholic families. So I was a priest. As much violence as they had committed, they were still capable of respecting the church of Jesus. They appreciated what the church was trying to do. They saw Jesus behind it.

The shootings between the gangs tailed off for a time, but then picked back up. But no more noncombatants were shot. We had no more shooting into darkened houses, no more gang initiations at the expense of innocent people. A very small step tending toward the kingdom of God.

The police gang unit complained to their commander that my friend and I obstructed justice in keeping them out of the meeting. These officers believed that a peaceful neighborhood would result simply from locking up every gang member. They were mistaken about that. For every gang member they locked up, another would be spawned by the smashed hopes produced by the dominant narrative.

The man who shot the mother lying in her bed may well have been in the church fellowship hall that night. When we asked the police to leave, we may have prevented them from identifying some gang members they had not previously made. We may have momentarily made it harder for the police to bring some of them to justice and to protect the community.

But all this depends upon how we define justice and how we decide what people are due. The man who shot the mother in her bed was due severe punishment from the criminal-justice system. But what else were the young men there due? What else were their families due?

The dominant narrative has a favorite put-down for those who aspire to be merciful. Bleeding heart. It is a phrase intended to discourage and devalue mercy. I aspire to be and have a bleeding heart. I wish my heart bled more than it does.

Why do young men join violent street gangs? Why do they subject themselves to that kind of violence? Based upon my getting to know many gang members during my time at that church, the answer lies in which young men join.

Is it young men from the inside who join? Sons of fathers who are bankers and CEOs and whose mothers are members of the Junior League? Young men who are assured of college tuition and careers in which they won't have to sweat and wear out their backs? Or even young men from lower-middle-class or even lower-class homes who still have the prospect of finding valued and adequately paying jobs? All of these already consider themselves to be "somebody." They have hope in their possibilities.

In my experience, gang members are born hopelessly off the playing field and away from the starting line of the race. These particular young men were Latino, but not merely Latino. I have met plenty of Latino young men who were born in radically different circumstances than these young men, from homes with tight families and with bright futures in professions, business or skilled trades. But the parents of these gang members were generally laborers, or shade-tree mechanics, or road-maintenance workers, or roofers, or maids, or low-wage assembly-line workers, or food-service workers, or yard men and gardeners. Their parents generally made minimum wage at insecure jobs with no health insurance. Their parents were one injury, illness or layoff away from destitution. They were hard, hard workers. But the system did not recognize and reward the value and dignity of their work. The prospects of these young men were no different than their parents' prospects. The myth is that people who are stuck in the lower classes are lazy. In my experience, this is an obscene lie told within the dominant narrative to obscure how brutally merciless the narrative is. Almost uniformly, these young men came from homes that valued hard work. It was the thwarted ambition of these young men to have a chance to be valued that led them into gangs. They saw that hard work was not going to free them from the grave of indignity and insecurity in which they were born, just as hard work hadn't freed their parents.

As I have written already, the dominant narrative is pervasive. These young men were taught multiple times each day, through TV and the radio, that a man's value is determined by what he acquires—stuff and pleasure. The car he drives, the home he lives in, the vacations he can take, the pleasures he can indulge. They are told by that narrative that a man is due what he can and does get, and not due what he cannot and does not. They are told by that narrative that a man with stuff and pleasure is a somebody and that a man without these is a nobody. They see that their fathers' experiences are generally of powerlessness, abuse and vulnerability at work, of the lowest ceiling on advancement, of a wage the family can't live on, of a body that breaks down after years of hard toil. Yet just like everyone else who is influenced by the dominant narrative, these young gang members wanted to be somebodies—respected and valued.

They want to be valued and respected members of a community, not just fungible, faceless, disposable costs of doing business, not just an economic competitor with a losing skin shade, accent, qualifications, and connections. What struck me most about the gangs themselves was what tight communities they were, almost a family. But they were communities that were mercilessly and criminally misdirected, projecting their resentments and frustrations on innocent people and on other gang members identical to themselves, assuring their own destruction and the insecurity of the neighborhood.

What are these young men due from others? According to the dominant narrative, nothing more than they were getting. In fact, they were due exactly what they were getting, no more, no less. And they aren't due any understanding or encouragement or a helping hand out of their graves. That is too much like mercy. No one is due mercy within this narrative. All they were due was the lives their parents lived and jail.

In my first story in chapter 1 of this book, I wrote about children who had little chance other than to climb on a conveyor belt of crime at the end of which was a prosecutor like I was, aiming to cage them until they were past their middle age. Here it was again.

I am not excusing the violence. There are men who are still in prison whom I put there because of their violence. But just putting violent young men one by one into prison will not stop the violence from continuing and growing from other young men born into the same merciless circumstances.

Bleeding heart. Consider closely that insult. How did we ever allow it to become an insult, even within the dominant narrative? Turning this into an insult is an attempt to discourage the mercy that the dominant narrative says is due to no one. Bleeding hearts can't run businesses and turn profits, says the dominant narrative. Bleeding hearts can't pursue progress and produce an increase in the GDP. Bleeding hearts can't defeat our nation's foes and secure our oil supplies and sea lanes. Bleeding hearts can't secure our borders and our streets. Bleedings hearts can't advance the work ethic among our class of cheap laborers. Turning bleeding heart into an insult is a transparent attempt to prevent us from seeing other people as members of a covenantal community, instead of just losers in an economic competition and beneath our concern. The prophet Isaiah wrote: "Woe to you who call evil good and good evil, who put darkness for light and light for darkness, who put bitter for sweet and sweet for bitter" (Isa 5:20). Turning into an insult having a heart that bleeds for people who are suffering and for children who are poor and born in a grave, is calling good evil, light darkness, and sweet bitter.

What are these young men due? Hope? Just prison? According to God's justice or the justice of the dominant narrative?

What are their families and neighborhoods due? The protections of the criminal justice system surely. But without ending the gang violence by giving these young men the hope and prospect of being somebody through some other avenue than gangs or the acquisition of stuff and pleasure?

**

On January 1, 2006, the Methodist Justice Ministry was founded. For more than a year, I was its only employee. My goal in starting the MJM was to be a free attorney and a pastor to indigent victims of family violence and child abuse. For the victims of violence, my hope was to obtain for them protective orders, custody orders limiting the access of the abuser to the children, and child-support orders so the victims could make new lives free of fear and violence. For abused children, my hope was to help family members or friends who would protect and nurture the children to obtain legal custody, and to provide financial and material support so these adults could care for the children.

About a year into the Justice Ministry, I obtained our first "put-out" protective order. A regular "stay away" protective order requires the abuser to remain at least 200 yards away from the residence and work place of the abused. The abuser can be held in contempt for entering that safety zone, even if he does nothing else wrong. And when the abuser lives in the abused's residence when the protective order is first granted, the court can order him "put out" of that residence, and thereafter he has to stay away.

A mother came to the Justice Ministry for help. She and her two small sons shared a house with the husband and father. The family lived in that house free of charge. The mother's parents had paid the lease for a full year.

The father was smoking crack in the house, sometimes in the same room with the two children. When the mother asked him to stop, he would slap and punch her. She said she wanted a divorce. He said she would have to move out then. He was staying put. And the sons were staying with him.

I had no difficulty obtaining the emergency *ex parte* protective order from the court, which included a provision that the man leave the residence immediately.

But putting the husband and father out was more of a challenge.

Our local sheriff's department and city police force will not execute such a put-out order. So there can be a long delay until the abuser actually gets out. The order has to be personally served upon him. Then, when he refuses to comply, a separate motion to hold him in contempt for failing to get out must be filed, a hearing on the motion has to be set, the motion and the notice of hearing has to be personally served upon him, the hearing has to held, and if he is held in contempt he will still likely to be given the chance to get out within a certain time before going to jail for willful disobedience of a court order. So an abuser can thumb his nose at the law for up to a month before he actually has to obey the original order and get out. Where was the woman to live during that period? It was just another reason for an abused woman not to turn to the law for protection.

I went to the house to serve the order on the abuser with the gentleman I was using as my processor server at that time. The good news is that he was a former U.S. deputy marshal. The not so good news was that he was in his 70s and was just returning to work from an illness. He did not carry a weapon, and I sure didn't. The man we were serving and trying to put out was 30 years old and had a number of criminal convictions for violence.

We found the man asleep in his bed. It was 4 in the afternoon. The former marshal woke him up, explained who we were and what he was being served with. The abuser cursed us and said he wasn't accepting any document and for us to get out.

I then told him that I was his wife's lawyer, that I was a free lawyer, that I was also a Methodist minister, and that my legal work was part of a ministry. I told him that I had filed divorce papers on behalf of his wife that day, that this protective order was signed by the court, and required him to get out of the house immediately and to stay at least 200 yards away or face contempt of court and jail time.

The young man got out of bed and started coming for me. "I said to get the hell out. Now I'm going to whip your and that old man's ass."

"No, you're not," I said. "You and I both know that the only people you ever whip are women." Every criminal conviction he had ever had was for assaulting a female.

He stopped dead in his tracks. He turned around and sat down on the edge of the bed. After a time, he started to cry.

"I'm nothing but a piece of shit."

"Word," I thought.

Eventually he cleared out to the curb with some of his clothes. My process server and I stood in the front yard and told him not to come any closer. He had called a family member to come get him. He was still crying and claiming that he would change his life and become a good father and husband. Then when his sister arrived to pick him up, he cursed me at the top of his lungs as they drove off.

I am not certain whether the tears and regret were genuine and the cursing was posturing for his sister, or whether the cursing was genuine and the tears and regret were posturing for me.

But my belief is that the tears and regret were really how he felt about himself down deep.

Was the loss of his family and another stint in confinement all he was due? On one level, he was due those. And his now ex-wife and his children were due a home that wasn't filled with cursing, violence, fear and crack smoke. But was that all they were due? For whom does that kind of justice work?

I have talked face to face with many abusive men over the last thirteen years. I have heard a lot of denials, a lot of resentment, and a lot of threats. But I have also heard evidence of a lot of self-hatred in them, which they project and inflict on their wives and children.

Are they due only loss of their family? Are protective orders and jail the total answer for the epidemic of family violence sweeping through the country? Are these even much of an answer?

I hope that I understand the impact and terror of family violence upon women and children as well as anyone who hasn't suffered it. These men must be held accountable for their conduct. In many cases, they were not held accountable soon enough by their own parents and even by law enforcement. Accountability is a form of mercy for the abused and can be a form of mercy for the abuser. Without accountability, there is no mercy for an abuser and no chance that he will become the kind of man he ought to be. But what he is due, to be made a better person, a person who is merciful to his family and to himself, is much more than the punishment that the dominant narrative would provide.

**

So many times in the last thirteen years with the Methodist Justice Ministry, we have convinced a judge to deny fathers any contact with their children because of repeated and unreformed abusiveness, untreated mental illness, and alcohol and drug abuse. In most of those cases, that man had witnessed as a boy another man abusing his mother and had even been abused himself. And he had been taught in a lost subculture that the tests of a man are control, abuse and violence. So many abusive men feel so impotent in their work and in their place in the society that they claim potency and value in their lives, assert that they are somebodies, by terrorizing their innocent partners and children. Home with their families feels like the one place that they can wield the dominance that the dominant narrative teaches is valuable. So often their anger and projected dissatisfactions with themselves, coupled with addiction and mental illness, get out of control. The lives of these men have often been tragic and manifestly unjust, inflicting wounds upon them that they were not due. So the boy becomes the father of the man.

I am not excusing the terrible conduct. We try to protect the women and the children. Much less is the woman due the terrible abuse received from the wounded man to whom she should be able to look most for love, support, and protection. And even less are the children due this violent home. So the justice of denying the father any access to the family is a kind of mercy to the woman and children as well. But human justice and mercy rarely fit together that neatly. Most often, the children still love the father deeply and have an almost inexhaustible capacity and urge to forgive him. They feel a hole in their lives when even an abusive father is taken away. Often the children believe deep in their minds and souls that they, the children, are somehow to blame for the violence and exile of the dad. And the mother loses the man to help in at least some parenting needs, which can be a particularly huge loss to a poor, working mother. Mercy might give the man another chance, albeit regulated. But is he due that chance as a matter of justice, after his failed second and third chances, and his unhealed, or at least untreated, underlying issues? How are we to "do justice" *and* to "love mercy" in this situation?

We deal with this dilemma daily in the Justice Ministry. Tell us, Jesus, I beg you. Tell us, Micah. How do we do justice and love mercy at the same time in these situations? How are we to be merciful to the wrongdoer and to the wronged, and just to them both?

Until we figure it out, we are placing our priorities on justice and mercy for the wronged. But everybody seems wronged in this situation. As I have already written, holding the abuser accountable is a mercy to him. It is the only possible start to his becoming the just and merciful person he should become. The accountability needs to be shaped in a way that doesn't only protect his partner and children. If possible, it needs to be shaped so that he is given an incentive and a possibility of restoration of relationship with his children. In the Justice Ministry, we have seen case after case in which children feel terrible pain and self-doubt at the loss of relationship with the worst of parents. No matter how badly she or he has been treated or neglected, the child wants to see the parent and know that the parent loves the child.

**

The entire Methodist Justice Ministry staff has come to know and love two special young women.

One is a beautiful, sweet, bright, hard-working, talented twenty-one-year-old who I will call "Mary." Mary had a painful, tragic, unjust and merciless childhood and youth. She only met her biological father when she was placed in foster care at the age of eight. Her mother was and always will be a meth addict, whether recovering or using. Together, she and her mother lived a relatively normal life until Mary was about five, although they did move many times. But when Mary was five, her mother turned to methamphetamine. Mary is not sure why. After her mother started using, Mary remembers being left by her mother at houses with women and men she did not know and her mother being gone for days at a time. Mary remembers seeing things in those houses that she shouldn't have seen, things she does not want to recount. She remembers being scared by the conduct of some of the men toward her. She remembers a loving third-grade teacher who wanted to know why she was missing chunks of time from school. She remembers her mother cooking meth on a burner in the bathroom of their house. She remembers riding her bicycle around her neighborhood one day and returning home to see her house on fire. Her mother had caused the fire by cooking meth. She remembers that was the incident that put her into foster care.

While Mary was in foster care for five years or so, her mother married, became clean for a time, and gave birth to three more children. Her mother regained custody of Mary. Then Mary's mother went back to meth, and the husband abandoned Mary and her half-siblings. While the mother was out looking for sex with high-school boys in exchange for meth, Mary was at home taking care of her three half-siblings. The family lived for a time in a trailer and when the mother brought boys home to have sex for drugs, Mary and her younger siblings could hear the sounds of sex through the thin walls. Mary was so devoted to her siblings, spending so much of her time mothering and protecting them, that she was in danger of failing her senior year in high school. A teacher convinced Mary to move out of her mother's trailer and in with a friend until she could graduate. The mother then took the three half-siblings, aged seven through five, to a distant relative in a distant city and dumped them. Soon, the mother was in prison again for methamphetamine possession.

Mary graduated from high school, moved alone to a nearby city, enrolled in junior college, and was working her way toward nursing school at two waitressing jobs. She had no help at all. She was alone in her rented home. Then she found out that the people on whom her mother had dumped her siblings had dumped them, too. Mary picked them up, took them in, quit school, sold her laptop to buy the children clothes, and became their mother. She was nineteen at the time.

When Mary first took possession of these siblings, she had no legal right to enroll them in school or to make medical decisions for them. The children were way behind on their vaccinations and one of the children needed psychiatric and psychological diagnosis and intervention for learning and behavioral issues. Mary needed to obtain legal custody of her siblings to be able to make parental decisions. The Justice Ministry was able to obtain this custody for her. But Mary and her siblings also needed a functioning vehicle, a healthy and safe place to live, a job that paid a living wage for Mary, and a way for Mary to continue her education. The MJM and my church were also able to help her obtain these things.

Mary is not only, as I already described her, beautiful, sweet, bright, loving, and hard-working. I left out one thing. She is also Anglo. Her ethnicity makes it easier for some insiders to see her as "deserving." To their credit, people with plenty of resources are giving Mary the help she and those children need, financial and otherwise. This help and attention has made a huge difference. It has shown how much of a difference that real help, not just a little bit of help designed only to make the helper feel good, can make. Mary is an easy young woman to help. Mary and those three children have a good chance for productive, loving, happy lives. Mary has obtained a remarkably well-paying job for her education level, an empathetic boss, good health insurance through her job, referrals to good medical care for her siblings, free education at the local junior college level, and is on her way to becoming a registered nurse. She has also found a fine young man of high character who is almost worthy of her and the siblings.

There is another young woman who is almost the same age as Mary. I'll call her "Carlota." Carlota is undocumented, which is not her fault. Let me repeat—*which is not her fault.* She was born in El Salvador and brought by her parents to this country when she was two. They were all refugees from the terrible gang violence there. Since then, Carlota has never been out of the U.S. If America isn't her country, Carlota doesn't have one. She recited our pledge of allegiance every school day through her public school career.

Her father was terribly abusive to her mother and fled to El Salvador to avoid prosecution, leaving his wife, Carlota, and four other children behind. He has provided no financial support since he left. The family doesn't know where he is to contact him. The other four children besides Carlota were born in the U.S. They are full American citizens, which is also no credit to them just like it is no credit to me or to anyone to have been born an American citizen. After Carlota had graduated from high school, she entered nursing assistant's school at the age of 19, still living at home with her mother and four younger siblings, and helping her mother care for them. But her mother walked out of a bar one night, tried to cross a highway on foot, and was hit by a truck and killed instantly. The oldest of Carlota's siblings was fourteen; the youngest was four. At nineteen, Carlota was the only "adult" available to take legal custody, care for them, and make parental decisions for them about education, health care, discipline. They have no other family in the United States.

The Justice Ministry helped Carlota get legal custody of her siblings so that she could make the necessary parental decisions. Formal legal custody led to an entirely new set of problems for her. Carlota could have declined to seek custody. Her siblings could have been placed into the foster care system. But there they likely would have been separated. Carlota was as poor as could be. She could reasonably have decided that she was not able to be a parent. As a legal custodian of four children, with the *legal* obligations to feed, clothe, shelter, educate, discipline, and obtain medical care for them, she was not going to have the time and opportunity to get the necessary training to make more than minimum wage. I discussed all this at length with her before she asked us to obtain legal custody for her. She really didn't hesitate. She felt that her siblings were due to be raised by someone in their family who loved them. They were not due the trauma of losing their father and then the shock of the death of their mother. They were definitely not then due the further trauma of being split up and raised by people whom they did not know, and who might or might not love them. So when we took Carlota on as a client, we knew we would be providing even more material and financial support to her and the children than we usually provide. We knew that we would be taking our own responsibility to stand with Carlotta. Not under the dominant narrative but under the counter-narrative of Jesus, she and her siblings were due all the mercy we could give them as a matter of justice.

Carlota has a bit of a learning disability. Like Mary, Carlota is also cute, sweet, caring and hard-working. But she is not Anglo, so we have had a much harder time getting help for Carlota and her four Hispanic-American siblings from generous insiders. We weren't able to get Carlota a good job that paid a living wage with an empathetic boss and good health insurance.

Two of Carlotta's siblings have a learning disability. One is starting to wander down the wrong roads. Carlota works behind the counter at a Taco Bueno. She makes seventy-five cents more than minimum wage. Her work provides her with no set hours and no benefits. She and her siblings survive on her meager wages plus food stamps. Her boss does not care what hours she needs to be home to care for her siblings or that the job doesn't pay enough for her to live even with the SNAP. If Carlota quit, her boss could quickly find a thousand other economically poor girls to take her place. The work schedule is put out for the boss's convenience and the needs of the business. So Carlota cannot be home consistently to ensure that her siblings come home from school on time, do their homework, turn off the TV and videogames, and stay away from the peers they need to avoid. Carlota can't afford child care, so the oldest sibling is supposed to be the sitter. That sibling is the one going down the wrong road.

Carlotta's old car kept breaking down. It had 160,000 miles on the odometer, but then the odometer wasn't working very well either. She had purchased it with a salvage title, which was resourceful of her. When the car would not start, Carlota was reluctant to call us for help again so she tried to arrange to get it repaired on her own. Carlota is very shy. She understandably lacks confidence. She is soft-spoken and appears younger than her actual age. The shade-tree mechanic she went to overcharged her to replace her battery. The problem was the alternator, not the battery, which the mechanic had to have known. After Carlota paid this mechanic, the car still wouldn't start. She was about to lose her job for lack of transportation, so she finally called us. We were able to call on the generosity of a mechanic who has helped many of our clients and who charges us nothing but the cost of the needed parts. We paid for the parts. The car was repaired, and Carlota was able to get to work and her siblings to school.

What happens to young people like Carlota who do not know people who know mechanics like this good man? They are losers in the *agón* of the dominant narrative. So are their children.

Carlota was still renting the same apartment in which she and the family lived when her mother was killed. It was a two-story, townhouse apartment. The air conditioner went out in the dead of summer, and water started leaking from the second floor to the first floor through the bathroom ceiling, making that bathroom unusable. The apartment manager promised Carlota that the needed parts were on order. But the manager did not get the problem fixed for half the summer. This same manager had previously removed the control knob on the temperature control for the central air conditioner to keep the family from effectively cooling the apartment. Carlota paid only rent with the electricity included in that monthly payment. The manager had a reason to keep the electric use down by removing the control knob on the thermostat. Only when we visited the apartment did we discover the problems. All the defects were fixed within 24 hours after we sent a formal notice and demand letter to the landlord.

Clearly, the employer, the original mechanic, and the apartment manager were taking advantage of Carlota because of her age and vulnerability. What they were doing was "just" within the dominative narrative. They were just eating what they could kill. They were winning the contest against Carlotta.

Carlota needed daily help. She met a young man who lived in the apartment complex. He had himself been in foster care throughout his teenaged years. He was the same age as Carlotta. He started hanging around the apartment and made friends with the siblings. He was allergic to employment, so had no place else to be. But Carlota was very grateful and came to depend upon him. Carlota was a young woman with a young person's needs. The young man started staying overnight, sleeping on the couch. Then he made his way into Carlotta's bed. He was persistent. At first she refused his advances. But he sulked and threatened to end his help. She gave in. She got pregnant. She gave birth. Then there were five children for her to take care of with a father and babysitter who could not find a hoe handle to fit his hand.

Unlike with Mary, we have not been able to find people to support and encourage Carlota and her family. I guess Carlota and her siblings are not as deserving. Such is the hit and miss character of charity within the dominant narrative. Mercy, after all, is only optional. And these children of Carlotta's are not due much at all as a matter of justice, according to the dominant narrative.

In ten years, we are betting that Mary will be a registered nurse and that her siblings will be productive and happy, given the mothering and example she has given them. In ten years, we are afraid that Carlota will still be working in the fast-food industry. Her siblings and her child . . . what can we reasonably hope for them?

**

"Cathy" was thirty-three years old when she hung herself. She climbed onto a kitchen table, looped a rope over a ceiling beam, tied the rope around her neck, and jumped off the table. It probably took her a while to lose all consciousness. Her three-year-old daughter watched as Cathy did all this.

Cathy had two other children, ten and eight. The three year old ran to get them. The ten year old later recounted that they arrived to see Cathy's body twitching at the end of the rope, her legs kicking, and her face blue. They called Cathy's mother. When Cathy's mother arrived, Cathy was already dead though her body was still warm. All three children were shooed out of the room when the EMT techs cut the body down.

Cathy had struggled with depression all of her life. She self-medicated with a lot of alcohol and boot-legged hydrocodone.

Cathy never married. Her three children had three different fathers. One of these fathers had himself committed suicide. All of the fathers had done time in prison for, among other offenses, drug possession. All three of the fathers had beaten Cathy. Cathy was petite, cute, depressed, desperate for love, and attracted to men who needed to dominate and hurt a woman.

CPS placed all three children with their maternal grandparents—Cathy's mother and father. The grandfather was disabled by a congenital heart condition, and had not been employed for many years. The grandmother had worked at Kmart for two decades. She had to quit her job to care for the three children after Cathy's suicide, all of whom were suffering from degrees of depression, anxiety, and post-traumatic stress disorder. These five people were living on a little social security disability, food stamps, and the biweekly sale of plasma by each of the grandparents. Plasma buyers would pay $20 for the first donation in a given week and $30 for the next donation that week. (I'm talking about plasma here, not whole blood. In your own city, consider the neighborhoods where the blood buyers are located. Invariably, it will be in poor neighborhoods. Near to the blood buyer you will also likely find a title loan or a payday loan storefront.) The family did not have the income to provide for themselves and the three grandchildren.

The ten-year-old child was in the worst emotional shape of the three children. He would sit for hours alone in a dark room, doing nothing, non-responsive to any conversation. He needed serious psychiatric intervention. Only a few pediatric psychiatrists in the area accepted Medicaid, so the wait for him was long between appointments. The grandmother gave up trying to talk this ten year old into returning to school after his mother's death.

The other two children fought constantly with one another and found it difficult to sleep. The three year old demanded constant attention. If the grandmother tried to leave the apartment alone for even a moment, even to smoke a cigarette outside the door, the three year old would scream and hold onto her leg.

The two grandparents and three grandchildren were originally crammed into a three-bedroom apartment. The apartment was further crowded by all of Cathy's belongings. The grandparents felt that throwing out any of these things was like throwing out Cathy.

None of the fathers was fit to take custody of these children. None wanted custody. None had been paying their previously ordered child support. All three of the fathers had multiple other children by other women who were not their wives.

The Justice Ministry was able to get legal custody of all three children for the grandparents. Through the help of one of our board members, we were able to get this family into a larger home and to provide them with used furniture. We were able to obtain fresh orders from the court requiring each father to pay their current child support and their child-support arrearages to the grandparents. None of them have paid a penny. A child support order is merely a piece of paper when its subject is a parent who works off the books and moves from job to job.

Years later, the children still suffer from serious emotional disruptions. The grandparents still can't find a responsive pediatric psychiatrist who takes Medicaid.

What are these children due within the dominant narrative, and from whom? Nothing from no one except their suffering and overmatched grandparents. All they can hope for is occasional, optional mercy.

Given the pervasiveness and power of the dominant narrative, what will these children ever be equipped to do or be? Given the depression that is a plague in their household and their own trauma, will they ever be able to work productively and to acquire the stuff and pleasure to be respected and successful within the dominant narrative? Will they ever even be "deserving" of help under that narrative?

**

"Abigail" was thirty-four years old and the mother of eight children. Three of these had been placed in foster care by CPS, and Abigail's most recent maternity had been legally terminated. Custody of one of the other children had been granted to that child's father who lived out of state.

Abigail's remaining four children were a girl aged ten, a girl aged eight, a boy aged two, and a boy aged four months. The identity of the fathers of the girls were unknown to Abigail. The father of the two-year-old boy was in prison in another state. The identity of the father of the four-month-old boy was known to Abigail, but his whereabouts were not. This father had choked Abigail when she was in the hospital recovering from the delivery of this youngest child. When the police were called, the father ran and has not been heard from since.

When the case about Abigail and her children came to us, Abigail was unemployed and pregnant with still another child, her ninth.

Abigail had once taken two of the children, the ten-year-old and eight-year-old girls, to live with her family in another state. While there, the ten-year-old, who was then six, was sexually assaulted by Abigail's brother who was convicted and imprisoned for his assault. Because Abigail's family was angry that Abigail had reported this assault, she moved with the two children back to the city where "Anne" lived.

Our client was not Abigail but Anne. Anne was fifty-two years old when we first started representing her. Her only income was from the sale of tamales that she made herself and from baby-sitting. She came to us seeking legal custody of Abigail's four youngest children.

Anne lived in a house with her sister, brother-in-law, and their two children, and with Anne's daughter Rachel and Rachel's two children. Rachel has a permanent limp because her father kicked Anne in the belly when Anne was pregnant with Rachel, injuring the child in the uterus. Anne and Rachel are undocumented. Anne brought Rachel to the United States when Rachel was one year old. Rachel went through every grade of public school here in the U.S. and graduated from a local four-year college with a degree in education. But she could not take a job as a teacher when we knew her because she did not yet have documents.

We represented Anne in her attempt to obtain legal custody of the four children. Anne had no blood relationship with Abigail, any of the fathers, or any of the children. Her initial relationship with them was that she was their babysitter.

Abigail had started dropping the ten year old with Anne for the day when the child was two years old. Abigail was spending the day with one of her men, and that man didn't want a child around when he and Abigail were doing drugs and having sex. Abigail would then pick the child up from Anne in the evening. Gradually, Abigail stopped picking up the child at the end of the day. That little girl would stay with Anne and her family overnight and then for days and then weeks and then longer without Abigail coming back. Then Abigail had another child, and another, and another. As soon as each of those children was discharged from the hospital after he or she was born (two had to remain in the hospital for weeks because they were born addicted to drugs), Abigail would drop the child with Anne. Abigail never paid Anne or her family. Anne came to consider these children part of her family.

When CPS was called in after the father of the youngest child choked Abigail in the hospital just after the delivery, Anne was referred to us to help her obtain legal custody of all four children.

So twelve people lived in Anne's house, including these four children. To call that house modest would be flattery. In winter, the inside of that house seemed colder to me than the outside. In summer, the inside seemed hotter than the outside. It is crammed full with human beings at any given moment. And it is crammed full of love. When you are invited in, the very first thing you notice is that the interior walls are covered, top to bottom, side to side, every room, with framed, black and white photos of all the children who live there. And the photos of Abigail's four children are as numerous and prominent as the children of Anne's daughter Rachel or the children of Anne's sister.

Anne is completely unselfconscious of her generosity. Those children had no one else besides her. "God placed them in my path. How could I pass by? Now I love them."

The dominant narrative would call Anne a fool and a sap. None of these strangers are due anything from Anne. By taking these children in, less foolish people would say that Anne is stealing resources and time from her actual children and grandchildren.

But the dominant narrative has no soul and no heart. Anne is one of the happiest and most satisfied persons I have ever known. She is merciful and just at the same time. She is adored by *all* of those children and her entire family. And by all of us at the Methodist Justice Ministry.

⁎⁎

"Julia" was born in Mexico City and brought by her mother and father to the United States when she was three. She has not been back to Mexico since she was brought here. She attended public schools here, graduating high school. When her graduating class took a cruise to Cancun as a graduation celebration, she could not go. She was still undocumented, "an illegal alien" within the system. After the cruise, Julia would not have been able to get back through U.S. customs and back to what is undeniably her home here in the U.S. And after her graduation, despite a 4.0 grade point average but without a social security number, she always had to work off the books and was unable to find a job making as much as minimum wage. She still worked steadily and hard for years. But she was unable to save any money. She resisted the temptation to marry an American citizen just to obtain a resident visa. Julia is a devout Christian, and believes that God will provide for her.

Julia's brother "James" was also born in Mexico City and brought to the U.S. when he was a child. James did not graduate from high school. He dropped out at age 15. He was big, strong and physically healthy, and was able to make good money as a roofer, working on crews of undocumented men, and using a bad social security card he bought at a *pulga*— a flea market.

James became a father when he was 17. The mother, "Annette," was 13 when James impregnated her for the first time. Annette was born in the U.S. Though they never married, James lived with Annette for seven years. They had five children together—two boys and three girls who were all born in the U.S.

James was an adequate material provider for Annette and the family, working steadily and bringing adequate money home for them. But he began to beat Annette. Julia and James's father had abused their mother before he abandoned the family, and James had witnessed the violence. Annette hadn't reported James's beatings to the police for fear that James would be deported and the family would lose its sole breadwinner. But during one particularly bad incident during which Annette was choked, a neighbor called the police. When the police arrived, James was still on the premises, and Annette's neck was already bruising and swelling. So James was arrested. A magistrate's protective order was issued forbidding him from coming within 200 yards of Annette and the family home for sixty days. James made bond on the family violence charge and tried to come back to the apartment. The same neighbor called the police again, and James was arrested for violating the protective order and kept in jail. The Immigration people then intervened. James was deported. He decided to stay in Mexico for a time. He did not send any money from Mexico to Annette to support the children.

Annette had not worked for many years. She found a job at a parking garage, but her income was certainly not enough to provide for herself and the five children. She began looking for a man to help her.

Annette started leaving the children with Julia and her mother "Emilia" while Annette was out looking for another man. Julia and Emilia's small apartment was close to Annette and the children's apartment and had served as a kind of haven for the children when James was being violent. Aunt Julia was someone in whom the children, and particularly the three girls, felt they could confide.

Annette found a new man named "Jake." Jake had at least two biological children of his own by two different women he had not married. He had been ordered to pay child support for each of those children but had refused. Jake was unemployed. He had been convicted twice of marijuana possession and of unlawful carrying of a firearm. Jake moved into the apartment where Annette lived with her five children. As soon as he did, he cut off all contact between Julia, Emilia, and the children. Julia would call Annette to ask to speak to the children, but there was never an answer.

When this was unfolding, Aunt Julia was 28 years old, single and still undocumented.

Four months into the relationship between Annette and Jake, Julia drove by their apartment. She saw the children through a second-story bedroom window. The oldest child, a boy who was then twelve, tried to mouth words to Julia. Julia yelled at him to open the window. He just shook his head. Julia could see the youngest child, a boy seven years old, crying in the background. Julia went to the apartment door and knocked. There was no answer. Julia went back to the window and gestured for them to open the front door. The oldest boy again shook his head no. Julia yelled, "Why not?" The boy yelled back, "We're locked in the bedroom."

Julia went to Annette's old employment at the parking garage but was told that she no longer worked there. So Julia went back to Annette's apartment and waited.

Jake arrived at the apartment two hours later. Julia intercepted him before he could climb the stairs to the apartment door. "Why are the children locked in a bedroom?"

"Who are you?"

"I'm their aunt. I'm their father's sister."

"I'm their father now. You can't talk to them. Stay the f*** away from here or I will call the police." He went into the apartment and slammed the door in Julia's face.

Julia waited for Annette to come home. More hours passed. A progression of men went to the door of the apartment, were let in, remained only a few moments, and left. Then Julia saw Annette walking to the apartment from a bus stop. Julia intercepted her. "Annette, I was here earlier and the children told me through the bedroom window that they were locked in the bedroom. And there have been a lot of men coming and going from your apartment. What's going on? "

Annette looked afraid. "You need to leave us alone." And she ran up the stairs and into the apartment. Jake came out and yelled at Julia to leave "or else."

Because she was undocumented, Julia needed to avoid any contact with police. But this time she called the police and asked for a child welfare check. While Julia waited in the apartment parking lot, the police arrived and knocked on Annette's apartment door. They knocked repeatedly, but there was no answer. As the two patrol officers were coming down the stairs, Julia approached them and told them her concerns. The officers told her that unless there was probable cause to believe that the children were in danger at that very moment, they could not force the door without a warrant. And based upon what Julia told them, they didn't think that there was enough evidence to obtain a warrant. They told her to call again if there was any more reason to think a crime was actively being committed against one of the children.

Julia didn't sleep that night. Every night thereafter, she would drive to the street next to the apartment building and park, hoping she could see that the children were all right, or see something that she could provide the police probable cause to enter the apartment.

Then one night Annette appeared at Julia and Emilia's apartment with all five children. They had walked over from their place. Jake had assaulted Annette. After he left in her car, she gathered the children and came over. She called the police from Julia and Emilia's apartment. An officer came and took Annette's statement and photos of the bruises and welts on her face. Then they went to arrest Jake.

That night, Annette and the children told Julia more of what had been happening. They denied that Jake was assaulting the children, but they said that he had assaulted Annette repeatedly in their presence. Annette worked all day. She had to be at the bus stop by 6:30 in the morning and did not get home until 7:30 in the evening. She had a car, but Jake demanded that she leave it for his use. When the children, who were then 12, 11, 9, 8, and 7 years old, arrived back at the apartment at the end of the school day, Jake would often lock them in a bedroom and then leave in Annette's car. The children had no access to a bathroom while they were in that bedroom. And he told them that if they got out, he would whip them when he returned.

When Julia asked why he would lock them in, Annette said she did not know. But the oldest child, the twelve year old boy, said he believed that Jake had drugs hidden somewhere in the apartment that he did not want the children to find. He said that when Jake was in the apartment when the children were there after school, random people would come in and out. When they knocked on the door, Jake would order all the children into the back bedroom while he was dealing with the visitors. The twelve year old thought he was selling drugs. Jake always had a wad of cash, but no job.

Julia asked Annette why she had tolerated this, and why she hadn't left or called the police before. Annette tried to tell Julia that Jake was a good person, and that she loved him. Julia told her that she had to choose between that man and her children. Annette said she had, which was why she was there.

Jake was arrested and charged with assault against Annette. A protective order was issued by a magistrate, directing Jake to stay away from Annette and the five children for sixty days. Jake found another place to live. Annette went back to her apartment with the children, and Julia started sleeping there as well at the two older children's request.

While Julia was staying with them, she noticed that Annette was distant and uninvolved with her children, barely paying them any attention. Julia was the one mothering them. Then Annette started coming home later and later, claiming that she had been working. Then she didn't come home at all. Two days later, Annette left a message on Julia's cell phone. She said she couldn't live without Jake. She was the one violating the protective order so Julia should not call the police. She said she would be coming to pick up her children in a few weeks, when things had calmed down and Jake was ready for them to come live with them again.

Julia told the oldest two children about her mother's message. They were afraid of going back to live in any home with Jake in it. They started opening up more to Julia and Emilia about what Jake had been doing. Jake called them "punks," "dummies" and "leaches." He threatened to knock out their teeth if they disobeyed him, even the youngest children. He told all of the children: "What happens here stays here. If you tell anyone what is happening here, I will shoot your mother and Julia. If you tell anyone about being locked in your room, you will see what will happen." The twelve year old described seeing Jake with a handgun with a scope. The three oldest children told Julia that when Jake locked them in the back bedroom, he left a piece of paper on top of the outside of the door. Jake told them that if they got out, he would know because the paper would have moved and he would beat them. Jake had broken a ruler on the oldest boy's wrist. He had left a bad bruise on the back of the seven-year-old's right thigh. The eight-year-old girl had had a bruise on her bottom and on her back. All of them described going hungry because Jake refused to let them eat when Annette was out of the apartment.

Julia and Emilia were staying with the children at Annette's apartment because it was larger than theirs and because the younger children were accustomed to it. Annette didn't even call to check on the children until she showed up to take the children with her. Julia refused to let them go. Annette demanded them. Julia slammed the door and activated the deadbolt. Annette pounded on the door. Julia asked the oldest two children, "What shall I do?" They told her they were afraid of what Jake would do to them if they went with their mother. So Julia called the police. By the time the officers arrived, Annette had left. The children described to the police what Jake had done to them. An officer called the CPS hotline in their presence to make an allegation against Annette for failing to protect her children. Then the officers drove Julia, Emilia and the children back to Julia and Emilia's smaller place. "Here," they said, "you can legitimately keep the mother and her boyfriend from entering. If they show up here, call us back."

Julia kept the children home from school the next day. A CPS investigator appeared at her door and questioned each of the children individually. The investigator took all the information Julia had on Annette and where she worked. Then she left, saying she would try to get Annette to agree to a safety plan voluntarily placing the five children with Julia and Emilia and banning her from letting Jake have any contact at all.

Julia suddenly remembered that she had not called her employer to ask for the day off. She worked off the books as a receptionist and part-time bookkeeper for a family-owned HVAC repair company. She received no benefits, and no paid vacation or sick time. She was paid less than minimum wage because she lacked papers. The owner told her that if she missed another day's work he would have to let her go. She tried to explain why she needed to be home for the children for a while. He said he was running a business, not a charity. Like a lot of companies, that one could always find another vulnerable, undocumented worker whom they could pay much less than a legal wage. After all, undocumented workers were not due being paid a legal wage because they aren't legal themselves.

And the employer knew that undocumented workers couldn't complain without fearing deportation.

Emilia had obtained a resident visa years before. She could work legally. No visa had been obtained for Julia because the lawyer had neglected Julia's case, and the family had no money to pay for another lawyer. Emilia was 49 years old. She worked on an assembly line, making about $9 an hour.

The CPS investigator returned to say that Annette had agreed to a safety plan placing possession of the children with Julia and Emilia for now and limiting Annette to visitation with the children supervised by Julia. She said that Annette agreed to this only because the children would be split up and placed in foster care with strangers if Annette did not agree. There were no other family members to take them in voluntarily.

Fresh on Julia's mind was her conversation with her boss. So Julia asked the investigator if CPS would be providing her and her mother with some supplemental income to help them feed and care for the children. No, said the investigator. The state can only pay foster families, not actual family members who voluntarily take possession. Can we be a foster family so we can receive some reimbursement? No, said the investigator. Why not? Because you and your mother have already taken the children in outside the foster system, and because the state wants to save money. Julia asked if they could apply for food stamps while they had possession of the children. Not until you obtain legal custody from a court, said the investigator. Can Annette be ordered to pay us child support to help us provide for her children? No, said the investigator. Not unless you obtain legal custody from a court. When can we do that? Not until we give Annette and Jake a chance to take our classes on parenting and family violence. Can you require Annette to give us her food stamps for the children? No, but you can ask her.

Annette and Jake refused to take their required classes. Annette lied that she was leaving Jake, but she was caught in the lie. Jake refused to let Annette give Julia the food stamp card for the children.

Julia, Emilia and the children survived, barely, until the Methodist Justice Ministry was able to get them legal custody. They survived on Julia's and Emilia's meager pay and by tightening their belts. And Julia took out a title loan on her car, which required her to pay back over time about 600 percent of what she had borrowed. That's not an error. About 600 percent of the principal she borrowed.

According to the custody orders that the court granted, Annette continued to be limited to supervised visitation with her own children for as long as she was still with Jake.

She is still with Jake.

Julia and Emilia have continued to live in their small apartment with the five children. For four years, Julia slept in a sleeping bag on the floor of the living room so the children could sleep on the beds and the couch.

Annette sees her children only intermittently. She pays very little of her court-ordered child support.

The children's father James has come back into the U.S. illegally and is making decent money again. But he is also paying very little of his court-ordered child support. He drives a very nice car. He sees his children only occasionally.

The children are 17, 15, 13, 12, and 11 as of this writing. The oldest boy has a job and contributes more financially to the family than either his father or his mother do. The children love seeing their actual parents. They love them very much, as children will, regardless of how they are neglected, abandoned, and abused. But they do not respect them. They adore their aunt Julia and their grandmother Emilia.

Julia is still an "illegal alien." Even if she did not have a voice or a choice in being brought here originally when she was three, she knows she is here illegally now. As I have heard it said by some advocates for the dominant narrative, we will "lose our country" unless we strictly "enforce our borders." Even if she knows not a soul in Mexico, they say that she must go back. Even if she knows no place there, she must go back. Even if the five children, who are all U.S. citizens, would lose one of the only two persons they have ever been able to depend upon, Julia must go back. And even if she is exactly the kind of loving, responsible, hard-working person every American ought to want as a fellow citizen, she must go back now. She sleeps on the floor in a sleeping bag so the children can have the beds and the couch. She put herself at some risk—risk from Jake and of arrest and deportation—to protect these innocent children. She selflessly delays the time when she can marry and have her own children. But, say the advocates of the dominant narrative, she must go back. She isn't due a place in our competition. The law is the law. She is not due anything at all from us because she isn't one of "us." Within the dominant narrative, she is not due to be here. And we can't undermine the power of the law with mercy. No matter how much she would suffer. No matter how much her mother would suffer. No matter how much the children would suffer. Within the dominant narrative, Julia, Emilia, and these children are due nothing more from us than the firm enforcement of the law without exception or mercy.

And the apologists of those who benefit the most from the dominant narrative use it mercilessly to scapegoat Julia and those in her status. To stoke up fear of "them" who are no threat. Of Julia! There are only so many benefits of our society to be divided up, the advocates for the dominant narrative say. This isn't just an *agón*. This is a zero-sum *agón*. For every benefit that Julia received within our system, one of us would be deprived of what was due us, they say. Nevermind that Julia receives no such monetary benefit. And she isn't depriving one of us of a job that pays less than even the legal minimum wage because none of "us" would want or take it.

But from the people of God formed by the counter-narrative of God and Jesus, what are Julia, Emilia and the children due? What is Annette due? What is James due?

**

"Nancy's" parents were methamphetamine addicts. Her father sold meth from the family home as Nancy and her brother were growing up there. The father injected or smoked his profits. So the family remained poor. Her father went to prison repeatedly. Her mother "Maggie" managed to avoid any criminal charges. The family moved from rented house to rented house. Their home was always dirty, cluttered and reeking of cigarette smoke. And there were always a lot of dogs and roaches.

Nancy's brother started using meth and cocaine when he was fourteen. He dropped out of school in the ninth grade. He turned to burglary to raise the money to buy his drugs. His parents were hardly in a position to push him in the right direction. The only line that they drew for him was that he couldn't get any of his drugs from them. When he started stealing from their inventory, they kicked him out. He went quickly from couch surfing at friend's homes to juvenile detention. Shortly after he turned eighteen, he landed in adult prison for the first time. He was eventually paroled, of course had no job prospects, and turned to armed robbery as a career. At the age of twenty-eight, he was sentenced to fifteen years in prison. By that time, he had fathered a son. The mother of his son was mentally ill and an addict.

Like so many addicts, Nancy's mother, Maggie, had realized that she had to kick drugs or die. Unlike so many addicts, she was able to quit for good. She's been clean for more than a decade now. Maggie gave Nancy's father an ultimatum: quit or I'll divorce you. He quit but quickly relapsed. She divorced him. The Justice Ministry helped Maggie obtain legal custody of Nancy's brother's son. Maggie's body was so messed up from her years of meth use that she developed a lot of collateral health problems. She was unable to work. She was able to qualify for disability. She and her grandson lived only on disability and food stamps. Her house was still dirty, cluttered, and reeking of cigarette smoke. But the house remained drug free.

When I asked Maggie why she had fallen so hard into meth, she said, "When life sucks so bad, and there's no chance of making things better, you might as well stay high. If you haven't tried it, you can't understand how euphoric and powerful meth makes you feel. It was only when I faced that I was going to die if I didn't quit that I was able to stop. I was more afraid of dying than I was of stopping. A lot of users would rather die than stop."

Amazingly, Nancy never used drugs until she joined the Air Force. She graduated from high school and enlisted, hoping to someday go to college on her military benefits. Her military specialty was security. She was part of the air patrol on an Air Force base in Virginia. She was planning to do her six years, earn her discharge and her benefits, and obtain a degree in criminal justice at a community college. Her goal was to work crime scenes as a police woman.

When she was on a weekend pass driving to Washington DC and back to hit some clubs, she was in a bad car wreck, breaking both legs. She was hospitalized for five weeks. One of the fractures didn't heal correctly at first and had to be surgically re-broken. Then she got an infection in that leg. After that was treated, Nancy was released from the hospital and returned to light duty at her original Virginia duty station.

She was prescribed Oxycodone for her continuing pain. She got hooked. She started lying about her symptoms to get more pills. When the Air Force doctors figured out that she was malingering for more pain meds, they cut her off. It wasn't a challenge to find illegal drugs on a military base. She turned first to cocaine and then to heroin. Then she turned to meth. Meth use ran in the family genes.

She was warned to quit and actually put through rehab by the Air Force. When she returned quickly to using, she received a general discharge under less than honorable conditions. The Air Force offered her that, instead of a dishonorable or a bad conduct discharge, to get her out quickly.

She went to live in Virginia with another Airman also just discharged for drug use, a man she had abused Oxycodone with while they were in. She got pregnant. She used heroin while she was pregnant. The baby was born addicted to heroin and remained in the hospital for two weeks after birth, going through withdrawal. Virginia Child Protective Services were called, and Nancy's newborn, a little girl, was placed in foster care. Nancy's maternal rights were soon terminated when she would not return to rehab and would not quit using.

She was twenty-one years old.

She returned to her mother's home because she had no place else to go. The tension between Nancy and Maggie was intense. Maggie knew firsthand what was driving Nancy to use. But when Maggie pleaded with her, trying to give her the benefit of her own experience, Nancy responded that her mother had no right to lecture her given her own past and the childhood that her mother had inflicted on her.

Nancy's self-loathing and her resentment of her mother contributed to her escaping to a succession of men who used her body in exchange for meth. Then her loathing for herself, for her weakness, for her past, her present and her hopeless future, and for the men who used her body would boil over into drugged arguments, insults, and mutual assaults. With fresh bruises and choke marks, she would return to her mother's home, having nowhere else to go, but more resentful, sullen and self-loathing than before.

Once when she returned to Maggie's home, Nancy found that she was pregnant. Maggie insisted that Nancy tell the father. The father was so moved to learn that he was to be a father for the first time that he resolved to sober up. Nancy resolved to do so as well for the sake of her child. She didn't want to have this child taken from her by the state. So Nancy and the father moved in with the father's mother. The father went to work at a Subway, eventually working himself up to manager. Nancy stayed with the father's mother until she delivered, taking some classes at a local community college. Nancy had a normal pregnancy and was drug free throughout. Her life was enlivened with some hope for the first time since she had been in the car wreck. She hoped that she and the father would marry, that she would be able to get her associate's degree, and that they would have a normal family life.

But then the father fell for a young woman who worked at the Subway. And he started using meth again. Nancy, the baby and the father were still living at the father's mother's home. He was staying out all night, claiming he was at work doing inventory, but in fact spending the night with the other woman. Nancy tried to teach him a lesson. When the baby was ten months old, Nancy left the child with the father's mother, found an old drug partner, spent the night with him, and did meth. But Nancy picked a drug-induced fight with the man in the early morning, hitting him in the face with a lamp. They made so much noise that a neighbor called the police, and Nancy was arrested and charged with assault. She didn't have the money to bond out and spent four days in jail before the man refused to press charges, and she was released.

By then, the father had decided that he wanted to raise Nancy's baby with his new girlfriend. He and the girlfriend rented an apartment. His mother provided child care during the day. The baby stayed with the father and his girlfriend at night. All of them forbid Nancy to come to the residences. Because she had no more right to the child than the father did, no custody court orders being in place, the police could not help her see her child. She would have to file a custody and visitation suit in family court to obtain any access. But of course she couldn't afford a lawyer.

Very quickly, the new girlfriend became pregnant. And this girlfriend and Nancy's baby's father married. Nancy's baby was only a year old.

Nancy returned to meth and to men who would use her body in exchange for meth. She returned to arguments, insults and assaults, and to her cycles of return to her mother's home. Nancy's self-hatred was at an all-time high.

An uncle stepped in. He gave Nancy a place to stay and some regular, physical work outdoors on his farm and plant nursery. His only requirement was that Nancy remain completely drug-free. Nancy was still young, and her body responded well to the rigor and to the work. She was over the effect of her car wreck. She loved the ranch work. And Nancy is smart. She learned quickly and loved learning.

When Nancy had been clean for more than a year and hadn't seen her child for longer than that, the uncle introduced her to a good friend of his who was the manager of a store with a plant nursery. The friend knew she was an addict. But his granddaughter was in trouble with addiction. He decided to give Nancy a chance after they walked through the garden shop, and she was able to demonstrate her knowledge about the plants in the inventory. The friend did require a drug test of Nancy's scalp hair, which will show any drug use for the previous four months plus. Nancy's test showed no drug use, and she was hired.

No one in that store knew her or her past. She was hard working, smart, and grateful to be working. There was a lot of turn-over at that store, which included a grocery, and she was soon promoted to the manager of the garden shop. In a year's time her uncle's friend was made a manager over seven stores. He promoted Nancy to night manager of her store. The store was open 24 hours a day. Nancy worked from 8 p.m. to 4 am. The grocery section was restocked beginning at 4 am every morning. Nancy was in charge of a crew that readied the merchandise for the re-stocking. She was given a decent salary with health insurance. And she had a real prospect of being made an overall store manager, able to work days instead of nights.

Her second child had never been far from her thoughts. I was introduced to Nancy through her mother, Maggie, whom we had helped obtain legal custody of her grandson. Nancy's income had recently risen above our income eligibility ceiling, which is 125 percent of federal poverty line. But I had the prerogative to waive that ceiling in selective cases. And in reality she could not afford a lawyer to obtain visitation rights with her daughter. I was so taken by her story—all she had been through in her life, how she had cleaned herself up, and how hard she was working. Nancy had made so many very bad mistakes. But I felt she had been more sinned against than sinning. And I felt she and her daughter were due our help and encouragement. Her daughter deserved to have a relationship with her mother. We filed suit and were able to obtain for Nancy shared custody of her daughter and regular possession rights.

Nancy's little girl was so very happy to have Nancy back in her life. Nancy was doing so well. It seemed that she had defeated her past. I suggested to her that she had a great deal to offer people who had been trapped in addiction. She had overcome such a difficult past and addiction that she could help other people to overcome their pasts, and their addictions.

More than a year later, I went by her the store to see how she was doing. We had moved onto other people's crises and had heard nothing from her or her mother. I was told that she had quit her job at the store three months earlier. I hoped she had found a better job with better pay, and better hours. Or maybe she had gone back to school to become a drug-addiction counselor. So I called her mother.

Maggie had been afraid to call me about what had happened. Nancy had been doing so very well. But then she met a young man who often came into the store. She fell in love with him. They started seeing a lot of each other, and then started living together in her apartment. One night he said he wanted to experiment with meth. He said he had never used it before. He lied about this. Unknown to Nancy he had done jail time for meth possession. He had been recently paroled and was unable to find a job. So he had fled from his parole officer and was hiding from a warrant out for his arrest. Nancy knew nothing of this. She and her new love used meth more and more. More and more of her salary went to buying drugs, and Nancy started missing work. Then she caught the boyfriend spanking her daughter with a wooden spoon. She kicked him out of her apartment. He took her car. She stopped using but sunk into depression. She got fired from her job.

She called an old drug partner, and he moved her to a small town south of here to live with him and his two young children. She soon found another source for meth. Her old drug partner, who was clean, kicked her out. She rented a dilapidated house in another even smaller town. She was selling drugs out of the house. I suspect she was selling her body as well. She was sharing that house with three men. There were only two bedrooms. She hadn't seen or tried to contact her second daughter in months.

Nancy's mother knew the name of the town but not the address of her house. Nancy wouldn't tell her. One Sunday morning, I drove to the town. It was a one-stoplight, one-convenience-store, and one-gas-pump metropolis. I spoke to the person behind the counter at the local convenience store and she had no difficulty telling me where Nancy was living. When I told her that I was a minister, she told me to be careful and that she had heard that the local sheriff had that house under surveillance.

I was able to convince Nancy to get out of that house. The hold-up was that she didn't want to go back to her mother's. She couldn't take the judgment. But she was able to get in touch with her good uncle who said she could crash at his place for a time. We spent four hours packing her things, cramming them into plastic bags. We loaded them into my little car and drove together to her uncle's about 150 miles away.

Part of the deal for her coming with me was that I would not ask her why she had gotten back into drugs when things had been going so well.

But I didn't feel that I needed to ask her. I have had so many conversations in the past thirteen years with psychologists, drug and alcohol counselors, recovering alcoholics and addicts, and people still abusing alcohol and drugs at the time. Clearly, by accident of birth Nancy had a genetic predisposition to addiction. Her exposure to her mother and father's drug use had made her own use more thinkable.

I knew from my past friendship with Nancy that she had a deep layer of self-doubt and self-hatred. She could never trust when things were going well for her. She didn't believe that she was due any happiness from life. She couldn't trust herself, and she couldn't trust the goodness of life itself. It was as if she had to sabotage things before she was somehow discovered as undeserving. She had to ditch that good life before that good life would ditch her.

And I believe there was another aspect of it. This dominant narrative's emphasis upon pleasure teaches that we must go from high to high, from extraordinary experience to extraordinary experience, to be truly alive. Just look at the advertising that drowns us. We need the thrills of life—the intense pleasure of this delicious, cheap, unhealthy food, this new truck or automobile that will take us into beautiful vistas for rendezvous with beautiful people, this resort vacation, this cruise, this wine, and this bedroom furniture. We need the beer of "the most interesting man in the world" to have an interesting life. And we live vicariously through athletes, the intensity and the immediacy of winning and losing, and the adoration the athletes receive. Or we live vicariously through celebrities who have talent for nothing other than attracting media attention. We are taught to mistake transient intensity for the enduring intimacy for which we really yearn in our souls. In my experience these yearnings for the immediacy of high after high are particularly strong for addicts. For a part of Nancy, when life was going so well—a decent job with an adequate income, benefits and a decent future, and mothering her daughter day to day with all those satisfactions and joys—life wasn't going so well at all. The highs weren't there. There was no risk. One day slid into another.

After I brought Nancy back to her uncle's, she worked there for a time and cleaned up again. She contacted the father of her daughter and arranged to see her. I was there when Nancy saw the little girl for the first time in months, and that child was so very happy to see her mommy.

The father had left his wife and other child. He had the same job as before, but was using meth periodically again. Nancy moved into his apartment to be able to be with her daughter. She started using meth with him. Nancy and the father got into another drug fight one night. The daughter, now two years old, was cowering in the bedroom while daddy and mommy threw furniture at one another. The police arrived. CPS was called, and they placed the little girl with the father's mother again. Nancy can't see her. That's where things stand as I am writing this.

In the world created by the dominant narrative, people like Nancy and Maggie are not due any help. They are defective losers who won't "just say no." The rest of us should avoid contamination by their uncleanness. If we are foolish enough to offer mercy, we are to give such people a maximum of one chance to fix themselves, maybe, if that. If they keep taking the wrong road, no matter what had been done to them as children and no matter their accidents of birth, they are due no more mercy. In the parable of the prodigal son, the prodigal made one mistake, left one time, saw his mistake and returned to the straight and narrow. If he left again, or if he hurt his father again, he was due no more mercy. And frankly, the dominant narrative would say in that situation the father was responsible for enabling the son's repeated mistake by taking him back so readily the first time.

In the world of the dominant narrative, Nancy wasn't due any more help or any more mercy. She is not a "deserving" poor person.

But her mother was once just as undeserving. And now, because someone did not give up on her even after many of her failures, she is sober and raising and protecting her grandson. The dominant narrative's justice did not do that. God's mercy did that. We are not giving up on Nancy.

**

"Lakeisha" met "Byron" in New Orleans when she was twelve years old. Byron sent her mother a letter saying he wanted Lakeisha to model for him. And he would drive by her house every day, and would follow her in his car as she walked to her school.

Byron was forty-two years old—thirty years older than Lakeisha.

Hurricane Katrina struck New Orleans in 2005. Thousands of citizens of that great city were transformed into refugees. Lakeisha and her mother were just two of them. Byron was one more.

Lakeisha encountered Byron again in a Jackson, Mississippi, shelter where they had fled. Then Lakeisha's mother rented a small house for a short time. Byron started talking to Lakeisha's mother about her. The mother invited Byron to the house. He came often. He kept asking her to call him her uncle. Then he started writing her letters, saying that he wanted to take care of her.

Lakeisha's mother moved to my city with a new boyfriend. Their old home in New Orleans was still uninhabitable because of the hurricane. The mother, boyfriend, and Lakeisha stayed in an extended-stay motel. Byron tracked them there, and moved into the same complex.

Lakeisha's mother started using crack cocaine again. She used so much and so often, as she had in New Orleans, that she was disabled. The mother was not paying any attention to Lakeisha. Byron took this opportunity to take over the care of Lakeisha. He fed her, bought her clothes, and drove her to school and back. Byron had found a job working night shift as a dispatcher for a trucking company. He was contributing money to Lakeisha's mother for her own needs. When the mother had the chance to return to New Orleans, Byron essentially bought Lakeisha, who was then fourteen. Byron paid the mother a sum of money and received a written document giving him the power to make all parental decisions in the mother's absence.

Byron found them a secluded house set well back from the street by a large yard. He made Lakeisha drop out of school. He drove away her friends. He isolated her completely. Her older brothers in New Orleans did not know she was living with Byron. Her mother told her brothers that she was living with a friend of hers. Lakeisha had never learned to drive, and Byron kept it that way. He denied her access to the internet, email, or any social media. They never went out. Lakeisha had grown up in so much poverty, a cocaine addict for a mother and an absent father, that she was happy at first with the arrangement. Byron was the caring father she had never had.

It started with oral sex performed by her on him. She was completely inexperienced sexually before then. Byron groomed her by having Lakeisha watch pornography. Byron waited until Lakeisha was sixteen before he had intercourse with her. He was impatient and insistent before then. But she was afraid, and he let her refuse. He finally raped her one night. She was crying, angry, and hurting. When he kept forcing himself on her, she was unresponsive and then withdrawn. He lowered her defenses by telling her that God had sent her to him and him to her, that God meant for her to be his wife and for him to be her husband and to free her from poverty. And as the wife God had selected for him, it was her duty to have sex with him. When she objected that he was too old and she was too young, he told her that the Virgin Marry was her age and Joseph was his age when they married.

Lakeisha became pregnant the first time when she was barely sixteen. Byron had her lie about her age when she received prenatal care and delivered her child at the county hospital, so he could avoid criminal prosecution. She became pregnant with a second child when she was seventeen and delivered just after she turned eighteen. He married her when she was eighteen, and he was forty-eight. She delivered a third child when she was nineteen.

As Lakeisha became older, she tried to be more assertive. She realized that what he had done to her was not only wrong but illegal, and she told him that. She rebelled at his trying to confine her to the house and to prevent her from telephoning her mother. He tried to control her with coercion and violence. He nailed the windows shut and locked her in the house when he was at work. On occasion he locked her in a closet when he took the children with him. He washed her mouth out with soap when she said he had raped her when she was a minor. He quoted Scripture to her that taught, he said, that her body belonged to him.

She was able to flee to New Orleans with the children. She had scrimped enough money together to pay cab fare and get herself and the children to the bus station. She called her mother collect and waited until her mother paid for the bus tickets online. She stayed with the children in her mother's house for three weeks. But her mom was selling crack out of her house, and Lakeisha knew she needed to get out of there. Lakeisha had a middle-school education and no job skills or work history. There was no way that she could find work and a place to live on her own. It was impossible for her to provide for the needs of her children and herself.

Trapped, she called Byron and negotiated with him. He promised to allow her more freedom, if she would come back and promise not to run away again. He also promised that she could have a computer and use the internet. He drove down to New Orleans and brought Lakeisha and the three children back.

Things between Byron and Lakeisha were better for a while. But soon he was accusing her of communicating with other men over the internet. The verbal and physical abuse resumed. The three children were acting out because of the violence they witnessed. One child was hitting Lakeisha in imitation of the father. Byron cut off her internet. But Lakeisha had already been communicating through the internet with a young man named "Alec" who was just a few years older than she. She explained her plight to him. So they arranged for him to help her escape Byron.

Lakeisha successfully fled with the children to Alec's apartment. This was her escape haven. She was ignorant of the existence of local women's shelters. She was still in the same plight as she was in New Orleans, unable to find work and provide for her children. Alec was a good-looking, strong, young man. He was pleased and surprised to see that Lakeisha was an attractive young woman. The inevitable eventually happened.

After three weeks, Lakeisha telephoned Byron and told him where she and the children were. He came over and pounded on the apartment door, demanding the return of his wife and children. Alec faced him down and told him never to return. Byron called the police. The police came, found that the children were in good health, told Byron that Lakeisha had as much right to possession of the children as he did, and that he would have to file suit in family court to obtain custody.

Byron filed a custody suit and had the constable serve Lakeisha. At the initial hearing, both parties represented themselves. Byron lied that Lakeisha was making money as a stripper and as a prostitute, and that she had moved her children in with her pimp. Lakeisha was overwhelmed by the court process and was unable to tell her side of the story. The associate judge granted primary custody of the children to Byron, granted Lakeisha only supervised visitation, and ordered her to pay child support.

Lakeisha was crying outside the courtroom after the hearing. A compassionate family attorney tried to comfort her. Though this attorney did not offer to represent her for free, she did tell Lakeisha that she had a right to request a new hearing before the district judge. The court coordinator helped her fill out the demand.

Lakeisha and Byron appeared before the district judge for a new hearing. When it became evident to the judge that Lakeisha was Byron's victim, she reset the hearing and had her court coordinator call the Justice Ministry.

I filed for divorce. At the rescheduled hearing, it was my pleasure to cross-examine Byron. I had arranged for a detective from the police department of the city where Lakeisha and Byron first lived and had sex to be in the courtroom. And I led Byron through all of the elements of proof of what is commonly known as statutory rape, all of which Byron arrogantly admitted.

The judge, of course, returned the children to Lakeisha. Byron was restricted to visits with the children supervised at the visitation center of the court house. The judge believed Lakeisha's testimony about Byron's violence and her captivity. The judge ordered him to give Lakeisha one of his cars, so she could have transportation for herself and the children once she learned to drive. And the judge ordered Byron to pay her $1,800.00 a month in child support.

The detective who listened to what amounted to Byron's confession obtained a warrant for sexual assault of a child. Byron was arrested, and an initial criminal complaint was filed by the local prosecutor. Byron was unable to make bond, so he sat in jail awaiting indictment and trial. Then, inexplicably, the grand jury refused to indict him.

As soon as the criminal charges against Byron were dropped, he moved back to Louisiana to avoid enforcement of his child-support obligation.

We set the final divorce hearing six months later. Though we gave Byron notice of the hearing, he failed to appear. He had paid no child support. In Louisiana, he kept quitting and taking and quitting jobs so we were always one step behind in arranging for mandatory withholding of child support from his pay. He had not tried to see or contact his three children. Lakeisha had heard from her mother that he had entered into another relationship with another young girl.

The final divorce decree denied him any access to his children and increased the ordered child support. To date, he has still not paid any.

Byron's avoidance of his child-support obligation left Lakeisha totally dependent upon Alec. Alec worked as an assembly-line worker for a phone manufacturer, making $10 an hour. His monthly take home was about $1,300.00. This was of course much less than what was needed to provide basic needs for him, Lakeisha, and the three children.

Lakeisha soon became pregnant with Alec's child. Alec really wanted to father his own baby. Lakeisha was afraid, with or without basis, that if she refused him he would throw out her and her children. Lakeisha had no place else to go. Her mother's home in New Orleans was not an option because her mother was still selling crack out of her house.

The new child ended any tiny chance that Lakeisha had to return to school to earn her high-school diploma and the nursing-assistant's certification she desired. And the new baby suffered from a congenital heart condition.

Alec suffered from some layoffs from his work. The family qualified for food stamps, but the waiting list was long for government subsidized housing. Every month was a financial crisis. The Justice Ministry paid their rent for months.

The trauma of her past, the stress of the poverty, the crowded two-bedroom apartment housing two adults and four children, and the constant needs of the ill newborn were too much for Lakeisha. She couldn't sleep. She began to lose her temper with Alec and her children unpredictably. She would lose control and throw things at Alec in the presence of the children. There was so much violence in the home that Child Protective Services became involved. Alec had to supervise all of Lakeisha's contact with her children, which kept him out of the job market. Lakeisha was referred by CPS for psychological assessment and was diagnosed with bipolar disorder and Post Traumatic Stress Disorder from the trauma of her entire history. She was required to attend parenting classes and anger-management counseling, and to take medication. She completed all of her services, and CPS closed its case and its supervision.

Then she got pregnant again. Alec left her. I put Lakeisha and her children on the bus to New Orleans. She had no place else to go, even though Louisiana is no place for her.

Lakeisha had been a victim since she was born. Her mother was a crack addict and a crack dealer. Her father was never involved or supportive in any way. A hurricane drove them out of their hometown and into the arms of a twisted stranger. Lakeisha was essentially a victim of sex trafficking. Her mother sold her to a twisted man thirty years her senior, who made her a sex slave, not a wife. When she woke up to all that had been done to her and ran for freedom, she also ran back to poverty. The man who did most of this to her has thwarted the law because of an unmotivated assistant district attorney or an uncaring grand jury, and an ineffective interstate child-support collection system. And Lakeisha has a child with an ongoing heart problem and her own mental-health issues. Now the father of her last child has bailed on her. So Lakeisha has taken her children into the home of a crack addict and dealer where she will remain until she meets another man who takes her and her children in and gets her pregnant.

How much of what happened to Lakeisha was due to her? How does the culture created by the dominant narrative respond to the utter injustice and mercilessness of her life? Food stamps and section 8 housing, if the waiting isn't too long. Medicaid. Nothing that will change her plight. Just maintenance in her poverty.

The dominant narrative teaches you and me to write her off, to shrug our shoulders and tell ourselves that she is beyond hope. This narrative gives us all the excuses we want to do nothing. She is not our problem. She just lost the *agón*. She made some mistakes. Why in the world would she allow herself to get pregnant again, as poor as she and Alec were?

But what are Lakeisha and her children due from the people of Jesus in the world being created by the counter-narrative of God?

The random merciless injustice of her life dwarfs any mistakes she has made. The specific ways her ex-husband preyed upon her is unusual. But the remainder of her plight is common among young women born into a grave of poverty and drug addiction. Why do we aspiring Christians care so little for the Lakeishas of our communities? We care so little because we are disciples of the dominant narrative, not of the counter-narrative of Jesus.

**

"Carolyn" is in her eighties. Her husband, also in his eighties, has Parkinson's. Their only income is a social security check in a small amount from each of their work. Their daughter died of cancer. Their granddaughter is a drug addict and mentally ill. At the Justice Ministry, we see drug addiction and untreated mental illness in combination regularly. The drugs don't cause the mental illness. The person tries to self-medicate the symptoms of her mental illness with the drugs. This granddaughter has five children by four different fathers. The granddaughter's relationships with all men have always been marked by violence.

CPS stepped in, and Carolyn's five great grandchildren were going to be placed in foster care. The granddaughter was leaving the children alone in her apartment to go out to her car to use meth. Then she'd fall asleep in the car and wake up not remembering where she was. The children weren't being fed or bathed. The granddaughter would beat her children with a belt, sometimes hitting them in the face, if they woke her up. If Carolyn didn't agree to become their legal custodian, the children would go into foster care and probably be separated. Carolyn couldn't say no.

The income of Carolyn and her husband was already well below the federal poverty line. Taking in five children would make them much poorer. Neither the granddaughter nor the fathers were ever going to pay any child support. All four fathers were in prison when the Justice Ministry filed the custody suits and obtained a court order appointing Carolyn managing conservator of these children. And we helped her with some of the material needs of the children.

I'm telling this story because it is one of the most frequent scenarios we confront, although usually it's grandparents, not great grandparents, who take custody.

We are seeing an epidemic of drug abuse by poor, young parents. We try to protect and place in protective homes child after child who is the product of a drug-induced hook-up between virtual strangers. We have had hundreds of cases in which a child was born addicted to drugs. We have interviewed, negotiated with, or cross-examined hundreds of parents who were abusing drugs, some while they were pregnant. The dominant narrative just condemns and discards these parents. And within this narrative their *conduct* is worthy of condemnation and deterrence. But the dominant narrative is as heedless of the welfare of the children as are the parents. The narrative's version of justice means no help or intervention is due them—parent or child. According to the dominant narrative, mercy is ineffective and undeserved. Ironically, there is a hopelessness, a cynicism, and even a nihilism in all this behavior and response—both the drug use and the lack of help and intervention from the culture shaped by the dominant narrative.

Much of this drug use is anesthesia against the pain of feeling worthless and hopeless within the culture. These young parents know they have no valued place. The dominant culture communicates through its entire media and through all its mouthpieces that a person's value and worth comes from the acquisition of stuff and shallow pleasures, and the honor that comes with those. Gratification must be immediate. As I have written, this dominant narrative doesn't really value and honor hard work at an honest job. The only jobs available to these young people are unvalued and belittling. They don't pay nearly enough for one person to survive. Many of the drug users are also involved in selling drugs to get stuff and pleasure.

An addict mistakes intensity and immediacy for intimacy. The entire dominant culture *prefers* intensity and immediacy to intimacy. The narrative teaches us to prefer stuff and shallow pleasures over community.

What are these children due within the dominant narrative? Or from within the world being created by the counter-narrative of Jesus?

From the beneficiaries and advocates of the dominant narrative? Or from the people of Jesus?

In the experience of the staff of the Justice Ministry, the *overwhelming* majority of the poor grandparents, great grandparents, aunts and uncles, and adult brothers and sisters in our city who take legal custody of these neglected, abused children, are devout Christians who give their faith as the deciding reason they are doing so.

**

The dominant narrative says that homeless people are homeless because they do not want to work and prefer being homeless. Thus, says this narrative, they are not due our mercy. When I served as chairperson of the local commission appointed by our mayor to draft a ten-year plan to end chronic homelessness in our city, I spent a lot of time on the street talking to homeless people, getting to know their names and their stories, and getting to know why individuals fall into and are then trapped in homelessness. I learned that the dominant narrative's claim about why people are homeless is dead wrong, as this narrative is about most things related to the poor. People are not homeless because they don't want to work; they are homeless because they cannot get enough decently paying work to get out of homelessness. They can't get that work because minimum wage is not nearly enough. They can't get that work because they are women with children who are homeless because they are running from family violence, and they have no child care. They can't get that work because they are men and women with a physical disability. They can't get that work because they are mentally ill, and part of the illness is denial and refusal to take medication. They can't get that work because they have a felony record for a serious mistake they made long ago—a mistake that will not be forgotten under the dominant narrative. Most homeless who are addicts become addicts after they become homeless. They lose hope and turn to drugs as anesthesia.

I met "Jane," a woman who had worked for years on an assembly line of a manufacturing company. She got out of her bed in her studio apartment one night to use the toilet, tangled her foot in her blanket, fell hard, and fractured her knee cap. The injury did not occur at work, so there was no workers' compensation coverage for her medical bills and no supplemental income while she was recovering. She had no savings

THE TOLL OF THE DOMINANT NARRATIVE 121

because her pay was barely enough to survive. Her employer provided her with no health insurance. While she was recovering, she was fired and told she could reapply when she was able to work again. When she recovered as much as she was going to, she had some lingering pain, so the employer would not take her back. The employer was able to hire a younger replacement at an even lower wage. She had no family left. She was evicted from her apartment for non-payment of rent. So she moved into a walk-in shelter for the homeless, one in which guests cannot stay during the day. Most sleep on mats on the floor, side to side and head to feet with the people sleeping around them.

When I met Jane, she was still living in that shelter. When she applied for a new job, she had to put down the shelter address as her residence and had to give the shelter's phone as a call-back number. When a prospective employer called and heard that she was living at the night shelter, they immediately lost interest in hiring her. She has been out of work so long that she is now trapped there.

This kind of story is far more common than the dominant narrative would have us believe. According to the dominant narrative, Jane is homeless because she deserves it. According to this narrative, Jane is homeless because she is lazy. According to the dominant narrative, Jane is merely a loser of the *agón*.

People prey upon the homeless in their need. In my city, the homeless are funneled into one neighborhood because all of the services and shelters are located there, and because they are shunned and coerced into being there. I would say that the homeless are treated like stray dogs, except that more people will help a stray dog than will help a homeless person. The fast-food places, gas stations, and convenience stores in "their" neighborhood regularly cheat homeless workers. They promise to pay them less than minimum wage. Then they pay them less than the amount they promised. Or they fail to pay them at all.

Almost all the able-bodied, homeless males in my city have used a private, for-profit labor pool operator to find work. The office is located on the edge of the homeless neighborhood. Homeless people line up well before dawn every day to try to be picked for work. The work is often "walking paper"—walking door to door in a distant neighborhood, stuffing flyers into front doors, with the promise of being paid pennies per page stuffed. So the operator looks for people who can walk fast and long.

One labor pool operator preyed upon alcoholics. This operator had contracts with local, professional, athletic venues to clean the spectator areas of trash after the evening sporting event had ended. The labor pool operator was paid a set amount to clean the entire venue. He hired the homeless to do the actual cleaning. He maximized his profit by keeping the amount he paid to the homeless as low as he could. This is of course just a good business practice according to the dominant narrative. He preferred alcoholic homeless for this work. He would pay beer vendors at the venue to keep their beer selling counters open. The workers were to be paid minimum wage of $7.25 an hour. But the operator would offer to pay them in beer. The going price for a jumbo cup of beer was $7.50 per cup. He would pay his homeless alcoholic workers one jumbo cup per hour. But the actual cost to the vendor, including the beer and the cup, was $1.50 each. The operator offered to pay the vendor $3.00 a cup of beer. The end result was that the operator in effect paid the homeless alcoholic $3.00 an hour. None of this was disclosed to the workers. A lot of alcoholic workers jumped at the chance.

The operator transported the homeless to the venues in vans. The workers sat in the back of the van on wooden benches that were not fastened to the floorboard and were without seat belts. The vans were death traps. At the Justice Ministry, we tried very hard to find potential plaintiffs to obtain an injunction against the use of these vans. None of the men I found who had ridden in the vans would lend their name and testimony to such a suit. They didn't want to lose the source of income.

Under the dominant narrative, it is only just that people are homeless and vulnerable. They are losers in the contest. And because they are losers, you and I needn't be concerned about the way they are preyed upon.

But what about under the counter-narrative of Jesus?

**

First, a parable.

A group of wolves conspired to dam a stream and create a pond of cool, clear drinking water. When a drought hit, as the wolves expected, they patrolled the pond and only let the weakest, most vulnerable, thirstiest sheep into the pond to drink of the cool water. When the sheep had drunk their fill, and were so filled with water they couldn't run, the wolves killed and ate them. And when the wolves were being criticized for preying on the sheep, they answered that they were providing a "needed service" to the sheep. After all, who else was supplying the thirsty sheep with water?

Second, a story.

We at the Justice Ministry represented a young woman named "Louise." Louise was thirty and had a son who was almost ten and a daughter who was twelve. The father of the children was "Roger." Roger refused to marry Louise. He supported Louise and the two children intermittently, just often enough to keep them dependent upon him. Louise had a high-school education but was unable to make the kind of money on her own to cover child care to enable her to work full time. So she needed his support, as unreliable as it was. Roger would show up at Louise's door with some cash, demand to spend the night in her bed, ignore the children and leave. She suspected he had the same relationship with other women who were also mothers of his children.

Roger was an alcoholic and a drug abuser. Even when he showed up drunk and high, she still felt she had to let him in to receive his money. He was verbally and physically abusive to her in front of the children. When the son started imitating Roger's behavior, Louise was moved to act. She called the police when he assaulted her the next time. She moved herself and her children to another apartment, the location of which was unknown to him. She carried through on the criminal prosecution. He pled guilty to the assault and received 90 days in jail, which he served on weekends. And she applied to the local District Attorney's Protective Order Unit. The DA's office obtained a two-year Protective Order for Louise. And the Unit referred Louise to the Justice Ministry so we could enforce the Protective Order when Roger inevitably violated it, and so we could obtain a child-support court order requiring Roger to pay a set amount of monthly support so Louise could try to make a new life free of him.

When Louise came to the Justice Ministry, she had not been able to work full time and her part-time job was low pay. Because Roger had not provided any money to her for many months, Louise had fallen behind in her rent payments. She and her children were in danger of being evicted and of having her old automobile repossessed. No car, no job.

Desperate, without family or friends in the area, she had turned to two national "pay day loan" companies.

The Methodist Justice Ministry monthly pays past-due rent for clients like Louise and her two children—if, that is, the landlord will not take our money and then evict the family anyway. We use money from contributions to pay rent and utilities to keep families from eviction and having to go back to their abusers. So we paid off the past due rent for Louise and her two children. The world of these children had been turned upside down enough, and we wanted to have the stability of remaining in their present, familiar home.

But that left the payday loans. In this case, Louise had two of these payday loans outstanding. If we didn't pay them off all at once, by the approaching deadline, Louise would default and be forced by contract to extend and increase the loans. More and more of her paycheck would be eaten up to service these loans, she would never be able to pay off the principle, and she would never be able to afford to support her own children.

One of the loans was for a principal amount of $571.00. Louise had borrowed this money for one month. At the one month anniversary of the loan by 5 p.m. sharp, she was required by contract to pay back the principal of $571.00 plus a "fee" of another $131.40. So she had received $571.00 from the company, and in one month, had to pay back $702.40. If she didn't make that full payment of $702.40 on time, that $702.40 would turn into the principal of another loan, with a still greater fee. And so on and on. This company was doing what these companies do—make money by defaulting, "extending," and increasing loans and "fees." All this when people couldn't afford the loan under its contractual terms in the first place. We were able to pay that first payday loan off by the first deadline, and get Louise and her children out from under.

The second loan for Louise was from another national company for a principal of $610.00. At 5 p.m. on the two-weeks anniversary of the loan, this principal of $610.00 plus a fee of $124.00 had to be paid. This fine company was charging Louise $124.00 for two-weeks' use of $610.00. Again, the full amount of $734.00 had to be paid off by 5 p.m., or the same kind of default and "extension" system I describe above would take effect.

I arrived at this second "loan" store at 4 p.m. on the day the two-week loan was due. I tried to pay off the full amount of $734.00 with a debit card. I got a lot of push-back from the employee behind the counter and plastic screen. There would be a large fee just for using a debit card. When I insisted on using the debit card anyway, she reported that her computer system had suddenly gone down, and that $734.00 *in cash* would be required to pay off the loan on time.

"What if your computer system doesn't come back on line by 5 pm?"

"The loan would automatically default and renew by contract."

"Even though I am here on time to pay it off in full?"

"You aren't here with cash. The contract says we are allowed to insist upon payment by cash. And you shouldn't have waited until the last second."

"How are people who need your loans in the first place supposed to come up with that kind of cash? The only place they can go for that amount of cash in a lump is here or a place like here."

"We make all this clear to them when we give them the money."

At this point, I had about 35 minutes to come up with $734.00 in cash. I got some help from the internet, sped to a bank that was fortunately only 12 blocks away, and got the $734.00 in cash.

I arrived back at the store. I tendered the $734.00 cash in the full amount.

"Our computer system is still down. I can't take the money."

"Why does the computer need to be up for you to accept cash? You told me 15 minutes ago that I should go get cash."

"I didn't say that I could accept cash without the computer being up. How I am supposed to know how much is owed without the computer?"

"You told me what was owed 15 minutes ago." And I showed her the note she had given me with the amount she had written on it. "You know how much is owed. And you can give me a handwritten receipt with the date and time of payment."

"I am not authorized to do that."

"So you are telling me that even though Louise is living up to the letter of her contract, through me, you are not authorized to accept this cash, and she will default on this loan as of a few minutes from now?"

"Are you always this rude?"

"Lady, I am just getting started."

I demanded the telephone number for her supervisor. I assume that she wanted me to be rude to someone else so she dialed the number for me and handed me the phone. I stood in front of this employee, who was trying to lock up, until I pleaded and threatened my way to a paralegal in their corporate, legal department. This legal assistant first told me that it was past 5 pm, so Louise was already automatically in default on the loan. This default had already been noted at 5 p.m. in their computer system.

"So, the computer is down when it comes to accepting a pay-off of a loan, but is still operating fine when it comes to automatically defaulting on the loan?"

I told this legal assistant who I was and what the Methodist Justice Ministry does, and told her that if Louise was defaulted and was then forced to extend and increase the loan, despite my being there on time tendering full payment for her, we would sue everyone involved. Then they would have to pay Louise's legal fees, which would amount to *a lot* more than the loan amount we were discussing. This legal assistant informed me that by contract any dispute had to be arbitrated. I told her that I would attack this arbitration clause as unconscionable. This legal assistant then seemed to put her hand over the mouth piece on her phone. I heard a muffled conversation on her end. Then the assistant asked me to hand the phone to the store employee. The employee listened for less than a minute and hung up. The employee then slid sideways—oh, I don't know, maybe three and a half feet—to another computer terminal to her right. You'll never guess what happened then. The computer system came back on line. A miracle! Hallelujah! And she took my cash and gave me a receipt: "Paid in full."

Here's the rest of the story. As I went outside the store, I found a middle-aged woman waiting for me. I had not noticed, I suppose because I was too busy being rude, that this second lady had come into the loan store, watched, and listened to what was happening. We'll call her "Ms. Maude." Ms. Maude waited outside to tell me, "Mister, almost every time I come in here to pay-off a loan, their computer goes down. But when I come in to make only a partial payment, or to take out a new loan, that computer is always working." "Ma'am, I have to ask. Then why do you come back?" "I got nowhere else to turn," Ms. Maude said. "I got grandbabies to feed and rent to pay."

I was trying to picture how folks without a law degree, without forty years of learning how to be rude effectively, deal with companies like these.

I wish this story was just another parable.

And, of course, these companies claim that they do provide a needed service to folks like Louise and Ms. Maude.

After all, sheep need to be sheared.

All of their contracts have arbitration provisions.

The justice of the world created by the dominant narrative is that companies like these are due whatever they can get under the rules. And then they hire lobbyists to make sure this is within the rules.

CHAPTER 7

God's Justice and Mercy Proclaimed in the Parables of Jesus

THE DOMINANT NARRATIVE'S TEACHINGS about value, meaning, honor, happiness, and particularly about justice and mercy, are shallow failures. These teachings are like "chaff that the wind drives away" (Ps 1:4). They do not satisfy and they do not serve the individual or the community. These teachings have created a closed nation of individuals who are alone, fearful, suspicious, and at war with every person and every nation for things and pleasures that do not satisfy, ennoble, or save. This narrative has created and been created by a society of strangers and mere competitors, not a community of neighbors. The narrative has created and been created by an insular, entitled class of the super wealthy who lack effective empathy for working or poor people. This narrative is responsible for the increasing inequality, immobility, injustice and mercilessness of this culture.

The counter-narrative of Jesus is starkly and thoroughly in conflict with this dominant narrative. God's justice and mercy, as set forth in Our Lord's narrative, would satisfy, ennoble, save and create the true *shalom* that the dominant narrative manifestly does not. The plights of the women, children, and men that I describe in chapter 6 would be radically different if American Christians first admitted the depth of the conflict between the dominant narrative and the counter-narrative of Jesus, and chose to follow Jesus' way instead.

We must turn from an "abstract concept" of justice and mercy to the revelation of God's justice and God's mercy in Scripture, and *particularly in the parables of Jesus of Nazareth*. My answer to the true nature of God's justice and mercy lies in discerning what Jesus tells us in his parables that all are due.

In this chapter, I wish to show that God's justice and mercy are not in opposition but are integral and complementary aspects of the same Truth and Way. Revealed in the parables of Jesus, what every child of God is due as a matter of justice is mercy and to be made merciful. It is the form of the mercy that changes in every situation. In the parables of Jesus, God's justice is always accompanied with God's mercy, as challenging and uncertain as this can be to discern and balance in a given situation. The criteria by which we are to determine what is due from whom and to whom is radically different than the criteria used by the dominant narrative of the secular culture.

We start with the parable of the sower from Mark, then go to the parables of Luke, and then to those in Matthew.

✶✶

The Parable of the Sower

1 Again he began to teach beside the sea. Such a very large crowd gathered around him that he got into a boat on the sea and sat there, while the whole crowd was beside the sea on the land. 2 He began to teach them many things in parables, and in his teaching he said to them: 3 "Listen! A sower went out to sow. 4 And as he sowed, some seed fell on the path, and the birds came and ate it up. 5 Other seed fell on rocky ground, where it did not have much soil, and it sprang up quickly, since it had no depth of soil. 6 And when the sun rose, it was scorched; and since it had no root, it withered away. 7 Other seed fell among thorns, and the thorns grew up and choked it, and it yielded no grain. 8 Other seed fell into good soil and brought forth grain, growing up and increasing and yielding thirty and sixty and a hundredfold." 9 And he said, "Let anyone with ears to hear listen!"

10 When he was alone, those who were around him along with the twelve asked him about the parables. 11 And he said to them, "To you has been given the secret of the kingdom of God, but for those outside, everything comes in parables; 12 in order that

'they may indeed look, but not perceive,
and may indeed listen, but not understand;
so that they may not turn again and be forgiven.'"

13 And he said to them, "Do you not understand this parable? Then how will you understand all the parables? 14 The sower sows the word. 15 These are the ones on the path where the word is sown: when they hear, Satan immediately comes and takes away the word that is sown in them. 16 And these are the ones sown on rocky ground: when they hear the word, they immediately receive it with joy. 17 But they have no root, and endure only for a while; then, when trouble or persecution arises on account of the word, immediately they fall away. 18 And others are those sown among the thorns: these are the ones who hear the word, 19 but the cares of the world, and the lure of wealth, and the desire for other things come in and choke the word, and it yields nothing. 20 And these are the ones sown on the good soil: they hear the word and accept it and bear fruit, thirty and sixty and a hundredfold." (Mark 4:1–20)

We start with this parable of the sower because the entire thesis of this book of the interconnection of God's justice and mercy collapses if Jesus actually said what is attributed to him in verses 10–12.

There is something of a disconnect between the parable itself set forth at verses 3 through 9 and the privileged secret provided in explanation to the disciples at verses 10 through 20. For me, the explanation is inconsistent with the parable itself and is also internally inconsistent. And there is a terrible disconnect between the utter mercilessness of verses 10 through 12, and the mercy so incarnate in Jesus' other teachings and entire ministry. Did Jesus mercilessly keep secrets from the hungry, ill, crippled, suffering, and outcast members of the crowds that followed him, and upon whom he otherwise poured so much mercy? Apart from his initial response to the Syrophoenecian woman reported in Mark 7:24–30—a merciless response that he quickly corrected with a merciful healing—when did Jesus ever refuse to eat, touch, or heal anyone? Don't the parables illumine instead of conceal? Verses 10 through 12 are among the most doubtful, pernicious, and merciless in all of Hebrew and Greek Scripture.

If we consider the parable itself at verses 3 through 9 apart from the verses 13 through 20, we are left with a burning question: Why would a sower spread his precious seeds on a hard path, on rocky ground, and among thorns, as opposed to spreading them all on "good soil?" Is there anything at all surprising about what happened with the seeds sown on these hostile topographies?

Is it surprising that a seed sown on a hard path would not germinate and grow before it was trampled on or eaten by birds? Wouldn't the surprise have been if it had flourished?

Is it surprising that a seed sown on rocky soil, with only a thin layer of soil over rock, would germinate but not be able to survive? Is it surprising that the rock would prevent the root from burrowing deep enough to find water? Is it surprising that the plant would die from scorching sun? Again, wouldn't the surprise have been if the germinated seed on rocky soil had flourished?

Is it surprising that seed sown among thorns would be choked off, that the tough thorns would hoard the water and the sun, and stunt the plant's growth? Again, wouldn't the surprise have been if the seed had flourished among the thorns?

Imagine that you have a garden in which you want to grow flowers or vegetables. Before you planted, would you examine the ground to ensure you weren't planting the seed in rock or thorn? Would you instead plant them in the prepared soil of the garden?

Now consider again that the seeds described in the parable were precious—the result of last season's hard labor—and that their flourishing was vital to the survival of the sower and his family. Seeds had to be set aside from previous plantings, preserved, and protected. Given the inherent uncertainties of farming in the best of circumstances—the risks of drought, disease, and birds, and the uncertainties of the market—every seed was precious, and none was to be wasted.

So wouldn't Jesus' listeners have been shocked by these choices by the sower in this parable? Indeed, wouldn't this parable have produced scorn and laughter from the listeners at the clownish fool who spread his precious, life-giving seed on such merciless grounds? What terrible stewardship! What terrible farming practice! What was this sower thinking? What was his goal? Who is he? How could he have survived even a second growing season as a farmer?

Surely the initial reaction of most who heard this parable was that the sower was a negative example. So when Jesus is reported to have said at the conclusion of the parable at verse 8b, "Let anyone with ears to hear listen!" what the hearers may well have heard was "Do not be a clownish fool by spreading your precious seed on a hard path, on rocky ground, or among thorns. Instead, spread the seed on good soil. Don't waste the seed, particularly when seeds spread on good soil have the potential to produce so abundantly."

But there are at least three problems to such an initial reaction as the understanding that Jesus intended.

First, such a reaction and interpretation does not allow for a surprise or a shocking twist in the parable. Surprises, shocks, and twists from the dominant narrative of the time were part and parcel of Jesus' parables. These surprises were some of the ways that he ensured that his parables would get under people's skins and change his listeners. Consider three of Jesus' best known parables. In the parable of the prodigal son, if the father had responded to the son's return by making him stay in the servant's quarters until the son proved himself and earned his way back into the family, would we remember this parable? Would it have challenged us and our usual way of thinking and reacting as it does? In the parable of the good Samaritan, wasn't it shocking to Jesus' listeners that it was the hated, alien enemy who was so merciful, and not the two professionally religious Jews? And in the parable of the workers in the vineyard, if the owner had paid the workers who were hired so late in the work day some fraction of a *denarius*, or if the owner had not made such a show to the longer laboring laborers of paying a full day's wage to the workers hired at the end of the work day, would this parable have gotten under the listeners' and the readers' skins as it has? So where is the surprise in the intended understanding of this parable of the sower that Jesus was merely telling us to be selective where we sow the word of God?

Second, wouldn't the listeners to the parable of the sower have known that Jesus sowed his word of mercy, his food, his healings, and indeed himself everywhere to everyone, no matter the ground? Wasn't this the crux of the controversy between Jesus and the religious insiders? In fact, didn't the Pharisees complain that he was sowing almost all of his seed in the most unsuitable places among the least-deserving people? Weren't the Pharisees and the scribes objecting that Jesus was wasting his words on sinners—the violators of Torah, the unclean, the impure, and the traitorous tax collectors? So was Jesus responding in this parable of the sower by telling his disciples and followers not to waste their time and their seed planting among Pharisees and the leaders of the synagogue, the Romans, and the wealthy because the planting would prove fruitless? But is this consistent with Jesus' other actions and teachings? How many stories are there in the gospels of him eating with, teaching, and being merciful to Pharisees, scribes, leaders of the synagogue, the wealthy, and even Romans and their collaborators the tax collectors? Jesus was indeed a sower like the sower in the parable, spreading his word of God's mercy and himself everywhere to everyone, despite the odds against an abundant harvest from some of the sown seeds.

So, third, wouldn't it have also occurred to the listeners that Jesus was describing himself and God as the sower? Didn't he imply in his admonition at verse 9 that the seeds were the words he was speaking? In the doubtful (to me) explanation starting at Mark 4:14, Jesus states that the seed was the word and thus implied strongly that the sower of the seed in this parable stands for Jesus himself. Jesus ("the Son of Man") describes himself as the sower of seed in Matt 13:37 and God as the owner of a vineyard in Matt 20:1–8. God is described as the planter of a vineyard in Isa 5:7 and Jer 12:10, and the sower of seed in Jer 31:27. These poetic metaphors had long been part of the culture of Jesus' listeners. Then how could an initial reaction have endured as a valid understanding of the parable that Jesus' followers were to be much more selective that Jesus was about where to sow his word?

Judging by verses 10 through 20, an explanation evidently spread among the early Christian communities that the parable should not be understood in a straightforward way. Instead, it had a private, privileged meaning disclosed in "secret" to those on the inside but withheld from the "very large crowd," or the "great crowd gathered and people from town after town" (Luke 8:4), who came to Jesus for teaching and for healing but who were still on the "outside" (Mark 4:11).

But how could that be? How could this Jesus described in all the other verses of the Synoptic Gospels want to hide "the secret of the kingdom of God" from those he came to save?

The justification given by the gospel writers relied upon Isa 6:9–10, quoted in Mark 4:12 and Luke 8:10. The argument was that Jesus' use of parables just followed Isaiah 6 "so that they may not turn and be forgiven."

There are many objections to this terrible distortion of Jesus' teachings and life. The main objection is that these brief verses place the most merciless of purposes in the heart and on the lips of the most merciful of beings. The best way to understand Jesus' parables is by reference to his life and ministry of mercy.

A related objection is that one of Jesus' main teachings was to repent and be forgiven (Mark 1:4, 1:15, and 6:12). But here, the gospel writer claims that Jesus chooses a mode of speaking intended to *prevent* people from understanding how to repent and be forgiven.

Another objection is that the verses from Isa 6:9–10, quoted in Mark 4:12, were spoken and written in a completely different setting than the setting of the ministry of Jesus. The call of Isaiah was radically different than the call of Jesus. When Isaiah prophesied, the LORD had firmly decided to punish the people of Israel for their violation of Torah, for their worship of other gods and for the exploitation by the wealthy of the poor. The LORD charged the prophet Isaiah to speak a word of judgment and eminent punishment to the people, but not in a way that would cause them to actually repent and avoid the punishment. Part of Isaiah's call was to "[m]ake the mind of this people dull, and stop their ears, and shut their eyes so that they may not look with their eyes and listen with their ears and comprehend with their minds and turn and be healed" (Isa 6:10). But Jesus came for the absolutely opposite purpose of calling and persuading God's people to turn and repent, saying, "The time is fulfilled, and the kingdom of God has come near; repent, and trust in the good news" (Mark 1:14–15).

Jesus' stated purpose in Mark 4:11 of using parables to ensure that his words *not* bear fruit with outsiders is inconsistent with the abundance of the harvest described at verse 20. In verses 10 and 11, Jesus allegedly describes his use of parables as an intended impediment to the flourishing of the seed. But in the explanation at verses 13 through 20, he describes "Satan," "trouble or persecution," and "cares of the world, the lure of wealth, and the desire for other things" as the impediments. So verses 10 through 12 are inconsistent with verses 13 through 20. And verses 10 through 12 are inconsistent with the parable itself, unless we are to count Jesus' use of parables as the thorns that choke the word of the good news.

The clear purpose and success of Jesus' use of parables was to grow the kingdom of God, to plant mercifully a growing seed of understanding, influence, justice and mercy in people's hearts, and not to hide mercilessly the kingdom, its presence, its further coming, and its nature from people.

This pernicious explanation of Jesus' use of parables—that the use was to hide and obscure—is radically inconsistent with his teachings. "But strive first for the kingdom of God and his righteousness . . ." (Matt 6:33). "So I say to you, Ask and it will be given you; search and you will find, knock and the door will be opened for you. For everyone who asks receives, and everyone who searches finds, and for everyone who knocks, the door will be opened. Is there anyone among you who, if your child asks for a fish, will give a snake instead of a fish? Or if the child asks for an egg, will give a scorpion? If you then, who are evil, know how to give good gifts to your children, how much more will the heavenly Father give the Holy Spirit to those who ask him?" (Luke 11:9–13). Strive for the righteousness of the kingdom, but the one who taught this then obscured that righteousness and kingdom with obscure and obscuring parables? Ask, search, and knock, but the teacher will respond by hiding from some that which was asked, sought, and knocked for?

As for the power and success of these parables, consider that we have no record that Jesus himself preserved his parables by writing them down. He just spoke aloud these amazing, enduring stories over a period of, according to the Synoptic Gospels, no more than a year. Surely he used somewhat different versions of them in different settings and before different groups. Perhaps a parable changed, grew, and flourished as he used it, like the seeds of this parable. Surely Jesus had a repertoire, if you will, of parables, from which he chose as he traveled from setting to setting teaching of the kingdom. These parables were brilliant, vivid, and fertile products of his experience, his mind, his breath, and his larynx. These parables were his performances, which included his delivery, his tone of voice, his facial expressions, his mannerisms, and his gaze at one or another of the groups in attendance as he spoke.

One would reasonably have expected that spoken stories would not endure and would have no further impact after the sound of the spoken words faded away in the air. But the power of these parables to teach and to transform people's lives was so great that followers remembered and wrote them down. Through the centuries, these stories have had greater impact upon individuals and cultures than any other collection of stories in all of recorded history, greater even than Homer's or Shakespeare's. That power has come from what these parables have revealed, not what they have obscured and hidden. Listeners and readers have been able to peel away their multiple layers of meanings in their own times and settings. If the use of parables was intended by Jesus to keep his truth secret and to prevent understanding and transformation, Jesus was the greatest failure as a storyteller in history. To claim that Jesus intended to teach in parables so that his audiences would "look but not perceive, and listen but not understand" (Mark 4:12), is demonstrably untrue by the nature and impact of these parables.

Fourth, such a claim about why Jesus spoke in parables is utterly out of place and in total conflict with the character and mission of Jesus revealed in these gospels. For instance, this claim that Jesus used parables to hide the truth of the kingdom from outsiders is also in the eighth chapter of Luke. Shortly after Jesus proclaimed the purpose of his ministry by reading from what we call Isaiah 61 in his home synagogue in Nazareth (Luke 4:18–19), he told the "crowds" who wanted "to prevent him from leaving them" that "I must proclaim the good news of the kingdom of God to the other cities also; for I was sent for this purpose" (Luke 4:42–43). Intermingled with healings, he continued to spread this good news. He taught while "Pharisees and teachers of the law . . . from every village of Galilee and Judea and from Jerusalem" listened to him (Luke 5:17). He preached his Sermon on the Plain (Luke 6:20–49), to "a great crowd of his disciples and a great multitude of people from all Judea, Jerusalem, and the coast of Tyre and Sidon . . . who had come to hear him" (Luke 6:17–18). Part of that sermon was: "Why do you call me 'Lord, Lord,' and not do what I tell you?" (Luke 6:46). "[Be] someone . . . who comes to me, hears my words, and acts on them" (Luke 6:4). Thereafter, Jesus healed the slave of a Roman centurion (Luke 7:1–10), and then raised from the dead a poor widow's only son (Luke 7:11–15), causing the word that he was a "great prophet" to spread "throughout Judea and all the surrounding country" (Luke 7:16–17). Later he ate with a Pharisee in his home, and welcomed and defended a "woman of the city, who was a sinner" who intruded into the dinner to minister to him (Luke 7:36–50). "Soon afterwards he went on through the cities and villages, proclaiming and bringing the good news of the kingdom of God" (Luke 8:1). The twelve disciples and many women were with him (Luke 8:1–3). Then, when another "great crowd gathered" (Luke 8:4), he told the parable of the sower. And just after Jesus allegedly claimed that he taught in parables to hide secrets from outsiders, Jesus exhorted his followers to put their light on a lampstand that all may see, not hide their light under a jar or a bed (Luke 8:16). Then, when his family came to fetch him home, Jesus said, "My mother and brothers are those who hear the word of God and do it" (Luke 8:21).

Does this sound like Jesus was trying to hide "the secrets of the kingdom of God" (Luke 8:10) from the crowds of people who came to hear him? How would using parables to hide the truth of the kingdom of God be "good news"? Why would Jesus teach people to "come to me and hear my words and act on them" and then hide the meaning of his calls to action? Why would Jesus teach that those "who hear the word of God and do it" are his family, and then hide from people what that word meant and required? Why would people flock great distances from everywhere to hear the words of a man who taught hidden truths in stories that only a few insiders could understand? When everything that Jesus did and

said was intended manifestly to save those whom the religious establishment considered outsiders and to break down the barriers to God erected
by these insiders, why would Jesus teach through a medium intended to
keep outsiders outside?

So these reasons are why I say the claim that Jesus taught in parables
to keep people from perceiving and understanding is inconsistent, per-
verse, and a dishonor to Jesus and to God. Again, these verses place the
most merciless of purposes in the heart and on the lips of the most merciful of beings.

Which brings us back to Mark 4:13–20, where Jesus is reported to
have provided a secret explanation to the insiders. The explanation is inconsistent with the parable itself and internally inconsistent.

In this explanation, Jesus first says at verse 14 that the sown seeds
are the word of God. But then he quickly shifts to referring to the seed
as the persons who presumably hear the word and respond differently.
The seeds are "the ones on the path." The seeds are "the ones sown on
rocky ground" who "hear the word [and] immediately receive it with joy"
but who eventually "fall away." The seeds are the "others" "sown among
thorns" and "the ones who hear the word" but whose "cares," "lures and
"desires" choke off the word. The seeds are the "the ones" "in the good
soil" who receive and accept the word and bear abundant fruit. The responses of the people hearing the word is likened allegorically to what
happened to the seed when it fell on the various ground.

In the parable itself, all the seeds of the word are identical. The same
word is spread to everyone in every setting. It is the topography that de-
termines whether the seeds will take root and flourish, not the seed. In
the parable, the sower can tell the characteristics of the ground on which
he sows as he is sowing. He can see that certain seeds sown on certain
ground are unlikely to live and grow, but he sows them there anyway. So
the blame, if there is any, for the dying or the flourishing of the word lies
with the sower. *But in the explanation,* the seeds are as different as the
hearers and their responses are different. The ground on which the seed
is sowed is compared to the response of the listeners to his proclamation. The characteristic of the ground, whether it is hard path or rocky or
thorny, is only known by the subsequent response to the sowing by the
hearer. The sower evidently cannot tell the characteristics of the ground
when he sows the word.

So the explanation blames the ones hearing the word for its failure or flourishing. Some listeners responded not at all. The word had no

attraction or power for them. Their hearts were like the path on which some of the seed fell. The response of the hearts of other listeners was at first receptive. But as the challenge of living out Jesus' proclamation of the kingdom grew evidently more challenging, the word died in them. They lacked the endurance and the courage to persevere. So their hearts are likened to rocks and thorns. But the hearts of others received the word and were changed by it into productive soil, so the word grew and flourished in their lives. "Let everyone who has ears to hear listen!" is a plea to listen and become "good soil," rather than hard path, rock or thorns. On this basis, when the word flourished and was productive, the listeners were due credit for the growth. And when the word died, it was because the listeners were due blame and even condemnation.

The explanation set forth in verses 13 through 20 turns the parable on its head. In the original, unexplained parable, it is hardly surprising what happened to these seeds—which seeds took root, thrived, and flourished and which seeds did not. It is a tortured explanation to make the persons on whom the seeds fell responsible for their flourishing or failing and not the sower who chose to sow on good and on inhospitable ground.

The key for me is in the parable itself, not in the appended explanation. The sower spreads his word to everyone in every setting, to the rich in settings of comfort and privilege, to the poor in settings of want and exclusion, and to everyone between. And the sower does so knowing that the word was much, much less likely to grow and flourish on some ground than the other. *But he sows everywhere to everyone anyway.*

As I read the parable itself, Jesus led the great, listening crowd to understand that the sower represented Jesus himself and that the seed was his word of the arriving kingdom of God's mercy. He described realistically the different way that his listeners could and would likely respond to the word, based upon their histories, families, economic situations, and social locations. *But Jesus, in his mercy, still sowed his word to everyone, everywhere.* He did not preach his word of mercy only to those whom he judged were due to hear it. He did not withhold it from sinners among the poor and the wealthy whom many believed were not deserving of mercy. He did not proclaim it only in a gathering of people allowed in after his disciples had screened and deemed them worthy or likely to respond productively. He did not proclaim it only among the Pharisees or the righteous few who claimed to live by every requirement of Torah, nor did he exclude those from his sowing. He did not proclaim it only to those who were already merciful to the poor, but also to the self-satisfied, the self-righteous, and even to the oppressors of the poor. He sowed much where his word of mercy was very unlikely to flourish. His sowing was a great act of non-judgmental mercy.

Jesus' words of mercy were part of his life of mercy. He lived out his words. He walked his talk. So we may also consider the seeds as acts of his mercy along with his healings, his feedings, his touchings, his inclusions, and his sharing of meals with everyone, no matter whether they were insiders or outsiders, Jew or gentile, male or female, and no matter whether they were considered clean or unclean, pure or impure, Torah righteous or Torah sinner, merciful or merciless, or rich or poor. He sows his words and acts of mercy on everyone in every situation, just as the foolish sower does in the parable. He speaks and acts out his words of mercy to everyone no matter their histories, families, economic situations and social locations. He did this even though the ground on which they found themselves, or had chosen, made it predictable how they would respond. But he did it out of mercy and because of the power of God to transform lives no matter the ground they are on. "'Indeed, it is easier for a camel to go through the eye of a needle than for someone who is rich to enter the kingdom of God.' Those who heard it said, 'Then who can be saved?' He replied, 'What is impossible for mortals is possible for God'" (Luke 8:25–27).

This understanding of the parable of the sower fits with the substance of Jesus' controversies with religious insiders and with his own followers. The religious insiders asked why he ate with sinners and tax collectors (Luke 5:30). They asked why he allowed a woman of the city and a sinner to touch him (Luke 7:39). And the crowds that followed Jesus asked him why he would eat with a chief tax collector and collaborator with the Romans (Luke 19:7).

In a sense, they were asking why he would waste his precious seed on ground that would surely produce nothing. And they were objecting, in their sense of justice, that these people were not due his words and acts of mercy. He responded through his words and actions that God's mercy is offered to everyone in every setting. He responded that God never gives up on anyone.

"Let anyone who has ears to hear listen," he says in Mark 4:8. Those who heard him should have understood that this was an admonition to be like the sower—to sow our words and acts of mercy everywhere to everyone. This was the surprise of this parable, the twist on what people would expect, because this was so in conflict with the dominant narrative of Jesus' time, symbolized by the foolish farming practice of such sowing. This is also deeply in conflict with the same dominant narrative of our time—a narrative that dictates that people must earn our mercy before we are merciful, and that our mercy must be due to them based upon their actions, their capacity for reciprocity, their relationship to us, or the likelihood that our mercy will bear fruit by causing them to fix their lives as we want them fixed. In this parable, Jesus is saying to you and me, "Sow mercy to everyone, without first assessing who is and is not likely to respond in the way you want, and without assessing who you judge to be due your mercy."

But the Methodist Justice Ministry and I do not act faithfully in light of this parable. We receive 20 to 25 new requests for free legal representation and help each week. We screen closely those who request our help. We have limited resources, and we are looking for the worst cases and the people who will benefit the most from our help. But one criterion we work by is not to take the case of an abused woman whom we can predict based upon hard experience is likely to return to her abuser. We make this assessment based upon a variety of factors, but the one we rely upon the most is whether the potential client has previously and repeatedly left her abuser but then returned to him. From working in this ministry, we hope that we have a good appreciation for why a woman returns, often with children, to her abuser's home. Often the reason is financial—because she cannot provide for herself and her children alone. Often it is because the psychological abuse she has endured has sapped her of her confidence, energy, and hope. Often it is because her abuser has kept her completely dependent upon him, and unable to make her own way. These are among the reasons why we provide free professional counseling and financial support to our clients.

But in assessing our screening practice in the light of this parable of the sower, I doubt that we are being faithful to the life and teaching of Jesus, who sowed his seeds of mercy everywhere and on everyone all the time. We don't take certain cases because we don't want to "waste" our seeds and because we want the twelve judges we practice before to rely upon our bringing only "good" cases to them. But an abused woman who has previously escaped and then returned to her abuser and then has escaped again is at least as much in need of our active mercy as one who is leaving an abuser for the first time. So perhaps we should just sow our seed and let Jesus determine what fruit it will bear. When Jesus says,

"Listen," I am hearing that we ought to be concentrating our seeds of mercy on the hardest paths, the rockiest ground, and amidst the thickest thorns.

Another great attraction of Jesus' own parable of the sower, as I interpret it, is its realism. Through this parable, Jesus tells us that everyone is vulnerable to forces and narratives that can and will kill mercy and mercifulness. What I hear as Jesus' original meaning was much more realistic, and much more in keeping with his other teachings, that the ground on which the listener found herself goes a long way to determining the receptiveness of her heart and how she is capable of responding. The ground on which she stood—her genetic inheritance, her history, her location, and her family, determined the receptiveness of her heart to the word and her capability to live it out.

The ground on which we comfortable people live *is* inhospitable to Jesus' word of mercy. Consider a child of a family in economically comfortable circumstances, a child brought up in a gated community in which everyone is a member of the same exclusive country club. Consider a child who attends a private school in which the students are carefully screened and come only from "good families." This child is likely taught that life is all about wealth, ostentatious consumption, comfort and freedom from risk. The only acceptable job is one that brings in lots of money. The child grows up associating only with people who think this way. The dominant narrative is utterly pervasive and judgmental. How hospitable could such ground be to Jesus' seeds of non-judgmental mercy?

Consider a child reared in a home in which the parents are constantly resentful and scapegoating others, and who model suspicion and condemnation. Consider a child reared in a home in which he is taught by his parents' words and actions to blame every poor person for their poverty, and to believe that everyone in need of the child's mercy is lying, lazy, and manipulative. How hospitable could that ground be to Jesus' seeds of non-judgmental mercy?

The ground on which the economically poor live can likewise prove inhospitable to the word of mercy. It is wrong to read Jesus' teachings as idealizing a life of poverty. A child born and reared in the ghetto is likely to have been exposed repeatedly to violence, anger, cruelty, exploitation, addiction, and hopelessness. That child will have experienced the random unfairness of life and the hypocrisy of a dominant narrative that asserts that she is to blame for the poverty into which she was randomly born. That child would have every reason to be bitter and angry. How hospitable could that ground be to Jesus' seeds of mercy?

But the response of people to Jesus' seeds of mercy can still prove something of a mystery. People do break free of the ground of their birth and of their present. Some children from wealthy families who are exposed to Jesus seeds of mercy do choose lives of service and modest comforts, as opposed to self-centered pursuit of stuff and transient experiences. The seed does sometimes transform the ground. It's a mystery which children from the thorny ground of wealth will choose the way of mercy. And some children from the ghetto or from rural poverty, raised on ground of hopelessness, do respond to the hard bitterness of their past with lives of hope and service. Some who are able to escape their poverty return to help the people left behind. It is a mystery which children will do this. Children from the same parents in any ground can have radically different reactions to the word of mercy and the ground in which they were born and reared.

**

The Woman of the City and the Parable of the Two Debtors

36 One of the Pharisees asked Jesus to eat with him, and he went into the Pharisee's house and reclined at the table. 37 And the sort of woman in the city who was a wicked sinner, having learned that he was eating in the Pharisee's house, brought an alabaster jar of ointment. 38 She stood behind him at his feet, weeping, and began to bathe his feet with her tears and to dry them with her hair. Then she continued kissing his feet and anointing them with the ointment. 39 Now when the Pharisee who had invited him saw it, he said to himself, "If this man were a prophet, he would have known who and what kind of woman this is who is touching him—that she is a sinner." 40 Jesus spoke up and said to him, "Simon, I have something to say to you." "Teacher," he replied, "Speak." 41 "A certain creditor had two debtors; one owed five hundred denarii, and the other fifty. 42 When they could not pay, he canceled the debts for both of them. Now which of them will love him more?" 43 Simon answered, "I suppose the one for whom he canceled the greater debt." And Jesus said to him, "You have judged rightly." 44 Then turning toward the woman, he said to Simon, "Do you see this woman? I entered your house; you gave me no water for my

feet, but she has bathed my feet with her tears and dried them with her hair. ⁴⁵ You gave me no kiss, but from the time I came in she has not stopped kissing my feet. ⁴⁶ You did not anoint my head with oil, but she has anointed my feet with ointment. ⁴⁷ Therefore, I tell you, her sins, which were many, have been forgiven; hence she has shown great love. But the one to whom little is forgiven, loves little." ⁴⁸ Then he said to her, "Your sins are forgiven." ⁴⁹ But those who were at the table with him began to say among themselves, "Who is this who even forgives sins?" ⁵⁰ And he said to the woman, "Your faith has saved you; go in peace." (Luke 7:36–50)

The sins of this woman were either known to this host, or he was merely prejudging her. All that is actually known of this woman from the story is that she lived in the city, was a *hamartolos,* a serious sinner, and loved Jesus with gratitude, devotion and sacrifice. Perhaps unfairly, she is presumed to be a prostitute, a woman who must sell her body to survive.

The intertestamental writing Sirach, known in Jesus' time, contains prohibitions against associating with a sinner, including a prostitute. "A prostitute is regarded as spittle. . ." (Sir 26:22; see also Sir 12:4–7, 13–14). Neither the woman nor the Pharisee makes a request for forgiveness. The Pharisee is proud. His welcome to Jesus is not loving. The woman is loving, grateful, courageous, and generous. Her response is the shadow of the Pharisee's. Which one needs the greater forgiveness? Jesus did say to her that her sins were forgiven. He did not say that to the Pharisee.

Jesus also said to the woman, "Your faith has saved you." The Greek word translated by the NRSV as "faith" is *pistis,* which could as easily be translated "trust." From what did her trust save her? From her prostitution? Or from her shame, her lack of self esteem, and her belief in what the Pharisee said about her? "Saved" is from the Greek *sōzō,* which means not only "to save or to rescue," but also "to protect, to heal, or to make whole." "Your own trust has made you whole" would be a provocative but fair translation. Jesus' words and actions emboldened this poor woman and inspired her trust in him and most of all in herself. Jesus welcomed her, allowed her to touch him, and accepted her tears and generosity. Before trusting herself, she trusted Jesus, his acceptance, and his love. She trusted that he would act toward her as she acted toward him, and that she could act toward him as he had already acted toward her. She trusted that Jesus believed and acted out that she was due his mercy. This trust, and Jesus' mercy, saved her from the contempt of others, self-contempt and so much else. Her trust, inspired by Jesus, "made her whole," just as the counter-narrative of Jesus seeks to create a world in which the poor and outcast of our time will be saved from the contempt of others and their own self-contempt learned from the dominant narrative of our time.

"Do you see this woman?" Jesus asks the Pharisee at verse 44. No, he does not. He does not see *her*. He sees only one of *them*. This unnamed woman could have been divorced, or widowed, or the daughter of an outcast. She could have been the daughter of a woman who was divorced and expelled by her husband, who then had to suffer in poverty and ostracism her entire life. She could have been born outside of marriage. Or her sin could have been violation of the purity laws of Torah, her failure to sacrifice or be cleansed after her monthly period, her eating of unclean foods in her poverty, or some sexual sins. The Pharisee is indiscriminate. A sinner is a sinner. She failed to perform the "thou shalts" and violated the "thou shalt nots." So he did not see *her*.

The Pharisee judges that Jesus is not a prophet. It was a given of that time that a prophet can see into the heart. The irony in the story is that Jesus could and did see into the heart of the woman and of the Pharisee. The Pharisee who cannot see thinks that he can.

This parable is about the interaction of God's justice and mercy. The Pharisee judges that the woman and Jesus are not due his mercy. He does not welcome the woman as a fellow child of God, as he did not welcome Jesus as an honored guest. His treatment of both shows he does not believe that they are due his mercy. He simply judges and condemns the woman as a sinner. And he judges and condemns Jesus for not judging and treating the woman as a sinner. According to the dominant narrative controlling the Pharisee, Jesus should have shared the Pharisee's judgement that the woman was not due to be so familiar with Jesus, to share his space, to touch him or to be merciful to him. In affording Jesus and the woman no mercy, the Pharisee renders onto them less than each of them are due under Jesus' and God's counter-narrative.

A decision we are called to make about this parable is who does the greater sinner of the parable represent—the woman of the city or the Pharisee?

The Pharisee probably heard the parable and concluded that it did not apply to him at all. If he recognized that one of the sinners in the parable represented him, he would have concluded that his sin was of course much less than the woman's. He would have concluded that he was in the position of the debtor whose debt was one tenth of the other debtor's. But even this—that he owed God for fifty sins—he would have resisted. And this was a great sin of his.

Jesus never explicitly identifies who the greater and the lesser debtors are. He leaves that to his listeners. Why do we assume that the poor woman is the greater debtor, when she was so much more loving, courageous, sacrificing, and merciful? We assume this because we are shaped by the dominant narrative of our time. But according to the counternarrative of Jesus, the mercilessness of judging that someone is not due mercy is the greatest of sins and creates the greatest of debts to God.

Jesus does say at verse 47 that the poor woman's sins were "many." But the fifty sins qualify as "many." Jesus does not say that her sins are more than the Pharisee's. With the Pharisee, we assume that she is the greater debtor and sinner. But in which narrative is this true? Is this assumption part of the Pharisee's sin and of ours?

Do the amounts of the debts of the two debtors provide a clue that Jesus is asking the Pharisee and us to see the Pharisee as the greater debtor? How could this poor woman possibly have incurred a debt of five hundred denarii, equivalent to five hundred days' work? Isn't it more likely that she could have run up fifty denarii in debt while the Pharisee was the one who could have accumulated five hundred? This Pharisee had a house in which to host meals. It would have been very difficult for this poor woman to have incurred or paid back a debt of fifty denarii. It would likely take a debt of five hundred denarii for the Pharisee not to be able to pay it back. Jesus was saying that it was the Pharisee who owed the greater debt within the meaning of the parable. In Jesus' time, commission of sins was considered to create debts to God. So the greater sinner would have incurred the greater debt. Within the dominant narrative of the Pharisee, this poor woman of the city was a much greater sinner than he was. But within the counter-narrative of Jesus, the Pharisee was the greater sinner for his mercilessness. I believe that Jesus is saying here that the Pharisee was the greater sinner for granting mercy only to those whom he believes mercy is due. This Pharisee was so given to condemnation to justify withholding mercy.

In the parable Jesus also says that love is inspired when crushing debt that could not possibly be repaid is mercifully forgiven (vv. 42–43). Therein Jesus teaches that the very purpose of God's forgiving sins is to inspire love of God and others. The question that Jesus asks his host immediately after he finishes telling the parable is "which of them [the greater or lesser sinner] will love . . . more?" (v. 42). The Pharisee is taken aback by the question, for he does not see that the purpose of forgiveness is to inspire love ("I suppose . . ." v. 43). Then Jesus says of the woman, "her sins, which were many, have been forgiven; *hence* she has shown great love" *(v. 47)*.

Why did Jesus represent this woman in his parable as a debtor who "could not pay" her debts, whether they were greater or lesser than the Pharisee's? Given the connection that Jesus makes in the parable between forgiveness of debt and the capability to love, this is the same as asking why she "could not love" until she was forgiven. Was it because her life had been so hard and unjust, because she had been so condemned and shunned? Was it because she did not trust herself and so was merciless to herself? This capacity to be merciful to herself was given back to her by Jesus' preaching, forgiveness, inclusion, and trust in her. She was freed to love by his mercy, and this merciful love poured back out of her in gratitude for the one who had saved her.

Why was it that the Pharisee is represented in the parable by a debtor who also "could not pay" his debts? This is also the same as asking why he "could not love." He could not love because he was trapped in a dominant narrative that devalued mercy and that made hard judgments of who was and was not due mercy. Given that he was trapped in this way of thinking and being, and that he resisted being saved from it, he would likely never be able to "pay" his debts to God.

The love this parable is about is mercy. Mercy is active, giving, compassionate, outpouring, and sacrificial love—a love that does not ask who and who is not due mercy, and a love that asks only what form mercy should take for particular persons in specific situations. In the story, the Pharisee showed no mercy to the woman at all. He barely tolerated her presence at the meal and probably did so because it enabled him to illustrate his condemnation of Jesus' association with sinners, adding to the Pharisee's sense of superiority. And the Pharisee showed no mercy in the form of true welcome to Jesus. He gave Jesus the bare minimum of hospitality. In the Pharisee's eyes, Jesus was due no more than this minimum as a matter of justice.

In clear and intended contrast, the poor woman was as merciful to Jesus as was possible for her. By her actions, she declared that Jesus was due all the mercy that she could give him in adoration and support. Jesus was due the courage she displayed in entering a private home where she knew she was counted as less than nothing. By this, she risked physical ejection and public shaming. She showed that Jesus was due the adoration of her body—her hair, her tears, her kisses—which was all she had. There is to me an undeniably erotic element to her love, which she also declared he was due. And she showed that Jesus was due sacrificial generosity through the expensive ointment she used to anoint his feet. She must have given all her material resources for that ointment. All this she did in gratitude and love for Jesus' rescue of her from public contempt and her lack of self-esteem. Perhaps she knew that Jesus was in a hostile place, among people who looked down upon Jesus as they looked down upon her. So she bravely entered and poured extravagant love upon him, showing the Pharisee how much Jesus was due. This poor woman was the lesser sinner, whatever her sins, because she was so merciful to Jesus and to herself.

By accepting her love and mercy, and by publicly welcoming her gifts, attention, adoration, and generosity, Jesus showed the world that this still unnamed, poor woman of the city—a woman of no account to the Pharisee—was due his respect, love, and welcome. He did not waive her away as unclean and unworthy to minister mercifully to him. He was not embarrassed because her ministrations came from one who was beneath him. He did not preserve his own honor and superiority by pulling his feet away from her touch. He did not try to reverse their positions, making himself the superior one who would minister to her because she was weeping. Instead, he was as merciful to her as he could be in that situation. He let her have the dignity and honor of being merciful to him. In the presence of the Pharisee, he declared that she had been forgiven, that she was *therefore* greatly loving and merciful, and that *she,* not the Pharisee, was the example for others to emulate.

This parable and the story in which it is embedded have so much to say to those of us today who want to live in a world being created by Jesus' counter-narrative. How many of us in the church will give our gifts to the poor whose faces we never see and whose lives we do not know—our back-to-school backpacks and clothes, our Thanksgiving baskets, and our Christmas presents—but would be embarrassed and scandalized if any of the poor presumed to give back to us or to join our inner circle? Under the influence of the dominant narrative of our time, we feel that they are not due inclusion in our circle. We think that the poor are not due the great mercy of our acceptance of their mercy to us. We think that they are not due being in the position of giver to us, and that we are not due being in the inferior position of recipient. Indeed, we feel that they have no mercy of value to give us. Yet so many economically poor people have taught and shown me so much about mercy and justice. The stories of some of them are in chapter 6.

According to the dominant narrative of Jesus' time and of ours, this poor woman was not due the mercy that Jesus gave her. She wasn't due being included or allowed into the Pharisee's house. She wasn't due being allowed to touch Jesus and minister to him. And under the dominant narrative of Jesus' time, Jesus wasn't due the mercy that the woman gave him. He was a poor, itinerant preacher and healer who seemed to be without income, who consistently violated the rules that determined who was deserving of being on the inside and who on the outside, who associated with the unclean and the immoral, who was a failure because he never accumulated any stuff, and who taught against the necessary basis for a functioning society. The dominant narratives of all times say that a necessary foundation of any functioning society is the distinctions that must be made among people who are and are not deserving of the society's goods and honor. But within the counter-narrative of Jesus, the necessary foundation of any covenantal community is for its people to be merciful to all. In the world being created by the counter-narrative of Jesus, what we are all justly due is mercy and to be made merciful. By Jesus' own mercy, example, and welcome of this "woman of the city," she had received the greatest mercy—to be made merciful. And this was the greatest mercy—to be made merciful—which the Pharisee refused.

⁎⁎

The Parable of the Good Samaritan

25 Just then a lawyer stood up to test Jesus. "Teacher," he said, "what must I do to inherit eternal life?" 26 He said to him, "What is written in the law? What do you read there?" 27 He answered, "You shall love the Lord your God with all your heart, and with all your soul, and with all your strength, and with all your mind; and your neighbor as yourself." 28 And he said to him, "You have given the right answer; do this, and you will live."

29 But wanting to justify himself, he asked Jesus, "And who is my neighbor?" 30 Jesus replied, "A man was going down from Jerusalem to Jericho, and fell into the hands of robbers, who stripped him, beat him, and went away, leaving him half dead. 31 Now by chance a priest was going down that road; and when he saw him, he passed by on the other side. 32 So likewise a

Levite, when he came to the place and saw him, passed by on the other side. [33] But a Samaritan while traveling came near him; and when he saw him, he was moved with pity. [34] He went to him and bandaged his wounds, having poured oil and wine on them. Then he put him on his own animal, brought him to an inn, and took care of him. [35] The next day he took out two denarii, gave them to the innkeeper, and said, 'Take care of him; and when I come back, I will repay you whatever more you spend.' [36] Which of these three, do you think, was a neighbor to the man who fell into the hands of the robbers?" [37] He said, "The one who showed him mercy." Jesus said to him, "Go and do likewise." (Luke 10:25–37)

In this very famous parable of Jesus—perhaps his most famous along with the parable of the prodigal son—the priest, Levite, and Samaritan speak mainly by their actions. By these they tell us their actual, lived versions of justice and mercy. Perhaps Jesus is telling us here that our loudest and most articulate speech is in our actions. Perhaps Jesus is telling us once again that discipleship is a matter of deeds of mercy, not words of belief.

But it is also true that the character of the man in need on the road is not allowed to speak by his words or by his actions. Here is another example of Jesus' creative genius, displayed in his parables. A critical aspect of the plight of the poor and needy in Jesus' time, as in ours, is that they are not allowed to be heard. Their cries for mercy and justice are not heard by the dominant insiders. They are kept out of sight and hearing, or their cries and sufferings are belittled and devalued. In this way the dominant narratives of Jesus' time and of ours deprives the poor and needy of their humanity.

If the man in need on the side of the road had been allowed to speak in this parable, what might he have said to the men who passed him by without justice or mercy?

Is it nothing to you, all you who pass by?
Look and see,
if there is any sorrow like my sorrow . . . (Lam 1:12a)

And so would the individuals whom I describe in chapter 6 speak to you and me, if we were to allow them to be heard.

The parable is quintessentially about justice and mercy. It reveals that mercy is a requirement of justice, and that God's mercy and justice are fused.

The root of the colloquy between the legal expert and Jesus was the legal command set forth in Lev 19:17: "You shall love the neighbor as yourself." We who are captive to the dominant narrative miss that this love of the neighbor is a *legal command*. It is not like our dominant narrative's view of mercy—optional, occasional, and disfavored. This love is not a feeling or sentiment. "Love" in Scripture is always active mercy. It is not just feelings of compassion and empathy. "Love" in Scripture is acted out compassion and empathy. Here, Jesus links the command from Deut 6:5 to love God with every part of our being with the command from Leviticus to love the neighbor as deeply and actively as we love ourselves. Jesus teaches us here that the only *way* we love God completely is by loving the neighbor and ourselves deeply. These two passages from Torah are declaring that just as God is due my active, merciful love ("you *shall* love the Lord your God"), and just as I am due my own active, merciful love ("You *shall* love . . . yourself"), the neighbor is due the same active, merciful love from me ("you *shall* love your neighbor as yourself"). Again, these are legal commandments and so a matter of justice. The teaching of Jesus is that the legal reward for obeying this law about what God, I, and the neighbor are due is eternal life (v. 25). By implication, what one is due for failing this command is eternal death. Inheritance (v. 25) of anything is a matter regulated by law, so even the use of the word "inherit" associates this Scripture with law and thus justice.

Many have tried to cast the lawyer of this encounter in a bad light, interpreting "wanting to justify himself" as a self-centered attempt to justify his own restrictions on who is and is not due his love. I interpret this differently. The expert on Torah was in fact asking Jesus whom he was required to love to become truly just. I have been taught that in Jesus' time and setting there was a debate between two major rabbinical schools about whether the "neighbor" who was due active mercy under Lev 19:17 was any Jew or only a Jew who observed Torah thoroughly. The lawyer was asking Jesus where he stood on this.

Jesus' famous parable explodes the limitations taught by the dominant narrative of that time and of our time about who is "due" our mercy. When the setting and meaning of this parable are understood in this way, the brilliance and creativity of Jesus as a storyteller is even more awe inspiring.

Focus first on what Jesus tells us, and does not tell us, about the victim. Jesus does not say whether he is just a Jew or a just Jew who scrupulously obeys Torah. He doesn't even tell us if he is a Jew. He is described only as a man. The only additional information that Jesus provides is that he is in need of mercy. His ethnicity and religious practice are not apparent to the other characters in the parable. He appeared as if he might be dead but was not. And Jesus does not provide the hearers of the parable any privileged information about the victim that was not apparent to the priest, the Levite, and the Samaritan. In this way, Jesus placed the hearer of the parable in the same position as the three passers-by. The persons hearing the parable were thus forced to make the same judgments about the victim as the other three men in the story.

The hearers of Jesus' parable would likely have expected the third passerby to have been a Jewish common man who was not part of the religious establishment. The entrance of the hated Samaritan in the place of the Jewish hero in the story would have been a shock and something of an outrage. Samaritans were the descendants of the citizens of the Northern Kingdom of Israel. They also worshipped YHWH. They also regarded Torah as Holy Scripture. But when the Northern Kingdom of Israel was destroyed by the Assyrians and when the leaders of the Southern Kingdom of Judah were later taken into captivity by Babylon, each group accused the other of taking advantage. Samaritans sacrificed to YHWH at their own temple in their capital of Samaria. Jews and Samaritans recognized the validity of only their own respective temple. Jews traveling from Galilee to Jerusalem to sacrifice and worship at the Temple on Zion mount had to walk through Samaria unless they chose to prolong the length of their trip by taking the long way around to the east. When Galilean Jews walked through Samaria, they were sometimes intercepted and beaten by Samaritans. Jesus' description in this parable of the "man" beaten by robbers could have evoked images of what sometimes happened to Jews at the hands of Samaritans, making it even more scandalous that a Samaritan emerges suddenly as the merciful hero.

In passing by the man in need of mercy, the priest and the Levite testified by their action what their version of justice was, just as we do today by our actions. They acted as if the victim was not due their mercy. They justified their mercilessness to themselves because they could not tell who or what the victim was. If they could not determine whether or not the victim in need satisfied their requirements, the person was not due their mercy. In order to be due their love, the victim had to be deserving within their requirements. It was not enough that he be in need.

Along comes the Samaritan. He knows no more and no less than did the priest or the Levite about the man in need of mercy. And he was bound by the same Torah—the same Lev 19:18. By his actions, he re-vealed his version of justice. He revealed that the neighbor due his mercy was anyone in need.

Arguably, the priest, the Levite, and the Samaritan all knew one additional fact about the man in need—that he was found in the land of the Jews. This would have made it likely that he was a Jew. This was not enough to cause the priest and the Levite to act mercifully and was not enough to dissuade the Samaritan. This reinforces that the person to whom mercy was due, in the eyes of the Samaritan, was any man in need of mercy, even a potential enemy.

The Samaritan was not merciful in a token or self-centered manner. Unlike the mercy shown by so many modern Christians, the Samaritan's love clearly was not acted out just to make the Samaritan feel good about himself or to achieve some moral status. The Samaritan's mercy extended to what was actually needed for the man to recover.

At the end of the parable, Jesus famously reverses the lawyer's question. The initiation of the legal discussion on the application of the law to love one's neighbor was the lawyer's question, "And who is my neighbor?" The implication of the question was that the person in need had to prove that he was within the requirements of being "deserving"—of being a neighbor—before being "due" any mercy. Jesus reversed the inquiry by asking who "proved to be the neighbor of the man in need?" Jesus placed the burden on the one encountering a man in need to be a neighbor, rather than demanding that the man in need satisfy the requirements of being a neighbor first.

How counter this narrative is to the dominant narratives of Torah, Jesus' time, and our time. This parable invalidates *any* judgments divid-ing those to whom mercy is due from me and those to whom mercy is not due from me. *Any* person whom I encounter in need of mercy is my neighbor and is due my mercy as a matter of justice. The only cri-terion that makes a person due mercy is his or her need for mercy. By this parable, Jesus allows for no consideration of whether the person in need could someday prove capable of helping us when we need mercy. Jesus allows no prudent consideration of self-interest by those called to act as neighbors. Jesus allows no limitation on the merciful action. Jesus allows no qualification or question about what foolishness on the person's part placed him in a position to be injured. Jesus teaches that the just obligations of all people to all other people are shaped by a universal, covenantal community of mutual love, justice, and mercy, not by the rules of competition of a merciless *agón*.

As I am going to repeat many times in this section, this parable teaches us about the nature and relationship of God's justice and mercy. What all people are due under God's justice are two things: mercy and being made merciful. The former seems obvious to me. As to the latter, consider that the very point of the commandment of Lev 19:17 was and is to make merciful the people of God. The very point of Jesus' brilliant parable of the Good Samaritan was to make the hearers just and merciful. Justice and mercy are fused. Could this be any more counter to the dominant narrative of our time?

**

The Parable of the Rich Fool

13 Someone in the crowd said to him, "Teacher, tell my brother to divide the family inheritance with me." 14 But he said to him, "Friend, who set me to be a judge or arbitrator over you?" 15 And he said to them, "Take care! Be on your guard against all kinds of greed; for one's life does not consist in the abundance of possessions." 16 Then he told them a parable: "The land of a rich man produced abundantly. 17 And he thought to himself, 'What should I do, for I have no place to store my crops?' 18 Then he said, 'I will do this: I will pull down my barns and build larger ones, and there I will store all my grain and my goods. 19 And I will say to my soul, 'Soul, you have ample goods laid up for many years; take your ease, eat, drink, be merry.' 20 But God said to him, 'You fool! This very night your life is being demanded of you. And the things you have prepared, whose will they be?' 21 So it is with those who store up treasures for themselves but are not rich towards God."

22 He said to his disciples, "Therefore I tell you, do not worry about your life, what you will eat, or about your body, what you will wear. 23 For life is more than food, and the body more than clothing. 24 Consider the ravens: they neither sow nor reap, they have neither storehouse nor barn, and yet God feeds them. Of how much more value are you than the birds! 25 And can any of you by worrying add a single hour to your span of life? 26 If then you are not able to do so small a thing as that, why do you worry about the rest? 27 Consider the lilies, how they grow: they

neither toil nor spin; yet I tell you, even Solomon in all his glory was not clothed like one of these. **28** But if God so clothes the grass of the field, which is alive today and tomorrow is thrown into the oven, how much more will he clothe you—you of little faith! **29** And do not keep striving for what you are to eat and what you are to drink, and do not keep worrying. **30** For it is the nations of the world that strive after all these things, and your Father knows that you need them. **31** Instead, strive for his kingdom, and these things will be given to you as well.

32 Do not be afraid, little flock, for it is your Father's good pleasure to give you the kingdom. **33** Sell your possessions, and give alms. Make purses for yourselves that do not wear out, an unfailing treasure in heaven, where no thief comes near and no moth destroys. **34** For where your treasure is, there your heart will be also." (Luke 12:13–34)

Was the timing of the rich fool's death merely a random coincidence? If so, this parable is merely a wisdom teaching that we cannot depend on our accumulation of many things for security and long life. If so, the main teaching here is that we can die at any time, despite our best calculations and accumulations.

Or was the timing of the rich fool's death—just after he had completed his new barns and vowed to take his ease, eat, drink, and be merry with his accumulation—a judgment and punishment for his greed (v. 15)? Was his death due him from his totally selfish hoarding of the abundant produce of the land, for his claims that the land had produced for his use alone ("*my* crops" in verse 17; "*my* barns," "*my* grain," "*my* goods" in verse 18), and for his idolatry in claiming that even his soul belonged only to himself and not to God ("*my* soul" in verse 19)? And was the timing of his death also an act of God to cause all of this produce and these goods to be enjoyed by the needy of the community? ("And the things you have prepared, whose will they be?" in verse 20b.)

I hear this parable as a judgment and a punishment, which are both justice issues. The rich fool was intending to use these abundant goods only for himself. Within Jesus' counter-narrative, the poor were due the rich fool's mercy, and his failure to be abundantly merciful with his excess caused him to suffer the just punishment of a quick death. The abundance of these goods would support a lifestyle of luxury for many years. The man was due judgment and punishment merely for failing to share his huge excess, even if Jesus does not state that he obtained that excess through cheating the poor of their land, seizing the land when the poor could not repay their debts to him, or underpaying his workers. Merely his merciless neglect of the needs of the poor was enough for him to be due this punishment. So this rich fool has much in common with the rich man in Luke 16:19–31.

Verse 21 is a key to interpretation here. Perhaps a better translation of this verse is: "So it is with those who are rich for themselves but are not rich for God." The "so it is" refers to their being punished. By being "rich for himself" the fool chose not to be "rich for God" through mercy to the poor. So he received quick justice.

I hear echoes of the Psalms—Ps 37:1–11, 20–29, and 34; Ps 49:1–11; Ps 52:5–6; and Ps 73:1–20—in this parable of the rich fool and in the teachings of Jesus in which the parable is set. The basic preconceptions, judgments, and hopes expressed in these psalms would have been shared by the poor who heard this parable. Present in these psalms are the issues of the evildoing of the rich by using all of their goods for themselves at the expense of the poor, the foolishness of this practical godlessness, the promise that God will judge the merciless rich with sudden, unexpected death in the midst of their greed, and the ultimate transfer of the land to the poor that God would bring about.

The parable and the teachings of Jesus in which the parable is embedded are dominated by the justice issue. The central questions throughout are who is due what from whom. What are the poor of the community due from the rich fool? What is this rich man's soul due from the total man? What is the total man due from the soul? What is God due?

Within the parable are two, wholly one-sided conversations. The first is between the man and his *psyche* in the Greek. "And I will say to my *psyche*, 'Psyche, you have ample goods laid up for many years; take your ease, eat, drink, be merry'" (v. 19). *Psyche* is translated in the NRSV as "soul." But the same Greek word is translated as "life" in the NRSV when it appears twice more in verses 22 and 23. Whether translated as "soul" or "life," *psyche* refers to that part of a human that is his essence, which is truly and eternally him, his true "self" and thus his best self, his true "life" and thus his best life, the aspect of the personality where the image of God dwells, the spark of the divine in all of us, and the part of each of us that most approaches God. The word implies a realistic assessment that the human person experiences inner conflicts between facets of the self and thus between judgments, urges, desires, and goals of these various facets. Jesus presents this man as a fairly rounded character who is capable of inner debate. The debate within this rich man was to decide whether to be "rich for himself" or "rich for God," and begins in verse 17 when he considered within himself what he should do with his windfall of abundance.

This conversation would have been a debate about what the man's soul was due from the other aspects of himself—the man's fears and appetites—and what the total "he" was due from and for his soul. Having said this, Jesus' parable describes a one-sided debate, because "he" didn't allow his *psychē* to be heard. The aspect of himself where fear, worry, greed, appetite, desire for pleasure, and ambition for personal honor reside—the place where the fool lives in all of us—shut up and out the aspect of himself where trust, faith, empathy, generosity, justice, and mercy reside. What the man in his totality decided that "he" was due was to use this abundance only for himself so he could be certain that he could "take his ease, eat, drink, and be merry" for the rest of his days. This man did not render what was truly due to his own soul and his own total self.

This moment of possible, actual dialogue in the inner decision making is described in this parable. In that moment there was the possibility of the rich man deciding not to be a fool, deciding instead to be merciful with his excess to those in need in his community, and deciding to be rich toward God instead of toward his appetite and fear of not having enough for himself. This moment of possibility was in a space between verses 17 and 18—an instant when his *psychē* could have spoken out for mercy instead of selfishness, and for trust in God instead of hoarding out of fear. It could have been more than a moment's space in time, more than a moment's pause. But in this parable, the *psychē* is either silent or was shut out before she could express herself. Perhaps in this man, his *psychē* was very weak from lack of nurture and from the destructive effects of the dominant narrative of that time.

This man depended upon externals for his meaning, honor, and satisfaction, upon his accumulation and selfish enjoyment of the abundant harvest, and the ostentation of tearing down and building new barns. The dominant narrative of his time taught him that these externals were the only sources of such meaning, honor, and satisfaction. So he shut out the urges to justice and mercy that were present within his own soul, and failed to find the greater meaning, honor and satisfaction that come from these internals. He failed to be just and merciful to himself. This failure is where all injustice and mercilessness to others begins. He was like an addict who fears that he cannot find happiness from the resources that he has within himself, and that he must turn to drugs for happiness. This rich fool feared he could not find happiness from the sources for mercy and justice within himself, and that he must turn to accumulation of even greater wealth for happiness.

The second one-sided conversation in the parable is between the man and God. That conversation was also about what the man was due from himself and what God was due from the man: "But God said to him, 'You fool! This very night your life [*psychēn*] is being demanded of you. And the things you have prepared, whose will they be?'" This is a very difficult sentence to translate. The NRSV translates it as stated above. But I prefer the translation "This very night these things will demand your soul of you," because it is closer to the literal. Such a life of selfish accumulation and hoarding is not satisfying or meaningful, because such a life is not one of giving and receiving what is justly due. This translation is consistent with Jesus' teachings elsewhere that greed and striving for possessions will kill the soul, and that a life preoccupied with accumulating and consuming is not a "life" worth living (Matt 6:19–21, 24–34; 18:22; Luke 16:13, 15).

In the encounter described in this parable, God tells the man that his soul, and thus his essence and true self, is due more than greed, comfort and the social honor of ostentatious displays of wealth. God tells the rich man that his soul is due the great mercy of being merciful. His soul was not due being rich for himself but being rich for God by using his riches for God's children in need. Thus did Jesus describe that God was justly due what the man's soul was due, and that the man's soul was justly due what God was due. Mercy and mercifulness.

"Whose will they be?" Based upon Hebrew Scripture that promises that the greedy rich will suddenly die and the needy poor will receive their land (Ps 14:5; Ps 37:3, 4, 9, 11; Ps 49:10–11; Ps 73:18), the answer to that question heard by Jesus' needy listeners would have been more than, "Not the rich man's!" The answer would have been heard as "God will see that the poor and needy righteous will receive the rich fool's wealth!"

In verses 22 through 30, Jesus also teaches that the soul is due the self's not worrying about what the body will eat or wear and even about the length of his life. The Greek word translated "worrying" in the NRSV in verses 22, 25, 26 and 29 has a nuanced meaning. The word root is *merimnaō*. It generally means being "made anxious from the distraction of being pulled in two different directions." Verse 31 is emphasized more sharply: "Instead, strive for the kingdom, and these things will be given to you." We should not be distracted from seeking the kingdom by worry about ourselves, our mortal lives, our things, and our status. Jesus teaches that the soul is due the self's not striving after these things. What is the soul due from the total self? The soul is due being allowed to grow in trust that God will provide what is truly needed. The soul is due the entire self's striving after God's kingdom (verse 31) over all else. The soul and the entire self are due being merciful.

What is God due? God is due that we place all of our energy in striving for the kingdom. God is due what our souls are due. God is due for us not to be distracted by other concerns. God is due for us to trust God rather than our appetites, fears, and accumulations. God is due for us to depend upon God's grace alone, rather than upon our own striving. God is due for us to use our possessions to be rich toward God through mercy to others in need, rather than to be rich toward ourselves through greed. In fact, the irony is that accumulating wealth for our own use is *not* being rich toward our souls. Being merciful is being rich to our souls. God is due for us to trust that being rich toward God through mercy to others is also being rich toward our own souls, and is the way to true life.

There is a fourth character present in this parable besides the man, his soul and God. It is the listening crowd. Luke 12:1, which is the beginning of this section of encounter and teaching, describes that the crowd gathered "by the thousands" to be taught, fed and healed by Jesus. We know from the gospels that the crowd following Jesus was largely comprised of those in great need and those considered by religious insiders as unclean "sinners." This parable of the rich fool was spoken in their hearing, though likely directed to the religious insiders who were also present. The rich man in the parable used his abundance as if the people in the crowd did not matter, much like the rich man did in Luke 16:19–31. The rich fool in this parable lived as if life were a contest in which all the characters were merely contestants. He did not live as if life were a covenant with God and with his neighbor. So he lived as if he was due whatever he could get and consume, and as if the members of the crowd were not due what they did not have. In short, he lived according to the dominant narrative of his time and of our time, not according to the counter-narrative of God.

The rich fool showed by his life that he believed he was due the consumption and use for his body alone of all that "his" land produced. And he behaved as if this was the sole meaning of life. He was already rich, and became even richer when his land produced abundantly. The abundance was so great that the multiple storage facilities that he already owned were not enough. Given that he was rich, we may understand that he already had stored away more produce than he needed personally. He could have added some additional barns to store his unusually abundant production. But instead he chose to tear the old ones down and build all new ones in an ostentatious show to secure even more status and honor. And even though he was so rich, he still was anxious that he would run out of things and doubting that he would be provided what he needed in the future. This focus on self, self-reliance, and accumulation of as many things as possible was and is the dominant narrative. Under that narrative, we can only rely upon and trust in ourselves. And when we rely and trust in ourselves alone, and such reliance and trust "produces abundantly," we are due to hoard and use all this produce for ourselves alone. In no parable is the conflict between the dominant narrative and the counter-narrative of God more starkly drawn.

Most remarkable about this parable is how it refutes and thus defeats the dominant narrative's dualistic thinking about justice and mercy. Through this parable, Jesus teaches that what the soul is due, what the needy crowd is due, and what God is due are all the same mercy and mercifulness. What is justly due is for the total self to allow the soul to be merciful, for us to be "rich toward God" by being merciful to those in need, and for the needy crowd to receive mercy and to then be made capable of being merciful. What is just is merciful. What is merciful is just. When the rich fool was merciless to the needy, he was merciless to God and to his own soul. When he was unjust to his own soul, he was unjust to God and to the needy. When he was not rich for God, he thought he was being rich for himself but he was not. When justice is merciful and mercy is thus just, the divisions and competitions between the soul and the self's appetites, between the self and God, and between the total self and the community are overcome.

Jesus tells us through these teachings why we are so anxious, distracted, and greedy, and why the dominant narrative is so attractive to the aspects of ourselves where our fears and appetites live. We do not trust God to tell us and to provide what we need to "live" truly. Instead we trust and follow the dominant narrative. Jesus tells us that if we strive for the kingdom, our material needs will be "given" to us by God (v. 31). The only requirement is that we strive for the kingdom. We will not be given what we truly need because we work hard and effectively, or because we are brighter, better educated, better connected, and more effective in our work. We won't obtain or earn what we need at all. If we strive for the kingdom, we will be given what we need. Luke 12:29–31 reads: "And do not keep striving for what you are to eat and what you are to drink, and do not keep worrying. For it is the nations of the world that strive after all these things, and your Father knows that you need them. Instead, strive for his kingdom, and these things will be given to you as well."

This is not just a startling affirmation because it is so counter to the dominant narrative of that time and our time. It is also startling because it is so challenging to trust like this as a practical matter. Jesus says here, "Do not worry and be distracted about material security and wealth, and do not be greedy . . . *because* God will provide what you need if you strive single-mindedly for the kingdom. You are free and able to render to all in need the mercy and generosity they are due—your neighbor, God, and even your own soul—*because* God will provide what you need if you strive for the kingdom."

Really? Is that the way it works in your neighborhood?

Why don't we trust God to decide what it is we truly need? Is it because we want to be the ones to decide what we need? (We think that we decide what we need, but, in fact, it is the dominant narrative that decides.) We don't trust God because we want the honor from winning the competition to take what the dominant narrative tells us we need and not to be given it with everyone else. The dominant narrative tells us that we will never have enough of what it dictates that we need. We do not trust God's counter-narrative that tells us what we truly need to make our lives satisfying and meaningful is no more than what we need to survive and be merciful.

Is it because our experience is that God will not give us the material things we need to live and be merciful? If we strive single-mindedly for the kingdom, will God then provide what we truly need? If we are not distracted from single-minded striving for the kingdom, if we do not fall into the worry and anxiety from the distraction of things and from transient pleasures, will God "give" us what we "need?" Have any of us tried this to be able to say whether it is true? Has the American church, cradled in the arms of the dominant narrative, shown or taught that this teaching can or should be followed?

Whether this teaching of Jesus, and the promise of God he communicates, are true depends upon (1) what we need, (2) what the kingdom does and would look like, and (3) how God gives. As to God "giving" our material needs to us, Jesus teaches us through both versions of the Lord's Prayer at Matthew 6:11 and Luke 11:3 to ask our Father to *"give"* us our "daily bread." "Daily bread" can also accurately be translated "enough bread for tomorrow." Surely Jesus would not teach us to ask God to give us our material needs if he did not believe that God in fact will and does do this. But how does God give what we need materially? And how does that giving involve the kingdom?

Perhaps the best known instance of God "giving" God's people their material needs is recounted in Exodus 16, when YHWH "gave" the Israelites their daily manna and quail in the face of their worry that they would not have what they needed to survive. All they had to do was to gather the bread and meat each day, but no more each day than they needed for that day (except on the day before the Sabbath). They were to trust YHWH to "give" them what they needed each day and so "not to leave any of it over until morning" (Exod 16:19–20). In their worry and lack of trust they hoarded more than they needed for the one day, and their excess turned foul and bred worms.

When Jesus says to us, through Luke 12:29–31, "[D]o not keep striving for what you are to eat and what you are to drink, and do not keep worrying. [Y]our Father knows that you need them. Instead, strive for his kingdom, and these things will be given to you as well," does he mean that we should sit down in total inactivity, so to speak, and wait for our material needs to appear from heaven, like manna and quail in the wilderness experience?

Jesus' teachings and actions reported in Luke's Gospel lead to a different understanding.

In Luke 4:4, Jesus is reported to have said to his tempter, "One does not live by bread, but by every word that comes from the mouth of God." He was quoting Deuteronomy 8:3, an additional account of the Exodus story of manna in the wilderness. Through this, Jesus and the author of Luke invoked the entire wilderness and promise-land story of Israel (Deut 8:1–5, 6–20) that resonated so powerfully with Jews in Jesus' time. In this story, God gave the people the land and the power to build their own houses, to plant and harvest the wheat for their bread, even to gain wealth for themselves, as long as they followed the LORD's commandments and remembered that their abundance came from and belonged to the LORD. Likewise, if the people disobeyed the commandments, the LORD would no longer give them the power to build their own houses, and to plant and harvest the wheat for their bread.

In Luke 9:1–6, Jesus is reported to have sent the disciples out to cure diseases and to proclaim the kingdom of God, relying upon those who welcomed them to shelter and feed them. And in Luke 10:1–9, he is reported to have given the same instructions to the "seventy," including to depend upon those who welcomed them for their material needs. Jesus did not tell the twelve and then the seventy to take no bread, and no money to buy bread and pay for lodging, because God would make their material needs fall from the sky like the manna and quail in the wilderness story. He instead told them, in effect, to strive for the kingdom. If they did, then God would give them their bread and material needs through the mercy of generosity of the people in whose households they were welcomed in the power and presence of that kingdom, whose counter-narrative included the mercy of generosity.

Between the two stories of the twelve and the seventy quoted above, and just after the return of the twelve from their mission, Luke reports that Jesus brought about the feeding of thousands of hungry people (Luke 9:10–17). This feeding story is proclaimed in all four Gospels. Clearly, sharing food and making sure that all had enough of their material needs to live were and are essential parts of the kingdom of God. Part of this feeding story is symbolic of the Eucharist and the abundant availability of that holy bread and cup to everyone. But the telling verse to me in all three versions in the Synoptic Gospels, particularly when read in conjunction with the missions of the twelve and the seventy, is "You give them something to eat" at verse 13 of Luke's version. The followers of Jesus will receive the bread, shelter, and their other material necessities when they strive single-mindedly for the kingdom, because the community of the strivers after the kingdom will share material necessities with others. This is an essential part of the striving and of the kingdom itself. (See also, among many teachings, Luke 6:30a, 35c, 38; 9:1b; 10:6–9, 34–35; 14:13; 18:22; 19:8–10; and Matt 25:3–36.)

So when Jesus says at Luke 12:29–31 "[D]o not keep striving for what you are to eat and what you are to drink, and do not keep worrying . . . [Y]our Father knows that you need them. Instead, strive for his kingdom, and these things will be given to you as well," he simply and confidently means that striving for the kingdom includes receiving the material things we really need and sharing our excess so that others can live and share. Part of the striving for the kingdom is this merciful sharing. The way that God will "give" what we truly need to us will be through the growing kingdom and through the others who are faithfully striving for it. Within the growing kingdom, we will all give and receive the mercy we need to live and be merciful, and we will all limit ourselves to the personal use of only what we need to live and be merciful. Within and through the covenant community Jesus calls the "kingdom of heaven," God will "give" us what we need.

The dominant narrative of our time is so insistent and pervasive that what each of us needs and must have to be satisfied is ever more stuff. The dominant narrative is likewise insistent that we are to win the stuff individually in the ongoing contest, and that we are then entitled to use selfishly for ourselves all the stuff we can obtain. Within that dominant narrative, the rich man in this parable was no fool. He was merely living successfully the American Dream. Within the counter-narrative of Jesus, he was a rich fool for failing to render what was due to others in need, to God and even to his own soul.

**

The Parable of the Wedding Banquet

1 On the occasion when Jesus was going to the house of a leader of the Pharisees to eat a meal on the Sabbath, they were watching him closely. **2** Just then, in front of him, there was a man who had dropsy. **3** And Jesus asked the lawyers and Pharisees, "Is it lawful to cure people on the sabbath, or not?" **4** But they were silent. So Jesus took him and healed him, and sent him away. **5** Then he said to them, "If one of you has a child or an ox that has fallen into a well, will you not immediately pull it out on a sabbath day?" **6** And they could not reply to this.

7 When he noticed how the guests chose the places of honor, he told them a parable. **8** "When you are invited by someone to a wedding banquet, do not sit down at the place of honor, in case someone more distinguished than you has been invited by your host; **9** and the host who invited both of you may come and say to you, 'Give this person your place,' and then in disgrace you would start to take the lowest place. **10** But when you are invited, go and sit down at the lowest place, so that when your host comes, he may say to you, 'Friend, move up higher'; then you will be honored in the presence of all who sit at the table with you. **11** For all who exalt themselves will be humbled, and those who humble themselves will be exalted."

12 He also said to the one who had invited him, "When you give a luncheon or a dinner, do not invite your friends or your brothers or your relatives or rich neighbors, in case they may invite you in return, and you would be repaid. [13] But when you give a banquet, invite the poor, the crippled, the lame, and the blind. [14] And you will be blessed, because they cannot repay you, for you will be repaid at the resurrection of the righteous."

[15] One of the dinner guests, on hearing this, said to him, "Blessed is anyone who will eat bread in the kingdom of God!" [16] Then Jesus said to him, "Someone gave a great dinner and invited many. [17] At the time for the dinner he sent his slave to say to those who had been invited, 'Come; for everything is ready now.' [18] But they all alike began to make excuses. The first said to him, 'I have bought a piece of land, and I must go out and see it; please accept my regrets.' [19] Another said, 'I have bought five yoke of oxen, and I am going to try them out; please accept my regrets.' [20] Another said, 'I have just been married, and therefore I cannot come.' [21] So the slave returned and reported this to his master. Then the owner of the house became angry and said to his slave, 'Go out at once into the streets and lanes of the town and bring in the poor, the crippled, the blind, and the lame.' [22] And the slave said, 'Sir, what you ordered has been done, and there is still room.'" [23] Then the master said to the slave, 'Go out into the roads and lanes, and compel people to come in, so that my house may be filled. [24] For I tell you, none of those who were invited will taste my dinner.'" (Luke 14:1–24)

I understand this parable by starting with (1) the hopes and expectations of an end-time banquet inaugurating a new, messianic age, and (2) the verses preceding this parable that condemn the insider/outsider system of the dominant narrative of Jesus' day.

Verse 15 is for me a reference to the eschatological banquet, the promised banquet announcing the end of the age when the world is broken. That banquet was to be a great and joyous celebration of the arrival of the time when this world would be restored to its intended form by the intervention of God. Isaiah 25 was a source of this hope and expectation:

[1] O LORD, you are my God;
I will exalt you, I will praise your name;
for you have done wonderful things,
plans formed of old, faithful and sure . . .

[6] On this mountain the LORD of hosts will make for all peoples

a feast of rich food, a feast of well-aged wines,
of rich food filled with marrow, of well-aged wines strained clear.

7 And he will destroy on this mountain
the shroud that is cast over all peoples,
the sheet that is spread over all nations;
he will swallow up death forever.

8 Then the Lord God will wipe away the tears from all faces,
and the disgrace of his people he will take away from all the earth,
for the LORD has spoken.

9 It will be said on that day,
Lo, this is our God; we have waited for him, so that he might save us.
This is the LORD for whom we have waited;
let us be glad and rejoice in his salvation." (Isa 25:1, 6–9)

Within his counter-narrative, Jesus' inclusion and eating with outsiders, sinners, the unclean, and "all" who would accept his invitation was
a sign that this intervention of the LORD had arrived. With Jesus, God's
promised banquet was beginning, which included "all" (vv. 6–8) and particularly the "poor" and "the needy in their distress" (v. 4) who had been
excluded from the banquets and celebrations of the dominant narrative.
God had come in Jesus to change the rules of life. "Distress," "tears," "disgrace," and even "the shroud of death" would be removed from "all." To
Jesus, part of that shroud of death in his time was the oppression and
exclusion of the poor, the needy, and the so-called unclean. In this new
age, "all" were offered acceptance, included, and saved regardless of merit
or deserving, and regardless of their righteousness, purity, or belief. God
was saving "all" through lavish mercy without calculation of who might
be due and who might not be due that mercy.

This vision of Jesus is of a new age based completely upon mercy
and not at all on calculations of who and who are not due inclusion, or
who and who might not reciprocate. In Luke 14:11–14 Jesus once again
criticizes the self-interest and lack of mercy in the dominant narrative of
the insider/outsider system. According to that dominant narrative, you
should invite only those individuals who can reciprocate in kind. You
invite people who are already included in your inside ("your friends or
brothers or relatives"), or you invite people in whose inside you wished
to be included ("your rich neighbors"). You do not invite people because
of their need for food, welcome, and inclusion. You do not invite them

to be merciful. But within Jesus' counter-narrative, you are called to invite people solely out of mercy and those people who cannot reciprocate. Within this new narrative for the new age, the people of God are called to "[b]e merciful, just as your Father is merciful" (Luke 6:36). Jesus calls us to eliminate insider/outsider considerations and the reciprocal benefit calculation. Verse 11 is a clear condemnation of calculations of who is due and who is not due. According to the dominant narrative of that time, a man strived for social honor by proving that he was due more honor than others were due. Jesus' teaching is: "He who claims that he is due more honor than another is actually due less. And he who refrains from claiming that he is due honor is due the most honor in the new kingdom."

Picture the setting for this parable of the great feast as a Sabbath banquet hosted and attended mostly by insiders. Many are gathered in the courtyard of the home of this leader of the Pharisees, reclining at a low table. The Pharisees and their guests are "watching [Jesus] closely" (Luke 14:1). Jesus was invited so that they might witness, hear for themselves, and have a basis for condemning his errors. Jesus was leading people astray, destroying the separation between the clean and holy, on the one hand, and the unclean and defiled on the other. He was making undue mercy primary, rather than obedience to the purity and holiness code in Torah. He was eating with sinners. What the Pharisees and their insiders did not see was that Jesus was eating with sinners at this meal with insiders.

Just as people were arriving, Jesus noticed that the guests were jockeying for the places of greatest honor at the table. Knowing why he had been included, Jesus himself started the debate about who is due the honor and admission into the "inside."

First, Jesus started the controversy by healing on the Sabbath a man with dropsy, an edema caused by an excess of fluid, perhaps caused by a kidney or a circulatory problem. The man happened to be present; there is no claim in the story that a Pharisee had invited him. Meals in that setting were often held in an uncovered courtyard, and passersby were able to stop and observe. What I read here is that Jesus saw this suffering man on the outside of the courtyard and brought him inside. He did this to confront the Pharisees about their priority of observing Torah Sabbath rules over the call of the Torah and the prophets to be merciful. Because this man's condition was not one from which he could die if not addressed that very Sabbath day, the Pharisees contended that there was no dispensation of the Sabbath prohibition against work. Within the dominant narrative of the Pharisees represented here, strict Sabbath obedience took priority over a merciful work of healing this man. Jesus was violating Torah by healing him that day. That Jesus had the power to heal this man was not what was important to the Pharisees! *When* Jesus healed him was what was critical. To the Pharisees, Sabbath observance was an essential aspect of what made a Jew one of God's favored insiders. Many of the Pharisees believed that the man's illness was a punishment for his sin and a sign of God's disfavor. To them, the man was not due Jesus' mercy of healing on any day.

Second, after the healing Jesus returned to the issue of the Pharisees' seeking the places of highest honor by poking fun at them. He told them how foolish they were, even within their own dominant narrative, for risking humiliation by claiming those places of honor (vv. 8–11).

Third, Jesus predicts a blessing in the eschatological end-time for those who are merciful and welcoming to the poor in the present (Luke 14:12–14). This prediction was a condemnation of placing Torah purity over Torah and prophetic mercy. And this was a condemnation of the view that the poor and the ill are poor and ill because of their sin, making them due their suffering as a matter of justice.

These three means of confrontation of Jesus led one of the dinner guests to exclaim in verse 15 how blessed will be the ones who will be included at the banquet that will mark the arrival of the messianic age. This dinner guest of the "leader of the Pharisees" was insisting that he and his fellow insiders would be included at that final feast, just as they had been included in this feast of insiders. His claim was that those who focus on observation of the holiness and purity provisions of Torah are and will be due inclusion in the banquet. This is a rebuttal to Jesus' actions and statements at verses Luke 14:1–14.

The end-time banquet when the kingdom of God is finally inaugurated was considered an aspect of heaven. Part of the good news of the gospel was that with Jesus the end-time banquet is already begun. So "all people" (Isa 25:6) are already being invited. Jesus ate with those excluded by the dominant narrative. The poor and excluded readily accepted Jesus' invitation. The rich and the insider did not. This guest was denying that it is the people whom Jesus describes in verses 13 and 14 who are and will be due inclusion. He is claiming smugly that just as he and his fellow guests are due their invitation to this banquet, they will be due inclusion in the end-time banquet.

Jesus will not relent. Too much harm was being done by this dominant narrative. So, fourth, Jesus tells the parable of the great dinner about
who is invited and who actually accepts the invitation to the banquet,
to bring this guest and all in attendance up short. It was surely a fourth
challenge to those who were so smug about being insiders.

A concern is whether it is *only after* the insiders are invited, accept initially, and then refuse to come that the outsiders—"the poor, the
crippled, the blind, and the lame"—are invited. But I finally understand
that Jesus told the parable in this way to heighten the criticism of the
failure of the so-called insiders to understand and respond to God's true
will. "Have it your way," says Jesus to the insiders. "You had priority. You
were invited first. But you failed to appreciate the value and meaning of
your invitation. You are too comfortable and smug. The world is all right
with you just as it is. You aren't hungry enough for the coming of the
kingdom to abandon your hierarchies to come to God's feast where the
world will be changed radically. So God turns to people who are hungry
and humble, and who will truly appreciate the value of the arrival of the
kingdom and the radical change it brings and requires."

In the parable, the "someone" is representative of God. The story
also assumes that the three persons described in verses 18, 19, and 20
had originally accepted the initial invitation, and that there was a delay
between the invitation, the acceptance, and the start of the "great dinner." Then those three offered weak excuses for backing out, showing that
routine activities of benefit to them were more important than the great
changes coming with the new age.

At least two of the excuses are weak. The first two even seem false.
Who waits until after he has purchased land to inspect it? Who purchases
five yoke of oxen and only then test drives them, so to speak? These excuses are flimsy attempts to get out of a previous acceptance, because they
decided they did not want the changes that will come with the banquet.

There is a parallel between the excuses of the three invitees and the
Pharisees' condemnation of Jesus healing the man with dropsy. The Pharisees claimed that the healing on the Sabbath was in violation of Torah
because there was nothing urgent in the man's condition that required
healing that day. In the same way, there was nothing urgent requiring
the man to go on the day of the banquet to see the land he had already
purchased, or requiring the man to go that day to try out the yoke of
oxen he already owned, or requiring the man to be with his wife that day
when he would enjoy a lifetime with her. Priority is the major lesson of

the parable and the entire encounter between the Pharisees and Jesus. The Pharisees believed the first priority was obeying the Torah's Sabbath prohibitions. For Jesus, the first, last, and only priority was mercy. Concerning the great dinner, the priority of the land owner, the oxen owner, and the husband were the self-serving affairs of their possessions and their family. For God, Jesus, the poor, and the suffering, the first priority was the end-time feast that would inaugurate a world without poverty, suffering, and death.

This parable is primarily about what the characters were due as a matter of justice.

What was the "someone" of verse 16 due? God was due for the three men to honor their previous acceptances of his invitations to his great dinner. God was due having his feast treated with the greatest priority and appreciation. God was due having his great dinner viewed and received as an astonishing act of undeserved mercy and grace. God was personally due the greatest fidelity, honor, and appreciation. Instead, the landowner, oxen owner, and husband acted as if God and the great transformation being worked by God were of no priority to them. Why? Because the world was so very good for them just as it was and as they were.

And what were the insiders—the first three invitees—due? Within their dominant narrative, they were surely due their invitations. Being invited to the great dinner was only just, given their well-deserved, insider status. So they were also due being able to decline for weak reasons and to come or not to come on their own whim. And they were due maintaining their favored, exclusive, insider positions, even if they did dishonor the "someone" who invited them to the great dinner. But within the counter-narrative of Jesus, these "insiders" were due no greater inclusion in the great banquet than the poor and suffering "outsiders."

And what were "the poor, the crippled, the blind, and the lame of the town" from "the streets and the lanes" due? And what were the same poor, crippled, blind, and lame of the rural "roads and lanes" due? They were due the mercy of welcome, inclusion, food, and the arrival of the new age. What they were due was based on their status as beloved of God—the only and same status that counted for the rich. All were in need of the mercy of the arrival of the new age. Because of their need, "the poor, the crippled, the blind, and the lame of the town" and of "the roads and lanes" responded to Jesus' invitation with gratitude and appreciation. In Luke's Gospel, the coming of Jesus and his ministry was the beginning of the eschatological feast in which God would begin to fix the world. The

Pharisees refused the invitation because the world was much more than alright with them. The poor, crippled, lame, and blind flooded in because for them the world was broken.

There is an interesting claim within the narrative of this parable as to why God invited the needy outsiders of the town and then of the country after the insiders backed out. Why did God not simply throw the food away? "'Sir, what you ordered has been done, and *there is still room*" (v. 22). "Then the master said to the slave, 'Go out into the roads and lanes and compel people to come in, so that my house may be filled" (v. 23). In the narrative, God felt a powerful urge to feed, to inaugurate the new age, to be merciful and to bring *all* people together. And no failure by the most privileged but unappreciative of people could thwart the feast giver's will.

As to the "compelling" ordered in verse 23, I view this not as force of violence but of the compelling power of the gospel—the good news of a transformed world for all people and particularly the suffering. "Compel" them refers to the urgency and attraction of the invitation.

Luke 1:50–53 is a precursor to this parable: "His mercy is for those who fear him from generation to generation. He has shown strength with his arm; he has scattered the proud in the thoughts of their hearts. He has brought down the powerful from their thrones, and lifted up the lowly; *he has filled the hungry with good things, and sent the rich away empty.*"

Is this parable also an expansion of the parable at Luke 14:28–31?

> 28 For which of you, intending to build a tower, does not first sit down and estimate the cost, to see whether he has enough to complete it? 29 Otherwise, when he has laid a foundation and is not able to finish, all who see it will begin to ridicule him, 30 saying, "This fellow began to build and was not able to finish." 31 Or what king, going out to wage war against another king, will not sit down first and consider whether he is able with ten thousand to oppose the one who comes against him with twenty thousand?

In other words, do not initially accept Jesus' invitation to join with him on his way without "first" considering whether you are willing to give up all else. Do not hypocritically say that you will come to his banquet but then balk when all that you must give up becomes real to you. Each one who refused to come had offers and opportunities that they did not turn down even though they had already accepted the banquet invitation. The banquet was not that important to them. But to the poor and the suffering, the invitation was such a great act of mercy that they came immediately. They did not have as much to give up. The rich did not follow through because they did not view the invitation as the great act of mercy that the poor and excluded did.

Why will God make the "feast of rich food" described in Isaiah 25 and invite "all" to enjoy, especially the poor in need of refuge from their distress, in need of shelter from the rainstorm, and in need of shade from the heat and the winter blast of the ruthless? Why did the "someone" of the parable instruct his slave to bring in the poor, the crippled, the blind, and the lame from the roads and lanes of the town and the country? Why did Jesus eat with sinners and minister constantly to the poor, the sick, and the possessed—in short, the outsiders? Could anyone claim that it was because "all" these were due this mercy because of their righteous conduct, their own acts of mercy, or their worship of the true God? How could "all" have been due this mercy?

Or is this the ultimate act of mercy—the mercy of rescue from the "shroud of death" (Isa 25:7) rendered by God to all people merely because all need the rescue and regardless of calculations of deserving? In the next chapter of Isaiah, at 26:12, is the phrase: "O LORD, you will ordain peace for us, for indeed, all that we have done you have done for us." Here, as in Isaiah 25, there is no claim of the gift of God being due only to those who deserve it. Instead, God's many gifts are given merely because God is merciful. This is true of the feast of rich food in Isaiah 25 and the great dinner of Luke 14. As in the parable of the rich man and Lazarus, there is no claim that those poor who are invited are righteous, orthodox believers, or merciful. They are just hungry and in need. As are we all.

While it is true that the insiders finally refused to attend the great dinner, they were still mercifully and repeatedly offered a place at the table with everyone else—not only in the parable but in Jesus' repeatedly eating and pleading with them. The mercy and inclusion of God is offered as if all are due it equally, and as if no one is due that mercy any more than anyone else. The rich, who are at least as much in need of the mercy of invitation and inclusion as the poor, exclude themselves. They think they can hold their own banquet. But they, as all of us, are in desperate need of the rescue from death that the banquet described in Isaiah 25 brings. Perhaps like the rich in our day, death and its fellow travelers are not always as with them as much as they are with the poor.

Clearly, the poor understand that they are being offered priceless mercy by their invitation. They have no claim to being due it under the dominant narrative. Under Jesus' narrative they receive it only because they need it—the welcome, inclusion, and the food. They are all Lazarus. But in the end some have to be compelled to come in because they have internalized the dominant narrative and would feel ashamed or embarrassed to come.

In the setting of Jesus' telling of this parable, was it also about who will accept the mercy and who will not? Is the paradox that those who believe they are due the mercy do not accept the mercy, while those who are told by the dominant narrative that they did not deserve it accept it eagerly? The rich do not appreciate that this offer of mercy is much, much more valuable than any of the goods and interests that motivated the excuse-giver not to come. Salvation from the shroud of death in all its forms is worth giving up everything else.

There is an additional way to interpret this parable. Maybe the dominant narrative of the time prevented the three original invitees from believing that a poor, itinerant rabbi who associated with the unclean and the sinner was the one described in Isa 11:1–9. Maybe the three original invitees just couldn't bring themselves to believe that the end-time when God would fix the world was beginning with this one Jesus and his banquet. Maybe they had experienced too much of the realities and struggles of real life to believe that a time would ever come when:

> The wolf shall live with the lamb,
>   the leopard shall lie down with the kid,
> the calf and the lion and the fatling together,
>   and a little child shall lead them.
> The cow and the bear shall graze,
>   their young shall lie down together;
> and the lion shall eat straw like the ox.
>   The nursing child shall play over the hole of the asp,
> and the weaned child shall put its hand on the adder's den.
>   They will not hurt or destroy on all my holy mountain;
> for the earth will be full of the knowledge of the LORD
>   as the waters cover the sea. (Isa 11:6–9)

And maybe they believed that the world was so stuck in its ways that only a warrior at the head an army empowered by the Lord of Hosts could truly hold the wolves, the leopards, the bears, the lions, the asps, and the adders at bay. Maybe they viewed Jesus and his promises not through the prism of Isaiah 11 and 25, but through Isa 61:1: "Who has believed what we have heard?"

Maybe they initially accepted the invitation to the Great Dinner because they too yearned for God to fix the world. But when the time came for them to actually sacrifice their daily and routine hedges against the suffering and injustice of the world, to sacrifice the security of land ownership and five yoke of oxen, or to sacrifice the happiness of a new bride, they couldn't bring themselves to do it. The promise of the great celebration when God would intervene to end the power of death, suffering, oppression, violence, injustice, and mercilessness just wasn't certain enough for them to give up their protections from want and suffering.

And to be fair to these characters, the food necessary to feed the poor and everyone else could only be grown on land. So however much the landowner was motivated by the desire for personal wealth in purchasing and inspecting new land, there was still a positive role for the common good being played by the land owner. If this land-owner were to stop his farming to rush to the Great Dinner of the Great Fix of God, and if he were to let the land lie fallow, who would grow the food to feed the children of God? Would God provide the food like the manna from heaven during the exodus from Egypt? The same questions could be asked about the owner of the oxen. This owner of so many oxen was surely very wealthy and either owned a great many acres of farmland to plow, or was accumulating considerable wealth by renting them for plowing or grinding. But whatever the man's personal motivation, his oxen played a needed part in production of food needed to sustain life for everyone. Was the owner of the oxen to abandon them, and leave all of the food production to the hand of God without human effort?

And the bridegroom of the parable could have been rich or poor, so this parable is not merely directed against misuse of the blessings of property to gain personal wealth. Marriage and family are the foundations of all human good. Yet the voice of the parable is critical of the bridegroom because he chooses to stay with his bride instead of rushing to the Great Dinner.

In your mind, change the activities and preoccupations of the three persons who were told that the Great Dinner of the Great Fix of God was finally ready. Imagine that the first person of the parable was a lawyer who argued in court in favor of humane treatment of suspected terrorists and of prohibition of interrogation by torture to save lives. But then this person hears the call of Jesus to drop all that and to come to the Great Dinner.

Imagine that the second person of the parable was a woman working on implementation of a plan to house all the homeless in a large city and to treat all of the causes of their homelessness. Years upon years of her efforts go without the numbers of chronically ill and disabled homeless being reduced. Then she hears the call of Jesus to drop it all and to come to the Great Dinner in which God will be the agent to house and treat the homeless.

Imagine that the third person of the parable had given up working and hoping and had just retired to the pleasures of family. Imagine that this third person was formerly the first person who fought against torture or the second person who was battling homelessness and its causes. And now that person has received the blessings of love in a marriage. But then he or she hears the same call of Jesus to leave the family and come to the Great Dinner.

What would that call mean today in these contexts? We know today that the Final Fix of God has not come as predicted and heralded by Jesus. So the call now is to do what . . . without the belief in the imminence of the Fix? To stop asking courts to prevent inhumane interrogation of suspected terrorists? Surely not. To quit trying to house and treat the homeless? Surely not. To quit strengthening the family? Most certainly not.

As many have said and written, including Albert Schweitzer in his *Search for the Historical Jesus,* Jesus' teachings look considerably different, and their application even more challenging, if we remove them from the context of belief in an *imminent* Day of the Lord.

But in the modern context, without this hope that God will soon or even ever bring the Final Fix, can or should we persevere in Jesus' way of extravagant mercy? Can we persevere in the way of Jesus without a powerful hope that God will someday bundle all our efforts with God's own into a Fix? Or do we just persevere through crisis after crisis after crisis until we are burned out? If we were to be offered a Final Fix now, if we would just leave everything we do and leave everything to God, would we go? Or would we hedge our bets and keep back a little means of working in a still broken world for ourselves, our families, and the suffering?

Doesn't the church's accommodation to the dominant narrative have at its foundation a doubt in the coming of this final, end-time fix by God of a broken world?

We in the comfortable American church try to domesticate Jesus—to make him into the ox that will plow our fields the way we want them plowed, and the ladder to get us into heaven without changing too much the earth on which the foot of the ladder rests. Part of that is turning Jesus into a twenty-first-century Anglo, middle- or upper-class American therapist, rather than a first-century itinerant rabbi, healer, and leader of an agrarian movement called the "kingdom of God" to transform a broken world. Part of this is softening the deep conflict between the dominant narrative of Jesus' time and of our time, and the counter-narrative of Jesus.

Given all this, why should we heed Jesus at all?

We should heed him because the conflicts he confronted through his life and teaching—worship of the God revealed in Torah and the prophets versus the worship of self and mammon; abject poverty versus self-indulgent wealth; elitism versus inclusion; judgment versus forgiveness; justice versus exploitation; and mercy versus mercilessness—are the conflicts we confront today. We should heed him because his life and teachings offer the greatest hope for our time just as they offered the greatest hope for his. We should follow him because living his life of humble, devout, hopeful, and sacrificial mercy offers us the deepest satisfaction and sustained joy. We should follow and worship him because his way resonates most deeply with the yearnings for God within all of our hearts and minds.

This parable is not an outlier in Jesus' teachings. Jesus clearly believed that the end-time described in the above passages of Isaiah 9, 11 and 35 was breaking into history with his own ministry. As a first century Galilean Jew, he believed in and yearned fervently for the Day of the LORD described by the prophets. He had received a vision that this Day of the LORD was breaking into time with his ministry (Luke 9:23–27; 17:20–21).

That meant that the dominant narrative of business as usual—the rules for buying and selling, accumulating, producing, consuming, seeking places in the pecking order of honor, and even surviving and procreating—was no longer authoritative.

As we have seen, this parable of the Great Dinner resonates with other teachings and demands of Jesus.

The landowner and the oxen owner of the parable were concerned to preserve their property and what that property could produce. But this concern with security and possessions, and the need for possessions to calm fear and defeat want, missed Jesus' point that the rules were changing radically with the arrival of the kingdom. Even a concern with family and a priority on family relationships was being eclipsed by the call of the arriving kingdom that was represented by the invitation to the Great Dinner (see Luke 8:19–21; 9:23–25, 59–62; 12:22–34; 14:25–33; and 18:26–33).

It is not Jesus' belief in an imminent apocalypse that most separates the comfortable American church from him. What separates us most from him is the intensity of Jesus' pain at the injustice and mercilessness of the human world and the dominant narrative of his time. Even though the fully incarnate Jesus was mistaken about how fully or soon the kingdom of God was to arrive to put things right, we are called to share his pain at this brokenness, and to see the world as he did and does. We are called to yearn as he did for a world that is born anew, and for the coming of a kingdom in which loving and sacrificial mercy reigns—not self-serving violence, avarice and mercilessness. In order for the eternal Word to be incarnate, that Word had to be enfleshed in a particular body in a particular place and time. In that place and time, the hope was widespread for the imminence of the coming day of the LORD, represented by a great banquet, in which the LORD would fix a broken world. But Jesus' life, yearning, and teaching of justice and mercy is not bound to a particular time and place. So we are called to lean into a kingdom in which justice and mercy reign, to live into it, to enflesh it now as best we can.

Even if the kingdom never finally comes, even if this out-of-whack human creation is never put back into whack by God, even if all we can do is to inject justice and mercy crisis by crisis into a world of injustice and mercilessness, we will still be living a more joyful and satisfying life than offered by any and all of the dominant narratives of the world. We will still be living the hope, faith, and love of Jesus. And we will still feel his mysterious presence in the acts of just mercy we carry out. We will see his mysterious presence in the eyes of the people to whom we bring Jesus' heart of just mercy.

✳✳

The Parable of the Prodigal Son

[11] Then Jesus said, "There was a man who had two sons. [12] The younger of them said to his father, 'Father, give me the share of

the property that will belong to me.' So he divided his property between them. 13 A few days later the younger son gathered all he had and traveled to a distant country, and there he squandered his property in dissolute living. 14 When he had spent everything, a severe famine took place throughout that country, and he began to be in need. 15 So he went and hired himself out to one of the citizens of that country, who sent him to his fields to feed the pigs. 16 He would gladly have filled himself with the pods that the pigs were eating; and no one gave him anything. 17 But when he came to himself he said, 'How many of my father's hired hands have bread enough and to spare, but here I am dying of hunger! 18 I will get up and go to my father, and I will say to him, "Father, I have sinned against heaven and before you; 19 I am no longer worthy to be called your son; treat me like one of your hired hands."' 20 So he set off and went to his father. But while he was still far off, his father saw him and was filled with compassion; he ran and put his arms around him and kissed him. 21 Then the son said to him, 'Father, I have sinned against heaven and before you; I am no longer worthy to be called your son.' 22 But the father said to his slaves, 'Quickly, bring out a robe—the best one—and put it on him; put a ring on his finger and sandals on his feet. 23 And get the fatted calf and kill it, and let us eat and celebrate; 24 for this son of mine was dead and is alive again; he was lost and is found!' And they began to celebrate.

25 "Now his elder son was in the field; and when he came and approached the house, he heard music and dancing. 26 He called one of the slaves and asked what was going on. 27 He replied, 'Your brother has come, and your father has killed the fatted calf, because he has got him back safe and sound.' 28 Then he became angry and refused to go in. His father came out and began to plead with him. 29 But he answered his father, 'Listen! For all these years I have been working like a slave for you, and I have never disobeyed your command; yet you have never given me even a young goat so that I might celebrate with my friends. 30 But when this son of yours came back, who has devoured your property with prostitutes, you killed the fatted calf for him!' 31 Then the father said to him, 'Son, you are always with me, and all that is mine is yours. 32 But we had to celebrate and rejoice, because this brother of yours was dead and has come to life; he was lost and has been found.'" (Luke 15:11–32)

For me, this parable could be entitled "the parable of the unjust and merciless father."

This parable was, I am sure, scandalous in Jesus' time. And it is scandalous now if we understand it correctly. The retelling and the rehearing of this parable has reduced its impact upon us. This parable is completely about justice and mercy, about what we think we and the wrongdoer are due, and about what we think we and the wrongdoer are not due. The father in this parable is a particularly rich and complex figure. Unlike so many commentators and preachers, I do not believe that Jesus intends to present the father in a totally positive light. And unlike the burden of Christian preaching and commentary on this parable, I do not find anywhere that Jesus intended that we should see the father as a complete or satisfactory symbol for God. I do not believe that Jesus intended any of the characters in the parable to be models for our own just and merciful conduct. I believe instead that Jesus told this parable with the intention that those who heard it would be troubled enough to question the justice and mercy of the father and to consider the complexity and goals of the mercy and justice to which we are called.

The beginning of the parable is filled with injustice—of a son demanding what was not due him, and a father giving what was not due to the son, of a son treating the father in a merciless manner that the father was not due, and the father treating the son in a way that was not due him, that was not going to benefit him, and that was therefore not merciful.

The younger son was only due the property he demanded when his father died. Verse 12 makes this clear in the son's demand: "Father, give me the share of the property that *will* belong to me." The property, which amounted to one third of the father's estate, would justly belong to him only when his father died and not a moment earlier. But the younger son demands it now, as if his father were already dead to the son. He thus treats his father in a way that the father is not due, and he treats him mercilessly. *Thus the parable teaches that injustice and mercilessness are aspects of the same conduct.* That the behavior of the son was tantamount to a claim that the father was dead to him is also shown in the language of verses 12 and 30. The Greek of verse 12 translates literally, "So he divided to them his life." The Greek of verse 30 translates, "who has devoured your [the father's] life with prostitutes."

Not only did the young son initially demand property as if his father were dead, but he then abandoned the father to go to a "distant country." Rather than staying so that he could be of merciful help to which his father would be due when his father began to age, the son left as if the father were already dead. This is more merciless injustice.

The father should have foreseen that giving the younger son what he asked would not make his son just or merciful, or even safe and satisfied. So the giving was not just or merciful to the son. So I do not believe that Jesus intended the father to be the thoroughly positive role model that most have seen in his character.

Jesus does not need to give the reasons the son treats the father in this manner. It is evident that it is because he is young, self-centered, unjust, and merciless. By the accident of his birth he had grown up in a wealthy family, and he was spoiled, selfish and head strong. This young son could fit right in to our own dominant narrative—a man who thinks he is due whatever he can get, regardless of the cost to the people around him.

Jesus does not make clear why the father would agree and thus enable the younger son's merciless injustice. The parable puts me in mind of Shakespeare's *King Lear,* when the old king foolishly divides his kingdom among his children before he is dead, thus enabling their unjust and merciless treatment of him. Just as King Lear's premature benefaction to two of his daughters and his merciless treatment of his third and innocent daughter did not serve any of them well, Jesus makes clear that the father's giving in to his son's unjust and merciless demand did not serve the son well. Perhaps the son had been selfish and demanding as he was growing up. Perhaps he had been such a constant embarrassment to his father that the father was relieved to be rid of him. Perhaps the father was so hurt and angry at the son's request that he was glad that he was leaving. Perhaps the father was so in need of this son's love and approval that he lacked the strength to deny him. Perhaps the father had always excused and indulged this selfish son. Or, in defense of the father, perhaps the father knew that this younger son would fail, and hoped that he would therefore learn his lesson and be reformed, like an addict who must hit rock bottom before seeing the light. Jesus leaves open for us this issue of why the father gave in to the younger son's selfish, unjust, and merciless demand. And by doing this, was Jesus inviting us to consider whether it is just and merciful for the father to give in? Is it sometimes just and even merciful to hold a person accountable for their wrongdoing? By holding a person to some accountability for their misconduct, are we not trying to move them to justice and mercy on their own?

The end of verse 12 states that the father divided his property "between them." I have heard many preachers interpret "them" to refer to the younger son and the older son. Based upon common practice from that time, the father could have assigned day-to-day control of two thirds of his property to his older son while maintaining actual ownership in himself. The older son would only inherit full ownership when the father died.

But this is a problematic interpretation because the father still seems to have full ownership and control of property to give his returning younger son. Upon the prodigal's return, the older son objects that he has continued to work for his father "like a slave" and has always obeyed the father's command (verse 29) after the younger son had left with his portion of the divided property. Verse 29 also states that the father had failed to give the older son even a goat for a party. In verse 30, the older son states that the younger son had returned to "devour *your* property," meaning the property of the father's. If the father divided all of his property between his two sons, why did the father still have total control of this property, including the fatted calf, the fine robe, the rings, and the sandals he gave to his younger son upon his return? And why could the older son not use his own goat for a celebration with his friends?

My reading of this parable is either that the "them" of verse 12 refers to the younger son and the father, or that Jesus is saying that the older son did not accept the division of the property before the father's death, because this son was a just and merciful man. It may be a stretch, but I prefer this latter interpretation. The older brother recognized that he was not yet due this two thirds of the property, and that his father was not due to be treated as if he were already dead. So his objection to his father's forgiveness and immediate restoration of his younger brother is all the more understandable. Under this reading, it was Jesus' genius to make this older brother the representative of the dominant narrative of Jesus' time. To this older brother, the father's mercy to the younger brother was scandalously unjust, just as the father's initial giving away of a portion of his property was unjust. The younger brother was not due this mercy of forgiveness and welcome, because he had been unjust and merciless to the father.

Before his return, the younger son wasted the property in degrading and undisciplined living. He had lived as if he was due immediately whatever he wanted to have and do. He behaved faithfully to the dominant narrative of his and our time. But by this behavior, he had treated himself unjustly and mercilessly. He did not treat his soul with the respect and nurture that his soul was due. And he did not use this property to be merciful to others in need. After nothing remained, he had nothing to provide his basic necessities when famine hit. Then he needed mercy, though by the dominant narrative of that time and ours he was not due it. In the land he had moved to "no one gave him anything" (verse 16). He had acted as if nothing was due from him to anyone and had effectively died to everyone else. He was among people who lived as if no mercy was due from them to him, thus bringing him close to death (verse 17). Jesus teaches us here that living as if justice and mercy are not due from us to ourselves and to others is like dying. This is the death that is the subject of the rest of this brilliant parable.

The younger son came to his senses. He realized that he has not treated his father with the respect, love and mercy he was due. He resolved to go back, not in the arrogant mercilessness of his initial demand for property. He realized that the justice of that time would not allow him to be treated as a son. He did not feel himself that he was due that restoration. He realized that he was due at most to be treated as a hired hand, given what he had done to this father. In the better translation of verse 19, he said: "I am no longer due [*axios*] to be called your son; treat me like one of your hired hands."

In one of the most memorable scenes in any parable of Jesus' and in all of Scripture, the father sees his younger son from afar—a return that resurrects them from their mutual deaths. The father runs to the son and kisses him. When the younger son, in his new sense of what was and was not due to and from him, repeats, "I am no longer due to be called your son; treat me like one of your hired hands," the father says to his slaves, "Quickly, bring out a robe—the best one—and put it on him; put a ring on his finger and sandals on his feet. And get the fatted calf and kill it, and let us eat and celebrate; for this son of mine was dead and is alive again; he was lost and is found!' And they began to celebrate."

Now the older son enters the story. He is angry that the younger son has received the mercy he was not due, and that he, the older son, has not received what he felt he was due for treating his father with justice and mercy. The older son complains that he had been treated unjustly like a slave and that the younger son was unjustly receiving the mercy of forgiveness, restoration as a son and a grand party. The older son's is at least the voice of the dominant narrative of Jesus' time and of ours.

In his outrage at the injustice in the ways he and his younger brother were being treated, the older brother treats the father in a way that the father is not due. In that time and place, fathers were due to be obeyed. The older son affirms this in verse 29. "I have never disobeyed your commands." But now he is refusing the father's plea to go in to the party in disobedience (verse 28).

But the father does not stand on his command and does not upbraid the older brother for being disobedient. Instead, he "pleads" (verse 28) with the older son. To do what? To act mercifully.

What does the father tell the older son that the younger son is due? He tells the older son that the younger son is due mercy, merely because of his need. In that sense, the younger son is like the man in need in the parable of the Good Samaritan, except that we know that the younger son's wrongdoing caused his need. So the sum of both parables is that the one in need is due mercy whether or not he is responsible for his plight.

And what does the father tell the older son that he is due? To allow himself to be merciful! Verse 32 is translated: "But we had to celebrate and rejoice . . . " Another good translation of the Greek is: "It is due (Greek *dei*) for us to make merry and rejoice." The father tries to help the older son to see and embrace this.

Again, this parable is scandalous. I believe that Jesus intended it to be so. We, like Jesus' listeners, should fear that excusing so easily the younger son's terrible injustice and mercilessness will only enable him to repeat these when he is no longer in need of mercy. The parable would be less scandalous to us if, say, the father had honored his younger son's request to be accepted back as nothing more than a hired hand, at least until the younger son had suffered a "just" consequence for what he had done, until he showed by his conduct that he had learned his lesson, and until he proved his repentance was genuine. The father's love was so overpowering that he himself lacked the will to treat his younger son with the justice he had requested. Instead, the father acted out not only unconditional love toward the younger son, he also acted out scandalously unconditional mercy. This was partly for the benefit of the older son, to teach him to be merciful. What Jesus teaches us again in this parable is that the justice we are each due is mercy and to be made merciful.

But the scandal of the parable remains. Isn't accountability sometimes merciful and just? Isn't holding someone justly accountable for their actions sometimes in their interest and thus merciful to them? Can the particular form of our merciful actions be conditional while our love is unconditional? Does not the mercy we are all due when we hurt others and ourselves include accountability? Was the father's immediate and unconditional forgiveness of the younger son upon his return as merciless as his giving into the younger son's initial demand for his share of the property that would be due him when his father died? Did either of these actions of the father teach the younger son to be mercifully just and justly merciful?

Another way to ask this question is to ask whether it is enough for us as Christians to strive to be merciful ourselves? Or are we also called to empower others to be merciful? And if we do not, are we truly being merciful and just?

These are questions I believe we must ask ourselves when we are confronted with wrongdoing. But we are not permitted to demand accountability that is merely revengeful and punishing. We are not allowed to demand accountability that forecloses forgiveness and the possibility of restoration.

I am attempting to be true to the counter-narrative of Jesus and not merely trying to make these parables palatable to lives shaped and lived by the dominant narrative. I am trying not to write as if I know better than my Lord. So I must attend to another teaching from Luke's Gospel which may well undercut my interpretation of the parable of the prodigal son:

> 3 "Be on your guard! If another disciple sins you must rebuke the offender, and if there is repentance, you must forgive. 4 And if the same person sins against you seven times a day, and turns back to you seven times and says 'I repent,' you must forgive." (Luke 17:3–4)

So was the father in the parable of the prodigal son simply being true to Jesus' teaching in verse 4, forgiving his prodigal son without regard for the justice and mercy of this unconditional forgiveness on his younger and on his older son?

If the counter-narrative of Jesus requires us to forgive and restore a wrongdoer to the former relationship merely when he *says* "I repent," then we must radically reform the practices of the Methodist Justice Ministry. We have obtained legal protections for hundreds of women and children against men who have been physically and emotionally abusive to them for years, but who become abjectly apologetic when the woman leaves them, promising to repent if the woman would just forgive and let them back into the home. Sometimes these men have actually quoted Jesus to their abused women that they are required to forgive and take them back. When the woman takes the abuser back, the pattern repeats itself. We try to persuade the woman that taking the man back is certainly not merciful or just to her children or to herself. And we try to convince her that taking him back is also not just or merciful to the man, because it does not move him to actually repent, change his life, and become the just and merciful human being he should become.

So does the command of verse 4 mean that just because a wrong-doer "says" he repents we are required to forgive and restore him to the same relationship? After all, the father in the parable of the prodigal son did not just forgive his son. He restored him immediately to his former relationship with the robe, the rings, and the fatted calf.

But verse 4 should be read in conjunction with verse 3. Together they are one teaching. Reading these two verses together as they should be, forgiveness is not commanded merely after the wrongdoer "says" he repents. In verse 3, forgiveness must be given if there is "repentance." Repentance requires true change in deed as well as word, not just saying "I repent." So only if there is true change in heart, mind, and deed is forgiveness to be granted. Jesus' parables were often scandalous to have effect. That a wrongdoer could sin against the same person, be corrected for his mercilessness, actually repent in word and deed, and be forgiven—and then repeat that cycle six more times that very day—surely was not presented by Jesus as a realistic possibility. In this regard verse 3 is like its own parable.

Given Jesus' overall teachings and these two verses taken together, forgiveness is a species of God's mercy and justice. Why is forgiveness to be offered to the wrongdoer? For the moral purity of the one who is forgiving? No. Forgiveness is to be offered to benefit the wrongdoer by inspiring him to act in a mercifully loving manner (see Luke 7:47). So when someone acts mercilessly, he is to be corrected (v. 3). Why? So the one correcting can be righteous? No. So that the wrongdoer can become the merciful and just person he should be. If he merely says he repents but does not actually "bear fruit worthy of repentance" (Luke 3:8), forgiveness is not to be offered. Why not? Again, because it would not benefit and thus be a mercy to the wrongdoer.

Forgiveness can take many forms and progress through many stages, depending on what is merciful and just for all involved, including the wrongdoer. A wrongdoer can be forgiven but still not be restored to the same relationship as before the wrong, particularly when to do so would not truly inspire the wrongdoer to become the person he can become. And forgiveness and restoration should be withheld when to forgive would not benefit others who could be hurt again or would not move the wrongdoer to become just and merciful. In the Methodist Justice Ministry, we have tried to help abused women and children to forgive their long term abusers—letting go of their fear, resentment, and hatred, and hoping for a transformed life for their abuser—without excusing and enabling the abuser to continue his abuse by letting him back into their homes. I cannot believe that Jesus would have them be unjust and merciless to all involved by forgiving and restoring such an abuser merely because he said "I repent."

**

The Parable of the Rich Man and Lazarus

19 "There was a rich man who was dressed in purple and fine linen and who feasted sumptuously every day. 20 And at his gate was laid a beggar named Lazarus, covered with sores, 21 who longed to eat what fell from the rich man's table. Even the dogs would come and lick his sores. 22 The poor man died and was carried away by the angels to be with Abraham. The rich man also died and was buried. 23 In Hell, where he was being tormented, he looked up and saw Abraham far away with Lazarus by his side. 24 He called out, "Father Abraham, have mercy on me, and send Lazarus to dip the tip of his finger in water and cool my tongue; for I am in agony in these flames." 25 But Abraham said, "Son, remember that during your lifetime you received your good things, and Lazarus in like manner evil things; but now he is comforted here, and you are in agony. 26 Besides all this, between you and us a great chasm has been fixed, so that those who might want to pass from here to you cannot do so, and no one can cross from there to us." 27 He said, "Then, father, I beg you to send Lazarus to my father's house—28 for I have five brothers—that he may warn them, so that they will not also come into this place of torment." 29 Abraham replied, "They have Moses and the prophets; they should listen to them." 30 He said, "No, father Abraham; but if someone goes to them from the dead, they will repent." 31 He said to him, "If they do

not listen to Moses and the prophets, neither will they be convinced even if someone rises from the dead." (Luke 16:19–31)

The rich man, who would have been the recipient of so much regard and
honor within the world created by the dominant narrative of his day and
whose name would have been well known by everyone in his community,
goes unnamed in the world of the counter-narrative of this parable. Over
the Christian centuries of preaching this parable, the anonymity of this
rich man has evidently been so unsettling to preachers formed by the
dominant narrative of their own times that they have given the rich man
a name, thus obscuring some of the genius and intent of this parable.
They utterly missed the point of Jesus' naming the poor man but not the
rich one. So the preachers have named the rich man *Dives*, with a capital
"D," from the Latin for "rich man" in the Vulgate Bible.

Under the dominant narrative of Jesus' time, the homeless beggar
named Lazarus by Jesus would have been ignored, blamed for his own
suffering, and avoided, just as homeless men and women are avoided under our own dominant narrative. The only attention the poor man would
have received would have been held noses, avoidance, derision, and condemnation. People would have averted their eyes from this man, refusing
to look him in the face for fear of being confronted by his torment and
of being asked for alms. His sores would have caused him to be shunned
all the more. In the world of that dominant narrative, no one would have
cared to learn his name.

So Jesus is making a sharp point in giving him a name. And not just
any name. Jesus called him "Lazarus" from the Greek form of the Hebrew
Eleazar, meaning "God helps." The irony of this counter-narrative could
not be thicker. The one whom the dominant narrative assumed to have
been blessed by God through wealth, honor, health, and ease is unnamed
and eventually condemned to an eternity of torment worse even than
Lazarus' suffering on earth. The one whom the dominant narrative of
Jesus' time assumed was being punished by God through homelessness,
sores, and lameness was named "God helps." And in the parable, God
eventually did.

Jesus tells us that the rich man was so rich that he was capable of
abundant mercy to Lazarus without sacrificing his own comfort. And
there is no claim that the rich man was due his riches by his hard work.
Jesus tells us instead that he was rich because his father was rich, an accident of the unnamed rich man's birth. Just before he died, the rich man

was not working, but only gorging himself every single day. Within the parable, the only talent he displayed was his hospitality to his social and economic peers and in his choice of luxurious clothing and rich food. He was excessively self-indulgent and unconcerned to share any part of his wealth, not even the crumbs from his table, with the homeless, suffering beggar who lay just outside the rich man's gate—a gate the rich man must have left and entered whenever he left his mansion. In this regard he was the most complete and vivid representative in the teachings of Jesus of the dominant narrative of our time. The only additional characteristic we know of the rich man was that he was a Jew, given the reference to Abraham in the parable and that he had been exposed to Torah and the writings of the prophets. Jesus also tells us that his five brothers were as capable of abundant mercy as the rich man was. But they also chose to live a life of wasteful, narcissistic luxury.

Jesus includes no background in the parable about how Lazarus came to be homeless, ill, disabled, and suffering. Nothing is said about his prior industry or laziness, his sinfulness or righteousness, his mercifulness or his mercilessness, or his justice or injustice. Jesus makes no statement that Lazarus was due his extreme poverty, his illness or his suffering. We are not told what kind of life he had otherwise led, whether he tried to live by Torah and the prophets or not. Thus there is no claim that Lazarus was due his suffering or due his being carried away to heaven as matters of justice. Jesus merely paints a vivid picture of Lazarus' present suffering. Lazarus has sores. Sores alone would have made him an outcast. His sores are being licked by unclean animals, an additional cause and evidence of his impurity. These could have been pressure sores, resulting from his immobility, or the sores could have rendered him disabled. This is like homelessness in our day. Illness and disability can cause a person to become homeless, and chronic homelessness will cause a person to become chronically ill and disabled. All we know about Lazarus, other than his poverty, his sores, his lameness (according to verse 19, Lazarus had been "laid" at the rich man's gate by others), and his hunger was that he had a Jewish name. The only basis for any "relationship" between the rich man and Lazarus was that Lazarus was in the rich man's path as he left and entered his mansion, much as the beaten man was in the path of the Good Samaritan. The absence of any reference to these means that they had no relevance to the rich man's duty to be merciful.

It is startling to us, and I believe that Jesus meant it to be so, that a man would be punished with the eternal torment of hell just because he failed to be merciful to another man who was not a member of his family or his close circle of friends. According to the dominant narrative of our time, there is generally no legal duty enforceable by punishment to come to the aid of anyone who is not in a very close relationship of dependence and vulnerability to us. For instance, the duty of a parent to a child to provide necessities is enforceable by criminal and family law statute in every jurisdiction in the United States. Within our dominant system, there are other voluntary relationships of dependence and vulnerability that can lead to a legally enforceable duty to be merciful by providing services and protecting the person. Examples are voluntary, mutual relationships between a doctor and patient, or between a lawyer and client, or within other fiduciary relationships. Even there, the punishments for failure to be merciful within those relationships vary in form and severity. But generally, as to every non-family member with whom I have not entered into such a voluntary relationship of dependence and vulnerability, my only just duty is not to harm them myself. Within the dominant narrative or our time, I have no just and punishable duty of rescue and provision. According to the dominant narrative of our time, if I were to provide for a suffering beggar at my gate, it would be a voluntary act of mercy on my part, not an act of justice due from me to the beggar.

Likewise, within the dominant narrative in which Jesus told this parable, the rich man and Lazarus were not family and had no voluntary relationship. Yet when the rich man died, he was sent to hell just for failing to be merciful to Lazarus.

Within the story world of this parable, the "Pharisees, who were lovers of money" (v. 14), did not accept that a man would be sent to hell for failing to be merciful to someone with whom they had no such relationship. The dominant narrative of that time was that a man could justly "love" his own money—which is to say, could justly spend 90 percent on himself and his own pleasure so long as he tithed. But Jesus' parable taught that God's counter-narrative was rooted in the Torah and the prophets, not the dominant narrative. And within God's counter-narrative, the rich man's punishment of hell was a just sentence for failing to obey Torah and the prophets to render the mercy that was due Lazarus within that counter-narrative. These legal teachings and commandments included:

> 4 There will, however, be no one in need among you, because the Lord is sure to bless you in the land that the Lord your God is giving you as a possession to occupy, 5 if only you will obey the LORD your God you by diligently observing this entire

commandment that I command you today . . . 7 If there is
among you anyone in need, a member of your community in
any of your towns within the land that the LORD your God is
giving you, do not be hard-hearted or tight-fisted toward your
needy neighbor. **8** You should rather open your hand, willingly
lending enough to meet the need, whatever it may be. **9** Be careful that you do not entertain a mean thought, thinking, "The
seventh year, the year of remission, is near," and therefore view
your needy neighbor with hostility and give nothing; your
neighbor might cry to the LORD against you, and you would
incur guilt. **10** Give liberally and be ungrudging when you do so,
for on this account the LORD your God will bless you in all your
work and in all that you undertake. **11** Since there will never
cease to be some in need on the earth, I therefore command you,
"Open your hand to the poor and needy neighbor in your land."
(Deut 15:4–11)

2 Yet day after day they seek me
    and delight to know my ways,
as if they were a nation that practiced righteousness
    and did not forsake the ordinance of their God;
they ask of me righteous judgements,
    they delight to draw near to God.
3 "Why do we fast, but you do not see?
    Why humble ourselves, but you do not notice?"
6 Is not this the fast that I choose:
    to loose the bonds of injustice,
to undo the thongs of the yoke,
    to let the oppressed go free,
    and to break every yoke?
7 Is it not to share your bread with the hungry,
    and bring the homeless poor into your house;
when you see the naked, to cover them,
    and not to hide yourself?
8 Then your light shall break forth like the dawn,
    and your healing shall spring up quickly;
your vindicator shall go before you,
    the glory of the LORD shall be your rearguard.
9 Then you shall call, and the LORD will answer;
    you shall cry for help, and he will say, Here I am.

If you remove the yoke from among you,
    the pointing of the finger, the speaking of evil,
10 if you offer your food to the hungry
    and satisfy the needs of the afflicted,
then your light shall rise in the darkness
    and your gloom be like the noonday.
11 The LORD will guide you continually,
    and satisfy your needs in parched places,
and make your bones strong;
    and you shall be like a watered garden,
like a spring of water,
    whose waters never fail. (Isa 58:2, 3, 6–11)

For me, Jesus' parable of Lazarus and the rich man resonates with this passage from Isaiah 58. The rich man failed to "share bread" with the hungry beggar and failed to bring this "homeless poor" man "into his home." Therefore, when the rich man calls from the "parched place" of hell, the LORD does not say, "Here I am." When the rich man was "parched" and asked only for Lazarus to bring water to drip on his tongue, the rich man was refused. The rich man failed to see to it that his servants brought to Lazarus the discards and crumbs from his table, which may be a reference to the Torah teachings not to glean to the edge of a field or harvest to the edge of a vineyard so that the poor may benefit from what is left (Lev 19:9–10).

The rich man did not claim to be wholly innocent when he asked for mercy from hell. He had evidently learned from his torment what he had not learned from Torah and the prophets before his death. Perhaps Jesus is saying that the rich man's first-ever experience of suffering made him appreciate how Lazarus had suffered. A claim of innocence would surely have been accompanied by a request to be freed from hell and to join Abraham and Lazarus in heaven. Instead, the rich man's excuse for not opening his hand to Lazarus before they both died was that he did not know that the poor were due mercy as a matter of God's justice. He was saying that he did not know that a Jew would be punished with hell for failure to be justly merciful to the poor. So he prays that Lazarus be sent to his five brothers to "warn" them that mercy to the poor was a just requirement of Torah and that failure to be merciful would result in being denied mercy upon death.

The rich man had merely lived according to the dominant narrative of his and our time. According to the dominant narrative of Jesus' time, a man's riches and health were blessings from God, and signs that he was favored by God. So the rich man believed that he was entitled by God to enjoy those blessings and favors for himself, his family, and his circle of friends. He had been seduced into believing that he was living a "good" life as a "good" man. According to that dominant narrative, a man's poverty and illness were curses from God, signs of God's disfavor. So, before his death, the rich man surely believed that Lazarus was due his plight as a punishment from God.

The rich man's unjust mercilessness was not simply that he failed to open his hand to Lazarus by sending him food. The greater sin was that he failed to open his gate to Lazarus—that he kept this barrier between himself and Lazarus. He followed the dominant narrative that this separation was only just because Lazarus was unclean and disfavored by God. Jesus does not describe the barrier where Lazarus was laid as a "fence," a *phragmos* in the New Testament Greek. He describes it as a *pylōna*, a gate. And a gate may be the way of welcome, rather than a barrier. The rich man chose that it would be a gate to his friends and family but a fence to Lazarus.

To comprehend the impact of this parable in Jesus' time, we need to appreciate the shock of the rich man when he found himself in hell and saw Lazarus in "the bosom of Abraham," a sign of the greatest intimacy and favor with God. We also need to appreciate the outrage that the Pharisees and the insiders would have felt in hearing this parable. This shock and outrage are heightened by the rich man calling Abraham "Father" and Abraham calling the rich man "Son." So even though he was a Jew who lived faithfully within the dominant narrative of his time, the rich man was sent to hell. By asking Abraham to send Lazarus to warn his brothers of the counter-narrative of God set forth in the Torah and the prophets, the rich man was expressing his shock and despair that the dominant narrative he had lived by was actually against the will of God and could have such terrible consequences. So the rich man says to Abraham, in effect, "Who knew?" And Abraham replied, "*You* knew, from Torah and the prophets."

The rich man's plea for the tiniest mercy (drops of water) after he died was denied because he had denied the tiniest mercy to Lazarus (table scraps) before both of them died. This seems also to be the justification for the eternal rewards and punishments meted out in Jesus' parable of the sheep and the goats at Matthew 25:31–46. The goats who had failed to be merciful during their earthly lives were denied mercy at their deaths. These two parables have strong parallel features, including that the punished in both parables claimed ignorance as their defense. The rich man claimed weakly that he did not know that Torah and the prophets required him to be merciful to Lazarus, and the goats claimed strongly that they did not know that Jesus himself was with and within the suffering people whom the goats had failed to help.

Indeed, what could be more counter to the dominant narrative of our time? Under the power of that dominant narrative, in order to be successful and valuable we must dedicate our lives to our increasing accumulation of things and our own greater experience of pleasure. But God's counter-narrative given in Torah, the prophets, and Jesus' teachings warns that if we live by this dominant narrative, we had best enjoy our merciless lives to the hilt before we die because we will be tormented for our mercilessness for eternity afterward. This is the point of the punishments described by Jesus in his parables of the unjust man and Lazarus, of the rich fool, and of the sheep and the goats.

What more can we make of the "great chasm" that prevented Lazarus from being merciful to the rich man? The Greek is *chasma*, which means a "chasm, a gulf, a gap or a wide space." This is the only use of this word that I have found in the New Testament. One understanding is that the chasm or gap between Lazarus and the rich man after both had died was like the chasm or gulf of the rich man's closed gate before both had died. The implication, again, may be that the barrier after death was justly due the rich man because of the barrier he had enforced before his death. So the sinful barriers of indifference created by merciless humans before we die are made permanent by God against merciless human beings after we die. It is too late to repent after we die, this says.

I have a very difficult time giving into this interpretation, though it is clear. It presents God as utterly merciful before we die and relentlessly merciless afterward. It presents a double standard for God's behavior and ours. And it seems inconsistent with the life and other teachings of Jesus.

For me, the spine of Jesus' teachings is that all in need are due God's mercy from all of us as a matter of God's justice. Thus are justice and mercy aspects of the same, single Truth in the counter-narrative and kingdom of God. The dualism of the claimed conflict between justice and mercy of the dominant narrative is negated. If we make judgments about which needy person is or is not due our mercy, we are following the dominant narrative and not the counter-narrative of Jesus. The central issue in the Christian way is not to whom we should or should not be merciful. The central issue is what form that mercy should take—what will and will not benefit them in the context of all the people impacted. In some instances, that mercy can be utter generosity; in others, that mercy can require accountability and correction. In every situation we are called to judge what form mercy should take for all involved. But we are called to hold a wrongdoer accountable only out of mercy. Clearly there are situations in the real world and in the midst of real wrongdoing when mercy for the victim forecloses meaningful mercy for the wrongdoer. I have lived those situations. For us, mercy for all must always be the norm, the standard, and the goal never to be foresworn.

Yet, does the criteria of punishment described by Jesus in the parable of the rich man and Lazarus mean that God lives by an utterly different standard than we are called to—denying mercy to those condemned to hell because they were merciless? Does God make a divine judgment that some are not due mercy at their deaths because they made human judgments during their life that some (or most, or all) needy were not due their mercy? Consider Jesus' classic statement that we are to follow God's own standards for mercy, that there is no double standard, is "Be merciful, just as your Father is merciful" (Luke 6:36).

Let me ask again a question that I personally do not recall ever hearing or reading. Why would a God who is described as so merciful to us before we die become so mechanically merciless after we die? In a faith that denies the great separation and difference between life and death, and that affirms both are merely different forms of life, what is so decisive about physical death? Why would God not allow us to repent after we die? Does the merciful and forgiving nature of God vividly described in Jesus' parable of the prodigal son change so radically after we die?

Because my heart and soul want to resist this interpretation, I offer the following desperate and perhaps untethered hopes.

Within the parable, the stated reason that the rich man could not be granted the small mercy of a little water for his tongue was not that Abraham and Lazarus did not want to be merciful to him. Indeed, the reason for denial of this mercy was not that God had judged that the rich man was not due mercy because he had not been merciful. What Jesus teaches us here is that the claims of the dominant narrative about justice and mercy had produced in life *and* death the great chasm between poor sinners and the dominant so-called "righteous," and likewise between

heaven and hell. The rich man and his close circle had separated themselves from Lazarus and other homeless because of their claim that they
were due God's mercies and blessings while Lazarus and the poor were
not. The reason that Lazarus in heaven could not bring the small mercy
of water to the rich man in hell was because "a great chasm" had been
fixed between them. The dominant narrative—the rich man's claim that
some are due mercy and some are not—had fixed the chasm, not God's
mercilessness. The point of the parable was to inspire the self-righteous
and comfortable to be merciful, not to describe the limits of our Father's
mercy.

Likewise, nothing is said in the parable that Lazarus had received
the greatest mercy of being "carried away to Abraham's side" because
he had been merciful in his earthly life. The only reason given was that
Lazarus was in need of mercy and had not received it in his physical
life. In verses 25 and 29, Jesus has Abraham repeat in the hearing of the
Pharisees the dominant narrative's claims about justice and mercy. To
paraphrase, "In eternity, you receive your just deserts based upon what
you did not do in life."

As to the rich man's other request that Lazarus be sent to his five
brothers to tell them that mercy to the poor was an essential requirement
of God's counter-justice, the reason that Lazarus would not be sent was:
"If they will not listen to Moses and the prophets, neither will they be
convinced even if someone rises from the dead" (verse 31). It would do
no good to send Lazarus to them. But notice also the irony here. Was the
reference to someone rising from the dead a reference to Jesus himself?
Through this parable spoken by Jesus before he was crucified and raised,
and through Luke's inclusion of the parable in his gospel, someone who
was raised from the dead *was* warning everyone who would listen that
mercy to the poor *is* an essential and just requirement of "Moses [To-
rah] and the prophets." Someone who had been raised from the dead
was warning them of the just consequences of failing to be merciful
within the world being created by God's counter-narrative. The parable,
with so many others of Jesus' teachings, motivates and inspires us to be
merciful in this life and to give hope to those who are in need of mercy.
This parable itself communicates the warning to the "five brothers," who
represent all of us.

I do not believe that the point is to actually describe what happens to
us after death. I have always wondered why a merciful God would make
a hard and fast decree that it is too late to repent of our mercilessness

after we die. Why would our callings and possibilities be so different in life than in death? What if people have been so victimized by a merciless, pervasive, dominant narrative that, like the rich man and the five brothers in the parable, they really did not know that mercy to the suffering is an essential, just requirement of God?

Given the frequent appearances and references to the merciless rich in Luke's Gospel, I infer that the dominant narrative of Jesus' time had distorted Torah's older dominant narrative. Torah does not condemn wealth and command that wealthy people share with the needy and suffering whatever they do not need to live. The dominant narrative of Torah instead merely commands that the wealthy give some of their excess to the poor. (See again Lev 19:9–10.) But at some point in time in Israel, the Torah narrative had been supplanted by a dominant narrative that taught that a wealthy person was due to use all of his wealth for himself and his family with no thought for the poor or the community, so long as the rich man observed the Torah's purity provisions and temple requirements. This more recent dominant narrative had caused the rich man described in this parable to violate the older Torah narrative by not sharing the discarded food from his table with Lazarus and by spending *all* of his great wealth on luxurious clothing and lavish daily banquets, with no provision for the needy. This distortion of the original, dominant narrative of Torah and the prophets into a dominant narrative of selfish use of wealth had a long history in Israel. (See, for instance, Isaiah 5, and Jeremiah 5:20–28, 6:13–15, and 7:1–11.)

Jesus brought a counter-narrative even more demanding than the old Torah narrative—a radical counter-narrative which required the rich to welcome the poor into their homes and banquets (Luke 14:12–14, 21–24), and accordingly to invite Lazarus into the rich man's home and lavish banquet. This radical counter-narrative called the rich to give up their wealth to the poor (Luke 18:22, 19:8) and to choose between serving God in Jesus or serving possessions (Luke 14:35, 16:13b).

As discussed above, Jesus' counter-narrative does indeed include promises of eternal reward for the one who is sacrificially merciful to the suffering, and warnings of eternal punishment to the individual who fails to be merciful. Luke 14:14, 16:22b–23, 18:18–23; Matthew 25:31–46. But do God and Jesus really want us to be merciful because we have a self-centered desire for eternal reward or a self-centered fear of our own eternal punishment? Or do God and Jesus instead want us to be merciful because we genuinely love God and Jesus and feel genuine empathy for

God's suffering poor? How deep and wide and rich, how genuine would a mercy be, that could actually be produced by selfish ambition or fear? To inspire mercy, doesn't Jesus' brilliant parable of Lazarus and the rich man rely much more upon graphic description of the suffering of pitiful Lazarus outside the rich man's gate than upon the threat of hell?

> And at his gate was laid a beggar named Lazarus, covered with sores, who longed to eat what fell from the rich man's table. Even the dogs would come and lick his sores.

Even the description of the rich man in hell is intended by Jesus to inspire empathy and mercy:

> In Hell, where he was being tormented . . . "Father Abraham, have mercy on me, and send Lazarus to dip the tip of his finger in water and cool my tongue; for I am in agony in these flames."

The one thing the rich man and Lazarus had in common in the parable was their suffering and need for mercy, albeit at different stages of their lives and deaths. What God would be unmoved by such suffering after someone dies? The God described and incarnated by Jesus? The God revealed by and in Jesus' life and teachings? Perhaps another point of the "great chasm" of the parable is that a person who is unmoved to feelings of empathy and acts of mercy by the sight of extreme suffering will not be moved to such genuine empathy and mercy by the prospect of personal reward of bliss or the threat of terrible, personal punishment.

Put another way, was Ebenezer Scrooge's heartfelt and heartwarming repentance in Dickens classic *A Christmas Carol* mainly a result of the threat of eternal punishment? Or was it inspired and produced by Scrooge's witness and experience of the poverty and suffering of the Cratchit family and of the homeless poor under a London bridge? And did Dickens receive an inspiration for his work from verses 27–28 of this parable?

Why is one person deeply moved to empathy and mercy in the presence of another's suffering, while another person dismisses that suffering by blaming the sufferer for their plight? Why is empathy an overpowering experience in one person and merely a vague idea to another? Why do some people seek out people who are suffering and need mercy, while the majority of others avoid and deny the suffering? Some have claimed it has to do with the suffering that a person witnesses and experiences in life, particularly in childhood. Yet, siblings who experience the same pain and deprivation in childhood commonly become adults with very different capacities for empathy and sacrifice. This is one of life's greatest mysteries. Is it partly due to the dominant narrative, and how much individuals embrace the world of that narrative?

In the parable, the rich man's only act of mercy was to ask Abraham to send a warning to his brothers of their own impending judgment and suffering. This came only after he himself had suffered. But through my work I have known hundreds and hundreds of men and women who have been so angered and embittered by their merciless and unjust sufferings that their capacity for empathy seems to have been buried in a grave within them. Yet I have also been privileged to know some of their brothers and sisters who have emerged with great sensitivity and compassion for those who are hurting and in need. Given how unequally and randomly we humans are endowed and nurtured with the capacity for empathy and mercy, how can a loving, merciful, and just God condemn those without that capacity to eternal hell and reward with heaven those who had received the gracious blessing of this capacity?

A greater mystery, central to the way of Christ, is *how* to inspire greater acts of mercy. Is the question of "nature or nurture"—genetics versus life's experience—the key? Neuroscience has located anatomically common seats of empathy and mercy in all of our brains. Perhaps one day this science will be able to determine that greater blood circulation or a larger number of neurons or pathways in those critical brain areas exist in some people, and that these differences result in greater capacity for empathy and mercy. Regardless, we Christians are called to do our best to inspire the greatest possible empathy and mercy in our communities, in others, in our children and in ourselves, through whatever means are available. This was and is much of the life work of Jesus. He attempted to inspire mercifulness by being merciful and by teaching these brilliant parables of mercy. His counter-narratives have inspired mercy in every age. Who has ever done more?

Despite all efforts to create, inspire, and increase empathy and mercy, some of us will feel great empathy at the sight of suffering and an urge to act out great mercy, and some of us will not. When powerfully experienced, these feelings and urges can be so great that there really is no choice except to act them out. At times these feelings and urges will seem like a blessing and at other times like a curse. Or perhaps blessing and curse simultaneously. Others of us will experience much less feeling and few urges, and no sight of suffering, threat of punishment, or brilliant parable will increase them. Who really knows why? Who am I to judge?

So what is the point in *teaching* empathy and mercy? What is the point of proclaiming a counter-narrative of mercy to a culture controlled by a dominant narrative of mercilessness? What is the point of repeating Jesus' vivid parables about mercy and justice, suffering and need, accountability and forgiveness that serve mostly to emphasize that justice and mercy and their absence are matters of life and death to everyone? One point is to counter the merciless and unjust dominant narratives of every age and place, as well as the injustice and mercilessness that lurks in all of us. The point is to inspire the greatest possible just mercy and merciful justice in each and all of us. The point is to get the greatest number of Lazaruses in every age and place fed, dressed, sheltered, healed, and welcomed. The point of telling and repeating these parables is to shape and change the heart and soul of the human community in every age and place, and thus to shape every possible individual's goals, yearnings, and ethics. Jesus' parables are a major part of God's counter-narrative. Narratives shape the collective mind and the way of being and acting of entire peoples. They are a strong part of the "nurture" in the "nature or nurture" issue.

Among the greatest failures of the American church is our blindness to how deeply counter Jesus' narrative is to our dominant narrative, and our attempt to take turns living by each narrative—by the dominant narrative of narcissistic wealth during six and 23/24ths days a week, and the counter-narrative of just mercy and merciful justice for one hour of one day per week; by the counter-narrative during the Christmas and Lenten seasons and by the dominant narrative the rest of the year; by the counter-narrative in our relations with our family and friends but by the dominant narrative in every other arena of our lives and particularly in our economic, financial, and political lives.

A person who lacks the urge to be merciful is justly due . . . mercy—the mercy of understanding, acceptance, and encouragement to be more merciful.

A person who has this irresistible urge to be merciful is justly due mercy. For a person with this blessing, being merciful can bring almost a high. There can be not just joy but profound pleasure and *shalom* in helping someone who is in need. Being merciful can be an addiction for some of us. Persons who have this urge can be merciful to everyone but themselves and their families. Persons with this urge can burn out, suffer compassion fatigue and loss of empathy, and lose the meaning of their lives. The mercy that the merciful are due is understanding and the encouragement to be merciful to themselves and their families, to "love themselves" as they have loved their neighbors. Jesus said "Blessed are the merciful, for they shall receive mercy" (Matt 5:7). For me, what Jesus was saying was and is that those who are blessed and cursed with a powerful urge and need to be merciful will receive a continuing and greater capacity to be merciful even after they burn out. This they will receive from the community of the counter-narrative of Jesus and from the Spirit of the risen Christ.

**

The Parable of the Unjust Judge

1 Then Jesus told them a parable about their need to pray always and not to lose heart. 2 He said, "In a certain city there was a judge who neither feared God nor had respect for people 3 In that city there was a widow who kept coming to him and saying, 'Grant me justice against my opponent.' 4 For a while he refused; but later he said to himself, 'Though I have no fear of God and no respect for anyone, 5 yet because this widow keeps bothering me, I will grant her justice, so that she may not wear me out by continually coming.'" 6 And the Lord said, "Listen to what the unjust judge says. 7 And will not God grant justice to his chosen ones who cry to him day and night? Will he delay long in helping them? 8 I tell you, he will quickly grant justice to them. And yet, when the Son of Man comes, will he find faith on earth?" (Luke 18:1–8)

Why would Jesus compare God to this judge? It seems to be damning God with faint praise. For me, the reason Jesus did this is that God did indeed seem to have two things in common with this godless and merciless judge. First, the judge, like God, had the power to do something about this widow's plight. Second, God, like the judge, was delaying in bringing justice and mercy to the widow and others in bitter need. So many of Jesus' followers and listeners were suffering and vulnerable, despite Jesus' own justice and mercy, and despite his affirmations of his *Abba's* justice and mercy. Jesus' suffering followers had to be wondering why God was not saving them from those insiders who exploited them so unjustly and mercilessly.

The key to this parable for me is the phrase in verse 7: "Will he [God] delay *long* in helping them?" (emphasis added). There, Jesus realistically recognizes that there has indeed been a delay. But he promises that God's delay was not due to God's lack of regard for them. He also promises that God's delay will not be long. Despite the delay, Jesus teaches his followers and listeners to be as persistent in pleading for justice and mercy from God as this widow was from the judge.

Regardless of the theological issue about God that is central to this parable, consider how very affirming and encouraging this parable would have been to those followers of Jesus who were as powerless and otherwise voiceless as this widow. This widow prevailed against her oppressors and against a merciless, unjust judge because of her courage and persistence!

The parable also affirms that God's justice and mercy are fused and that both are aspects of what is due even to the vulnerable and unprotected.

The main character is of course a widow. In Israel, the word "widow" was not used merely for a woman whose husband had died. While women could not inherit from their husband's estates, it was customary for a husband of any means to provide for the continued financial support of his wife after his death. If the deceased had done this in his life, the male who inherited the deceased husband's estate was obligated to provide for the widow. Even if a woman's husband died penniless, if she was protected and provided for by his or her family, she was not a "widow" in the sense of the Hebrew Scripture or this parable. A "widow" as used here was a woman whose husband had died without leaving her any financial support *and* who had no male to protect and advocate for her. A "widow" had no patron. She was like an orphan or an alien.

In the Hebrew Scripture, "widows, orphans and aliens" were a triad of persons who were representative of all those within Israel's covenantal community who were treated by the dominant narrative of that time as non-persons. They were treated as if they were due nothing from anyone. So Torah and the prophets contain many Scriptures specifically forbidding this oppression. (See, for example: Deut 24:17, 27:19; Isa 10:1–2; Jer 7:5–7; Zech 7:9–10; Mal 3:5.) These protections and admonitions were extraordinary, even unique, in the laws of the ancient Middle East. The inclusion of these protections for the poor and vulnerable reveals how different the people of YHWH were called to be, and how deeply counter the narrative of God was to the dominant narrative of the time. That there are many of these prohibitions and admonitions shows how often

defenseless people were oppressed and cheated within Israel by the dominant classes. Jesus' telling of this parable of the Unjust Judge shows that
despite God's counter-narrative against oppressing the powerless and the
voiceless, the dominant culture did just that. The plight of this widow
would have been well-known to Jesus' listeners.

There is an Old Testament Scripture and a Deuterocanonical writing that resonate so much with this parable that they may have served as
foundations:

> 4 Jehoshaphat resided at Jerusalem; then he went out again
> among the people, from Beer-sheba to the hill country of
> Ephraim, and brought them back to the LORD, the God of their
> ancestors. 5 He appointed judges in the land in all the fortified
> cities of Judah, city by city, 6 and said to the judges, "Consider
> what you are doing, for you judge not on behalf of human be-
> ings but on the LORD's behalf; he is with you in giving judg-
> ment. 7 Now, let the fear of the LORD be upon you; take care
> what you do, for there is no perversion of justice with the Lord
> our God, or partiality, or taking of bribes." (2 Chr 19:4–7)

> 14 Do not offer him a bribe, for he will not accept it;
> 15 and do not rely on a dishonest sacrifice;
> for the Lord is the judge,
> and with him there is no partiality.
> 16 He will not show partiality to the poor;
> but he will listen to the prayer of one who is wronged.
> 17 He will not ignore the supplication of the orphan,
> or the widow when she pours out her complaint.
> 18 Do not the tears of the widow run down her cheek
> 19 as she cries out against the one who causes them to fall?
> 20 The one whose service is pleasing to the Lord will be accepted,
> and his prayer will reach to the clouds.
> 21 The prayer of the humble pierces the clouds,
> and it will not rest until it reaches its goal;
> it will not desist until the Most High responds
> 22 and does justice for the righteous, and executes judgment.
> Indeed, the Lord will not delay,
> and like a warrior will not be patient
> until he crushes the loins of the unmerciful

²³and repays vengeance on the nations;
until he destroys the multitude of the insolent,
and breaks the scepters of the unrighteous;
²⁴until he repays mortals according to their deeds,
and the works of all according to their thoughts;
²⁵until he judges the case of his people
and makes them rejoice in his mercy.
²⁶His mercy is as welcome in time of distress
as clouds of rain in time of drought. (Sir 35:14–25)

In this parable, the widow had no one to protect or plead for her. Not one male would stand for her and protest the injustice that was being done to her. Not one man who was in the dominant inside would intercede even privately with the man who was exploiting this widow. She had no patron who would take her side. She was so alone and vulnerable that the only male to which she could turn was this merciless and unjust judge. But in refusing to call her case for consideration, he treated her like she was due no attention. She was of no account—a non-person. She was like a person in our time who had suffered a great injustice that did her great harm, but who could not find a lawyer because she could not pay, and who could not get a judge to hear her case because she did not know the proper procedure.

Perhaps this judge ignored the pleas of a widow because he had been bribed, or because the man who had treated her unjustly was a member of the same insider group as was the judge. The judge was showing partiality to this wrongdoer because they were friends and colleagues. Perhaps the wrongdoer was a merchant who had taken the widow's outer garment in pledge for food she desperately needed and was refusing to give it back. Perhaps the man was a landowner who had hired her to perform some task, and he was denying her some portion of what he agreed to pay her. Perhaps the man had taken something that belonged to her, like a goat or a donkey, claiming that she owed it to him, or that the animal had trespassed on his land, or that it was his not hers. Perhaps the landowner about whom she complains was the owner of a large amount of land in the region of this city. Suppose he habitually violated the protections afforded to the poor by Lev 19:9–10 by reaping to the very edges of his field, or gathering the gleanings of his harvest, or stripping his vineyards bare, or gathering the fallen grapes of his vineyard, depriving the poor of these leftovers. And suppose this widow had the pluck to try to stand up to him in the city gate where legal disputes were heard and decided in Israel's cities. Or perhaps some male who was in the dominant inside had sexually assaulted this widow. And she had the courage to try to sue him and expose the truth about him. Perhaps this man believed that he was invulnerable to justice because this widow was a voiceless nobody whom no one would help. Perhaps this man was so proud of his reputation and position that he was insulted that such a nobody would have the temerity to question his behavior publicly. Because she had done so, she had to be put in her place. Perhaps the judge was friends with this wrongdoer or was just a member of the same insider group and wanted to be loyal to his friend and his class by keeping this widow in her place—on the outside and voiceless. The judge likely felt that the oppressor was due respect and protection, and that the widow was due nothing. Within the dominant narrative of that time, the widow was due nothing from anyone. So the judge would not even allow her case to come publicly before him.

Picture the scene. Courts were not held in separate buildings in Israel at that time. Courts convened in the open at the city gate. Here, there was one judge empowered to decide lawsuits. Elders of the city would take their places to watch and hear the proceedings. We may be sure that the hearing of legal disputes was a source of entertainment and interest for the city, particularly for elders who were effectively retired. We also may be sure that there were "lawyers"—scribes or experts in Torah—who were hired to plead people's cases. And because these suits were based upon Torah, every Jewish elder there would have had their own learned opinion on what Torah required in a given case.

So at the assigned time of day the judge would take his place on the judgment seat, and men, represented by lawyers or by themselves, would come forward with their disputes to ask for a just judgment—a *mishpat*—based upon Torah. No doubt many of these disputes were known in advance to the watchers. One thing is certain: there would have been no women in that place, and certainly no women bringing their own suit.

But in this parable, in the midst of this patriarchal setting, this poor widow kept crying to be heard. Perhaps everyday she was crying out her allegations and the passage from Torah upon which she relied. Day after day the judge refused to hear or even acknowledge her. But she herself kept appearing and demanding that her suit he heard, because she had no one else to whom she could turn. Surely many elders at the gate were variously angered, amused, or scandalized by her conduct. Surely some inquired about the truth of what she claimed. Surely the man against whom she sought justice was embarrassed and angry, and mounted his own gossip defense to her claims. Surely his friends spread false rumors about her—her immorality, incredibility, and ignorance. Slander was added to the merciless injustice she had suffered. But she kept coming back and coming back, as lonely and vulnerable as she had to have felt. Perhaps she developed a small following of elders who believed privately that she had been treated unjustly and mercilessly, but who still did not have the moral courage to stand and speak for her.

Eventually, the judge gave in and heard her case. Why? She was not going away. She was disrupting the proceedings. She was calling into question the legitimacy of the entire court. He gave her the "justice" she wanted to shut her up and make her go away.

Who knows what happened to her after she received her vindication. The parallels between this parable, 2nd Chronicles 19 and Sirach 35, are striking. In 2 Chr 19:7, the king instructs the appointed judges to "let the fear of the LORD be upon you; take care what you do, for there is no perversion of justice with the LORD our God, or partiality . . . " Yet the judge in Jesus' parable had no fear of God and no respect for this widow. He was partial to the oppressor and was perverting justice. The writing from Sirach, an intertestamental writing known in Jesus' time and place, contrasts God as judge with humans as judges, just as Jesus' parable does. In Sir 35:16b–17, the Lord "will listen to the prayer of one who is wronged. He will not ignore the supplication of the orphan, or the widow when she pours out her complaint," in contrast to the judge in the parable who ignores the widow's supplications for so long. In Sir 35:21–22, "the prayer of the humble pierces the clouds, and it will not rest until it reaches its goal; it will not desist until the Most High responds and does justice for the righteous, and executes judgment. Indeed, the Lord will not delay, and like a warrior will not be patient until he crushes the loins of the unmerciful." Just as the "prayer" of the humble poor in Sir 35:21 would not "desist," so the widow in the parable "kept coming" until justice was granted. Just as the Lord in the passage from Sirach would "not delay" or be patient in repaying with vengeance, so God in Jesus' parable would not delay in granting justice (Luke 18:8).

There is at least one other striking parallel between the parable of Jesus and this passage from Sirach 35. In the parable at verses 7 and 8, the Greek word *ekdikēsis* is used, which I believe is the only time this word appears in any parable. The NRSV translates the phrases that include this critical word as "grant justice." But I believe that the sense of the Greek is more than justice. The sense is that the widow had been done a greater harm than a mere injustice. The deeper translation would be "vindicate me," or more accurately, "avenge me." So in verse 3, the widow asks the judge repeatedly, "Avenge [*ekdikeó*] me." And in verse 5, the judge gives in to be rid of the persistent widow, saying "I will avenge [*ekdikeó*] her." Translated this way, verses 7 and 8 of the parable read: "Will not God avenge his chosen ones who cry to him day and night? Will he delay long in helping them? I tell you, he will quickly avenge them." This is just as in verses 22 and 23 of the Sirach 35: "The Lord will not delay, and like a warrior will not be patient until he crushes the loins of the unmerciful and repays vengeance on the nations."

And in the passage from Sirach which seems to me to provide a foundation for Jesus' parable, the justice that God grants to the widows and orphans—the vengeance he grants against the wrongdoer—is called "mercy."

> 24 until he repays mortals according to their deeds,
>   and the works of all according to their thoughts;
> 25 until he judges the case of his people
>   and makes them rejoice in his mercy.
> 26 His mercy is as welcome in time of distress
>   as clouds of rain in time of drought. (Sir 35:24–25)

What was the specific injustice done to the widow of our parable? It would necessarily relate to her vulnerability as a widow. Because she was so poor, something was taken from her that she needed for her very survival. She was not persisting in demanding just vindication for the principle of it. She was in need because of the merciless injustice done to her. Its loss made her even more in need of mercy. So in the passage from Sirach and in this parable, there is once again no difference between God's justice and God's mercy. The widow was due justice and mercy at once, one and the same.

This justice is the opposite of the justice of our American culture's dominant narrative: "She is not due whatever she cannot get" in the competition.

And holding the wrongdoer accountable is also a form of mercy for him, as well as for the widow. To have overlooked his calloused and merciless treatment of the widow would have excused, reinforced, and enabled it. It would have left the wrongdoer in his self-justification and denial. Of course, justice to the widow was a great mercy to her. But the only chance the oppressor had in being transformed into a person who would turn from the conduct taught by the dominant narrative to become merciful would be to hold him accountable through the widow's suit. The appetite for power being what it was and is in some human beings, and the power of the dominant narrative being as pervasive as it was and is, it seems unlikely that the victory of the widow would begin to transform her oppressor. Through the Justice Ministry, we have represented very many such widows seeking justice and mercy against their abusers from the court system. We have had an easier time obtaining vindication than the widow in this parable. The immediate reaction of the abusers has almost always been to rail at the system and accuse the victim of lying and worse, even though we have tried to treat the abuser with respect and encouragement to repentance. Being held accountable did not seem to start a process of transformation for the abusers in most of our cases.

But there are always two parts of merciful justice and just mercy. One part is the offer; the other is the acceptance. Whether the oppressor in this parable or the abusers in our family violence suits will likely accept the just mercy of accountability being offered them, under the counter-narrative of Jesus they are still always due the offer. Whether an individual accepts is something of an *agón* between him and the dominant narrative, and God.

**

The Parable of the Pharisee and the Tax Collector

9 He also told this parable to some who trusted in themselves that they were just and regarded others as of no account: 10 "Two men went up to the temple to pray, one a Pharisee and the other a tax collector. 11 The Pharisee, standing by himself, was praying thus, 'God, I thank you that I am not like other people: thieves, rogues, adulterers, or even like this tax collector. 12 I fast twice a week; I give a tenth of all my income.' 13 But the tax collector, standing far off, would not even look up to heaven, but was beating his breast and saying, 'God, be merciful to me, a sinner!' 14 I tell you, this man went down to his home justified rather than the other; for all who exalt themselves will be humbled, but all who humble themselves will be exalted."
(Luke 18:9–14)

We have been conditioned to believe the Pharisees were evil people, because they are presented so consistently in the Gospels as bitter opponents of Jesus. But most people of Israel in Jesus' time would have viewed them in a more positive light—as just and obedient to Torah.

The Pharisee in this parable seems to be an arrogant braggart, self-deceived about his own virtue and justice, claiming superiority by condemning others, and blind to his own sin. But his prayer of thanks to God that he is not like the extortionist, the unjust, or the adulterer is no worse than the claims of the psalmist in Ps 17:3–5, or the claims of Job at chapter 29. The issue is whether he is being truthful in his claims about his own behavior.

There is nothing in this parable that suggests that the Pharisee is being untruthful in his claims that he fasts twice a day and tithes from all of his income and property. If he is indeed being truthful, then he has been unusually merciful to the poor. Fasting twice every week is more than is demanded in Torah. The purpose of fasting was not merely spiritual discipline. Fasting was a means of mercy—the denial of one's appetite to give the money not spent on food, or the food not eaten, to the hungry. Tithes were not given merely to support the temple and its Levite staff, but also to be merciful to the poor and needy. (Consider Deut 26:12–15.)

This Pharisee stood apart ("by himself") to pray. There is no basis for claiming that his prayer was a loud show of public piety. Only God was hearing him, which is perhaps another reason to conclude that Jesus is telling us that the Pharisee believes what he is saying about his own conduct. And through the language of his prayer ("God, I thank *you* that I am not like other people . . ."), he does not claim that his virtue is self-made, but attributes it to God's influence upon him. This is something like Jesus' response at Luke 18:9 when the rich young ruler calls him "good," and Jesus replies that "only God is good." Finally, if indeed this Pharisee is truthful about how much he gives to the poor and needy, he truly is not like an extortionist, a person who fails to render to others what they are due, or an adulterer, and there is no good reason to believe from the parable that he is like them.

So what is this Pharisee's sin? Through this parable Jesus tells us that the Pharisee was incompletely merciful and just. His mercy and justice were not rendered to enough people in enough ways. The Pharisee did not appreciate the extent of the mercy that was due from him to the tax collector, the extortionist, the rogue, the adulterer, and to himself. The Pharisee's prayer is dripping with irony from the perspective of the

counter-narrative of Jesus. The word "rogue" of the NRSV is a translation of the Greek *adikos*. The Greek literally means "unjust." The Pharisee
thanks God that he is just while the *adikos* is not. But within the counter-
narrative, he fails to render the mercy to the *adikos* and the others that
they are due as a matter of God's justice. So indeed the Pharisee is unjust.

The Pharisee was quite merciful to the poor—the orphan, the widow, and the alien. The justice taught by Torah was that the orphan, the
alien, and the widow were due the Pharisee's tithes, and he obeyed. So he
was simultaneously just and merciful to them. But he did not accept that
his mercy was also due to "thieves, rogues, adulterers," and the "tax collector" in the parable. The sin of all those people was a failure to render
unto vulnerable people the mercy they were due as children of God. But
in judging who was due his mercy and who was not, the Pharisee was also
guilty of a lack of justice and mercy to thieves, rogues, adulterers, and
tax collectors. By his sense of superiority, his self-righteousness, and his
condemnations, he turned these children of God into "them." His judgment was that his own mercilessness toward "them" was not sinful, while
their mercilessness toward others was sinful. But all were guilty of the
same sins of injustice and mercilessness. As stated in verse 9 of the parable: the Pharisee trusted "in himself" to decide who was due mercy and
who was not. He was guilty of the same sin of lack of mercy as the others.
But unlike the tax collector in the parable, the Pharisee did not see his
sin, confess it, and repent of it. So he did not go down from the Temple
Mount acquitted of the sin. The sin continued.

What was the mercy due from the Pharisee to thieves, rogues,
adulterers, and the tax collector in the parable? To accept them as fellow
children of God, and to try to help them become merciful. Not just to
condemn and exclude, which would accomplish nothing for them. Not
just by keeping himself pure and separate, "standing by himself" (verse
1). Mercy toward the thieves, rogues, adulterers, and tax collector would
come from being in relation with them—befriending, mentoring, and
helping them find the way to being merciful through being merciful to
them. In this relationship, all could help all to be more merciful. This was
what Jesus did and taught. Mercy toward "them" would be to sit at table
with them, as Jesus was criticized by Pharisees for eating with tax collectors and sinners. (Luke 5:30.) The Pharisee seems to have been more
concerned with his own complete holiness than with his complete mercifulness. He thus created a false duality of holiness versus mercifulness.

As for the tax collector who "went down to his home justified," it is important not to read a Pauline meaning into the Greek word *dikaioo*. Tax collectors in that time and place took whatever they could from their victims. They were under contract to pay the Romans a certain amount, and whatever they extorted in excess of that amount was their profit. They were collaborators in the Roman oppression of Israel, and lived by the dominant narrative of Caesar and the Empire. Here, "went down to his home justified" does not mean this tax collector was only "reckoned" just by God because of momentary, though heartfelt, remorse and confession of sin. The tax collector became just because he had resolved to stop treating people mercilessly by extorting more money from them than he was due from them.

By calling himself a "sinner" in his prayer before God, the tax collector admitted that he had been merciless. The description of his actions—"standing far off, would not even look up to heaven, but was beating his breast"—shows how deep and genuine was his remorse, moving him to plead for God's mercy. Growing out of this remorse, he committed to being merciful himself and to treating others with the mercy with which they were due.

This story resonates with two other stories in Luke about repenting tax collectors; the story in which John told tax collectors who asked how they should repent: "collect no more than the amount prescribed to you" (Luke 3:13); and the story of Zacchaeus, who became just by resolving to give half of his possessions to the poor and to pay back fourfold whatever he had defrauded from any victim (Luke 19:8). In the Zacchaeus story, Jesus responded to the tax collector's repentance by saying, "Today salvation has come to this house . . ." (Luke 19:9). Similarly, in our parable of the Pharisee and the tax collector at Luke 18, Jesus responded to the tax collector's repentance by saying that the tax collector "went down to his home justified." I cannot believe that Jesus meant for us to understand that this deeply remorseful tax collector would leave the Temple Mount to return to his former unjust and merciless extortions.

Both characters had also been merciless to themselves. Only the tax collector repented of this. The Pharisee failed to recognize his continuing mercilessness and repent of it. He failed to recognize that every child of God is due mercy as a matter of God's justice, so he failed to see that he was counted among the *adikos*. He also failed to see that he himself needed the mercy of being made more merciful. His justice and mercy were incomplete. He was still under the dominant narrative, deciding who was due mercy rather than deciding the specific form of mercy that everyone was due under the counter-narrative of God. In his pride and self-satisfaction, he was not rendering unto himself what he was due—to become a thoroughly merciful person. The tax collector recognized his previous mercilessness and repented of it. The tax collector went from the temple resolving to treat the people vulnerable to him with the mercy they were due. In doing so, he rendered unto himself the greatest mercy—allowing himself to become a merciful and therefore just person.

Very many more Pharisees than tax collectors are in the modern American church and secular society. We follow the dominant narrative, deciding who is due our mercy and who is not, and who is and is not due being in our presence and in a relationship with us. Like the Pharisee, we believe ourselves to be due more of God's regard and protection than the people we see as rogues. We believe ourselves to be superior to others because of our accidents of birth—our families, our networks, our inherited positions, and our capabilities. And we believe ourselves to be superior to others because of their conduct, never asking what in their lives brought them to the conduct we condemn and fear. We give thanks to God that we are better than those who live the plight of the homeless, the addict, the convicted felon, the registered sex offender, the undocumented alien, the minimum wage earner, the recipient of food stamps, the unemployed, and the unmarried mother with children from multiple fathers. So we keep ourselves separated. We never learn what the lives of "them" are actually like. And we withhold the great blessings of our stunning virtue and shining personalities from them. In thinking and behaving in this way, like the Pharisee in the parable we deny the mercy that is due to them and to us. We remain complacently in our own mercilessness. The dominant narrative wins in our lives again.

∗∗

The Parables of the Lost and Strayed Sheep

12 "What do you think? If a shepherd has a hundred sheep, and one of them has gone astray, does he not leave the ninety-nine on the mountains and go in search of the one that went astray? 13 And if he finds it, truly I tell you, he rejoices over it more than over the ninety-nine that never went astray. 14 So it is not the

will of your Father in heaven that one of these little ones should be lost." (Matt 18:12–14)

Now all the tax collectors and sinners were coming near to listen to him. 2 And the Pharisees and the scribes were grumbling and saying, "This fellow welcomes sinners and eats with them." 3 So he told them this parable: 4 "Which one of you, having a hundred sheep and losing one of them, does not leave the ninety-nine in the wilderness and go after the one that is lost until he finds it? 5 When he has found it, he lays it on his shoulders and rejoices. 6 And when he comes home, he calls together his friends and neighbors, saying to them, 'Rejoice with me, for I have found my sheep that was lost.' 7 Just so, I tell you, there will be more joy in heaven over one sinner who repents than over ninety-nine righteous persons who need no repentance." (Luke 15:1–7)

Under the dominant narrative of that time, the forgiveness lived and taught by Jesus was manifestly unjust. Such forgiveness undermined true justice by excusing and thus enabling wrongdoing. Within this narrative, Jesus' species of forgiveness was a moral weakness—a failure to render the consequences due a wrongdoer before forgiveness and reconciliation are even considered. Jesus' forgiveness is a violation of the basic justice standard of an "eye for an eye, a tooth for a tooth, a hand for a hand, a foot for a foot" set forth at Exod 24:21. In fact, under the dominant narrative, forgiveness even after repentance encourages and enables more wrongdoing. This is the implied criticism by the elder son of the father in Jesus' parable of the prodigal son, also appearing at Luke 15. This is the scandal in Jesus' admonition to Peter at Matt 18:21–22 to forgive a person even after his seventy-seventh sin. This is the outrage, according to the dominant narrative, in Jesus' plea to the Father to forgive those who were torturing him to death (Luke 23:34), an act Christians believe was as unjust as any in history. Jesus did not say to his Father, "Forgive them after they have repented and made amends."

My reading of the Gospels is that Jesus did not teach that repentance was required *before* forgiveness and restoration was offered a wrongdoer.

Jesus of course did call for repentance. (See, for instance, Matt 4:17, Mark 1:15, and Luke 5:31–32.) In Luke 17:3–4, Jesus is quoted as saying that if a wrongdoer sins against you seven times a day but says "I repent" after each sin, Jesus' followers are required to forgive.

But I do not find in the Gospels that Jesus taught that repentance *must* always come *before* forgiveness and restoration. The consistent criticism of him by the Pharisees and religious insiders is that he associated with people who were still sinners—who had not yet repented and reformed their lives. Jesus' saying in Luke 5:31–32 was a response to Pharisees who were complaining that he was eating with unrepentant sinners. Jesus was associating with those sinners by sharing a meal with them in order to move them to repent. He did not require them to repent before he would eat with them.

Through the Lord's Prayer, Jesus teaches his followers to pray: "And forgive us our debts as we also have forgiven our debtors . . . For if you forgive others their trespasses, your heavenly father will also forgive you. But if you do not forgive others, neither will your Father forgive your trespasses" (Matt 5:12, 14–15). Jesus said nothing there about repentance by the wrongdoer to the wronged before the wrongdoer is due forgiveness.

In Jesus' teachings repentance would not just mean thinking differently. Repentance would require that one's entire purpose and life would change. But I find no strict *quid pro quo* requirement in Jesus' teachings that restitution be made, that the victim be compensated, that what was lost be restored, or that an eye be given back for every eye taken before the wrongdoer is due to be restored to relationship and given a new start. Jesus' emphasis was upon letting the wrongdoer up, letting her start over with a fresh chance, letting her get beyond the past, and letting her be "born anew." For him, there was no requirement of repentance first, no requirement that the wrongdoer first recognize and acknowledge that what she had done was wrong and hurtful, no requirement that she first apologize and ask for forgiveness, and no requirement that she first promise not to repeat the hurt. Jesus' focus is upon the future, not on the past. And the focus of Jesus' life and teaching was for his followers on his way to be merciful to a wrongdoer by freely giving her the mercy of forgiveness and restoration.

But according to the dominant narrative of Jesus' and of our time, setting aside a hurtful wrong without punishment and restitution is not only unjust but also scandalous. Only after the victim has received in full what is due from the wrongdoer, only after the wrongdoer has paid an equitable price, and only after justice is therefore done should there be a chance for forgiveness and restoration to relationship. And this forgiveness and restoration, like all mercy, was and is optional. In no area is Jesus' narrative more counter to the dominant narrative than in the justice and mercy of repentance and forgiveness.

The parable of the strayed sheep is remembered and reported in slightly different versions in Luke's and Matthew's Gospel. The common features are much more significant than the disparate ones. My interpretation turns upon (1) why and how the one sheep was "lost" or "went astray" and (2) who the one sheep and the ninety-nine sheep represent.

In one view, the lost sheep needed to repent and be rescued from the consequences of its sin. The ninety-nine were the righteous. In Matthew's Gospel, the one sheep "went astray." The Greek translated in the NRSV as "went astray" is *planao,* which could more fully be translated as "strayed from truth or virtue" or "erred." In Luke, the parable was given in response to the Pharisees' criticism of Jesus for eating with tax collectors and sinners (Luke 15:1–2). In Luke, the one sheep was "lost" (verse 4). The parable progresses with Jesus comparing the "lost" sheep to a person who needs repentance. So the sense in both versions is that the one sheep for which the shepherd searches is lost or strayed in sin and disobedience, and is in need of rescue and repentance.

In Matthew's version, the ninety-nine sheep who had not strayed were left "on the mountains" while the shepherd went to find the strayed one. In Luke's, the ninety-nine not in need of repentance were left by the shepherd "in the wilderness." In neither version were the ninety-nine virtuous sheep taken to a comfortable, safe place before the shepherd left them in search of the strayed or lost one. In neither version is there any hint that the ninety-nine were left in the care of other shepherds. The sense in both versions is that the shepherd gave more attention and care to the one sheep that had strayed than to the ninety-nine who had remained faithful. In Matthew's version at verse 14, the one strayed sheep is called "one of these little ones." In verse 10, Jesus had stated that the angels of "these little ones" "continually see the face of my Father in heaven." God "willed" (verse 14) that the guardian angels of the lost sheep report continually to God on the welfare of these little strayed ones. And this favoring of the sheep that need rescue and repentance over the many that do not is clearly revealed in the greater joy from the recovering of the strayed and lost sheep than in the constant faithfulness of the ninety-nine (Luke 15:7; Matt 18:13).

In both versions, the lost, strayed sheep had done nothing to repent before the shepherd went in search of her, unlike in the parable of the prodigal son in Luke in which the strayed son had begun to repent and had almost returned to the father when the father ran to greet him. The shepherd abandoned the ninety-nine faithful sheep to search for the sinner with no assurance that the sinner would respond with repentance. The shepherd went anyway, taking all of the initiative and with the evident intention of inspiring the strayed sheep to repentance by the shepherd's merciful and risky love. This is much as Jesus was eager to eat with sinners before there was any sign of their repentance.

This is not the justice of the dominant narrative, then or now. Within our dominant narrative, the ninety-nine faithful, obedient sheep were due more protection and more attention, not less, from the shepherd. In fact, they were due all of the shepherd's protection and attention. The one strayed sheep was due nothing, because he had strayed. Within the dominant narrative, it's up to the strayed sheep to un-stray himself, to find his way back, to repent first, and to pull himself up by his own hoof-straps, before any welcome and restoration is due to this sheep from the shepherd and the other sheep. In the meritocracy of the dominant narrative, the faithful, obedient sheep were due the rewards of their faithful obedience. In the dominant narrative, the shepherd's abandonment of the faithful ninety-nine in a place of risk was an outrageous injustice. Under the dominant narrative, the faithful ninety-nine are the "little ones" who are due having their guardian angels continually in God's presence, not the faithless sinner in need of repentance.

But there is an additional view of this, which is even more provocative to our time and situation. It is suggested by Jesus' use of the "one" compared to the "ninety-nine."

The Pharisees and their followers, not Jesus' sinners, were in the numeric minority in that time. Josephus, the Jewish historian and collaborator with the Romans in the first century, estimated that there were perhaps 6,000 Pharisees in all of the Holy Land during this period, among between 1.5 and 2 million Jews there. Regardless of the exact numbers, the Pharisees were a tiny minority. The word "Pharisee" is believed to have been derived from ancient Greek and Aramaic for "separated." The Pharisees insisted that Torah required all Jews to "separate" themselves from all gentiles and even from non-righteous Jews by strictly observing Torah Sabbath, purity and tithing regulations. Pharisees believed in an oral Torah through which strict religious observances were expanded into every area of life. The vast majority of Jews who did not, and could not because of their poverty, observe all of these regulations were "sinners" with whom Pharisees avoided contact. Because of their disobedience to these regulations, the Pharisees considered that these "sinners" had strayed through sin. These sinners had lost themselves. The Pharisees were few in number but relatively powerful in impact. The "sinners" whom Jesus rescued and redeemed were among the overwhelming numerical majority.

So could the ninety-nine to one ratio of the sheep in the parable mean that Jesus was saying the Pharisees were represented by the one lost and strayed sheep and that the vast numbers of the ones the Pharisees called "sinners" were represented by the ninety-nine sheep?

Jesus clearly believed that the Pharisees, the Torah experts, and the scribes were the ones who had "strayed" or were "lost" in their oppressive interpretation of Torah and their condemnation of the masses (Matt 23:1–12, 15, 23, 27–36; Luke 11:42–54).

If the lost and strayed sheep in Jesus' parable represented the Pharisees, what was the Pharisees' great sin? It was mercilessness. By their judgments of condemnation and exclusion of the poor and the so-called unclean, and by their loading burdens upon the backs of the poor, the Pharisees put up false barriers between God and God's children that God did not will. The Pharisees' dominant narrative made themselves the superior insiders and made everyone else the inferior outsiders. According to Jesus' counter-narrative, they denied to the vast number of "sinners" the merciful rescue and inclusion they were due under God's justice.

Ironically, under one application of the dominant "eye for an eye" version of justice of that time advanced by the Pharisees, the one strayed and lost sheep representing the Pharisees was not due rescue because of the great harm Pharisees were doing. And yet, in how many stories in the Gospels does Jesus interact with these Pharisees, eat with them, try to teach and correct them, and tell them parables, all to try to move them to repent? Jesus' interaction with the "lost" Pharisees was merciful, just as his interaction with Zacchaeus was merciful (Luke 19:1–10).

The Pharisees, who had "strayed" so radically from the essence and goal of Torah, would of course never admit that they were the ones who were lost. Because of their arrogance and self-righteousness and their view of Torah and of sin, they had excluded the followers of Jesus from what the Pharisees claimed erroneously was the true flock of God. They had separated themselves from the ninety-nine because they had judged and excluded the masses unjustly and mercilessly. "But woe to you, scribes and Pharisees, hypocrites! For you lock people out of the kingdom of heaven. For you do not go in yourselves, and when others are going in, you stop them" (Matt 23:13).

Jesus' strident condemnations of the Pharisees, the scribes, and their lawyers from Matthew 23 and Luke 11 seem anything but merciful. Perhaps these bitter condemnations more reflect the controversies between the communities of the early followers of the way and the synagogue in the remainder of the first century after Jesus was crucified. But accountability in the form of hard-spoken, truthful judgment can be merciful. And the repeated actions of Jesus in teaching and interacting with the Pharisees were undeniably merciful. This mercy, given the great damage that the Pharisees were doing to so many people because of their condemnations and exclusions, was certainly not due them under the dominant narrative of that time.

Another approach to this parable of the sheep can be rooted in the Book of Ezekiel. Regardless of whether the one lost or strayed sheep represented the Pharisees or the larger number of persons regarded by Pharisees as "sinners," passages from Ezekiel 34 have important language in common with Jesus' parable of the lost and strayed sheep. This may have provided Jesus with a resonate foundation for his parable.

1 The word of the Lord came to me: 2 Mortal, prophesy against the shepherds of Israel: prophesy, and say to them—to the shepherds: Thus says the Lord God: Ah, you shepherds of Israel who have been feeding yourselves! Should not shepherds feed the sheep? 3 You eat the fat, you clothe yourselves with the wool, you slaughter the fatlings; but you do not feed the sheep. 4 You have not strengthened the weak, you have not healed the sick, you have not bound up the injured, you have not brought back the strayed, you have not sought the lost, but with force and harshness you have ruled them. 5 So they were scattered, because there was no shepherd; and scattered, they became food for all the wild animals. 6 My sheep were scattered, they wandered over all the mountains and on every high hill; my sheep were scattered over all the face of the earth, with no one to search or seek for them.

7 Therefore, you shepherds, hear the word of the LORD: 8 As I live, says the Lord God, because my sheep have become a prey, and my sheep have become food for all the wild animals, since there was no shepherd; and because my shepherds have not searched for my sheep, but the shepherds have fed themselves, and have not fed my sheep; 9 therefore, you shepherds, hear the word of the LORD: 10 Thus says the Lord God, I am against the shepherds; and I will demand my sheep at their hand, and put a stop to their feeding the sheep; no longer shall the shepherds feed themselves. I will rescue my sheep from their mouths, so that they may not be food for them. 11 For

thus says the Lord God: I myself will search for my sheep, and will seek them out. ¹² As shepherds seek out their flocks when they are among their scattered sheep, so I will seek out my sheep. I will rescue them from all the places to which they have been scattered on a day of clouds and thick darkness. ¹³ I will bring them out from the peoples and gather them from the countries, and will bring them into their own land; and I will feed them on the mountains of Israel, by the watercourses, and in all the inhabited parts of the land. ¹⁴ I will feed them with good pasture, and the mountain heights of Israel shall be their pasture; there they shall lie down in good grazing land, and they shall feed on rich pasture on the mountains of Israel. ¹⁵ I myself will be the shepherd of my sheep, and I will make them lie down, says the Lord God. ¹⁶ I will seek the lost, and I will bring back the strayed, and I will bind up the injured, and I will strengthen the weak, but the fat and the strong I will destroy. I will feed them with justice.

¹⁷ As for you, my flock, thus says the Lord God: I shall judge between sheep and sheep, between rams and goats: ¹⁸ Is it not enough for you to feed on the good pasture, but you must tread down with your feet the rest of your pasture? When you drink of clear water, must you foul the rest with your feet? ¹⁹ And must my sheep eat what you have trodden with your feet, and drink what you have fouled with your feet? ²⁰ Therefore, thus says the Lord God to them: I myself will judge between the fat sheep and the lean sheep. ²¹ Because you pushed with flank and shoulder, and butted at all the weak animals with your horns until you scattered them far and wide, ²² I will save my flock, and they shall no longer be ravaged; and I will judge between sheep and sheep. ²³ I will set up over them one shepherd, my servant David, and he shall feed them: he shall feed them and be their shepherd. (Ezek 34:1–23)

This passage reflects that the dominant narrative of Israel in Ezekiel's time, the narrative advocated by the dominant classes, was very similar to the dominant narrative of Jesus' time and of our time. Within this narrative, life within the "flock" was a competition—an *agón*—between the shepherds and the sheep, and among the sheep. Of course, within this writing the shepherds represented the dominant classes of Israel—the royal and priestly families, the rich and the privileged. Israel in the prophet's time was not a community of covenant. These shepherds believed that they were due being allowed to eat the fat, clothe themselves with the wool, slaughter the fatlings, and rule forcefully and harshly over their sheep. The shepherds believed they were due to prey upon their sheep. To the shepherds, the sheep were *not* due to be fed, protected from predators, strengthened, healed, and searched for and brought back when they strayed. The sheep were not even due to be kept together by the shepherds. And between sheep and sheep, each animal was due to compete to feed on good pasture and drink from clean water while spoiling the pasture and the water supply for other sheep. Within the dominant narrative, each animal was due to be able to push the other animals away from good food and water with flank and shoulder, to butt the weak animals, and to scatter them far and wide.

Within the counter-narrative of the prophet Ezekiel—within the counter-narrative of God—the life of the flock was to be a community of covenant, not an *agón*. Just obligations were placed upon the shepherds and were due from the shepherds to the sheep. Because each sheep was in a relationship of trust with the shepherds and with the other sheep, just obligations were placed upon each sheep which were due to the shepherds and to every other sheep. These mutual, just obligations grew out of the relationships within the community, not from any competition. These were mutual, just obligations *to be merciful*.

The shepherds were *not* due to eat the fat of the sheep, to clothe themselves with the wool, to slaughter the fatlings, and to rule with force and harshness over their sheep. The shepherds were *not* due to prey upon their sheep. From the shepherds, each sheep was due to be protected from predators and from other sheep, and to be fed, strengthened, healed, searched for, and brought back when they strayed. Each sheep was due from every other sheep not to have their pasture and water source fouled, and not to be pushed away from pasture and water by the flank and shoulder of stronger sheep.

This writing from Ezekiel about the dominant narrative and the counter-narrative of God is relevant to our time. Consider the shepherd CEO of a large corporation with many sheep employees. Under today's dominant narrative, the CEO is due to eat of the fat created by the employees, and due to rule over them harshly by keeping their wages as low as he can while still maintaining a competent work force, by laying off large numbers of workers to maximize profits, and possibly even by closing their particular workplace to reduce labor costs further.

Within the setting of Jesus' telling of this parable, which was a response to the Pharisees' questioning of why Jesus spent so much time with and attention to sinners, Jesus was being asked about justice issues similar to the ones raised by the parable. Why are the sinners due so much more of your attention, protection, and encouragement than those of us who are righteous? Why are sinners due any of your attention and care at all? Why aren't we who are trying to be righteous due more of your love than sinners who scoff at God and righteousness? You are abandoning us to be with them. These are the same objections that the ninety-nine sheep might have asked the shepherd.

In this view, what Jesus teaches is that the lost and strayed "sinner," the excluded outsider, is due mercy from the shepherds and from the other members of the covenant community—the mercy of being searched for and rescued even before the sinner has repented, and the mercy of being welcomed back. This mercy is due because of relationship. The flock is a community, not a merciless contest. Each and every sheep is a member of the community. Both the sinners and the righteous are equally members of the same flock. So the sheep in need of more mercy because she is "lost" is due that mercy merely because she is in greater need. This mercy is just, and this justice is merciful, because of the relationship of all within a covenantal community created by the counter-narrative of God.

A large issue in the parable focuses on the hearts of the ninety-nine sheep that had not strayed, whether they represented Pharisees or sinners. This is much the same as the issue with the elder brother in the parable of the prodigal son. In the parable of the strayed sheep, the other faithful sheep were indeed left in a vulnerable position because the shepherd left them to seek the sinner. A shepherd has only so much time and attention to give. By leaving in search of the strayed and lost sheep, the shepherd was indeed paying more attention to the sinner than to the faithful. The most hurtful to the ninety-nine was that the shepherd rejoiced more at finding and bringing back the sinner than at the fidelity and obedience of the faithful. All this appears to be a violation of the trust due between the shepherd and these faithful sheep. But that all depends upon what is due. Consistent with Jesus' other teachings, what was preeminently due to the faithful sheep was for them to be inspired to be merciful, not to be kept safe and comfortable. When a faithful one supports the search for a lost and strayed one, the faithful one is being selflessly merciful. When the shepherd leaves the faithful ones in search of the lost one, the shepherd is teaching the faithful to be merciful.

Within Jesus' counter-narrative, it is not enough for the shepherds not to drive sheep away from the flock of insiders. The sheep are due more than not being led astray or preyed upon by the shepherd. And it's not enough to forgive after a sheep repents, finds his own way back to the flock, and conforms to the flock's image of a righteous and proper sheep.

The strayed sheep is due more than withholding forgiveness until after an act of repentance that satisfies the flock and that includes a promise to conform to the flock's view of righteousness. Under the above passages of Ezekiel and Jesus' parable, any sheep is due being protected from any other sheep that would push her out. Any sheep is due being searched for even if the sheep chooses to stray. Any sheep is due rescue just because she is a cherished member of the flock. Jesus teaches that there is a just obligation to search mercifully for all the lost, excluded, and separated.

Perhaps the sheep was lost and strayed because she was judged, excluded, and separated. Perhaps she was lost because she was "pushed with flank and shoulder, and butted . . . until scattered . . . far and wide" (Ezek 34:21). Perhaps she was lost because of the oppressive theology and ethic of the dominant narrative of her time by which she is declared to be impure and defiled. Perhaps she was pushed out because she did not have the resources to observe the purity provisions of Torah. Perhaps she strayed by not accepting the mercilessness of the dominant narrative. To Jesus, the Pharisees and their victims were lost. To the Pharisees, Jesus was lost and Jesus was causing his followers to be lost. In this sense, this parable dovetails with Jesus' parable of the wheat and weeds (Matt 13:24–30). Who are we to judge who is weed and who is wheat? So who are we to "push with flank and shoulder" until others are "lost" and "strayed"? All are to be sought after and reunited, regardless of who is judged as having strayed or having remained faithful. No one is due exclusion from the nurture and protection of the flock.

Jesus also addresses whether the faithful ninety-nine sheep actually want the "lost" and "strayed" brought back to their flock. Probably the ninety-nine did not want their shepherd to act like God depicted in the passage in Ezekiel 34. It was a matter of "us" versus "them," of "ours" versus "theirs." Consider that a strayed sheep has likely been changed by the experience of being lost. The world will look and feel differently to that sheep after the experience of exclusion and separation, and perhaps after experiencing the thrill and cost of the freedom of cutting loose. That lost world may always beckon. The excluded-and-then-rescued sheep will be seen by himself and other sheep as different from the members of the flock. The returned sheep may even not agree that he was lost. He may not agree that he sinned by leaving to take another path while the sheep of the flock played it safe in their version of righteousness. Perhaps the lost sheep strayed because he had issues with the self-righteousness of the flock. Upon his return he may not agree that the sheep that remained in the flock are as virtuous as they see themselves. Within the story world of the parable, I can picture the faithful refusing to join in the rejoicing of the shepherd over the homecoming of the strayed, much as the elder brother refused to rejoice over the homecoming of the prodigal brother. They may nurture their own resentment that the sinner was brought back by the shepherd into their community before repenting to conform to the way of the righteous. And I can picture the rescued sheep being resentful and resistant at being constantly reminded that he sinned and strayed.

Jesus tells his followers that we must lose our lives to gain them, and that we must pick up his cross. He promises us great risk on the Way, not comfort and safety. He promises that on his Way we will feel as if we are last, not first. We are in the position of the ninety-nine sheep in this parable. We identify with these faithful sheep. We feel we are not getting the mercy and attention that we are due because the shepherd is chasing after those who are not due his attention as much as we are. But what we are actually due is to be made more merciful—to be made more and more compassionate to the lost by supporting the lack of attention of the shepherd to our own safety and comfort. Those of us who fancy ourselves as righteous are called to stop thinking of the mercy that is due us and instead think first of the lost and suffering, and the mercy that is due them simply out of their need. By being made more merciful, we will receive the greatest mercy Jesus and God can give.

Through this parable, Jesus may also have been saying that the Pharisees, who bitterly criticized his eating and associating with unrepentant sinners and his offering free forgiveness without purification, were the bad shepherds. Jesus may have been saying to these Pharisees that their system of justice and mercy, in which only those who were righteous in the Pharisees' view were due mercy, was the cause of so many sheep being lost. The dominant narrative of the Pharisaic system, as described in the passages about Jesus' conflicts with the Pharisees, was essentially merciless. Only those who were due mercy could receive it, effectively changing mercy into something other than grace. Only those who were pure and holy were due to eat with a child of God. But many who are lost then and now do not admit or even know that they are lost. Many stray in a negative reaction to a merciless god acting through a merciless hierarchy of insider and outsider, of pure and impure, and of clean and unclean. The Pharisaic system, as depicted in the Gospels, featured many merciless judgments of who deserved mercy and who did not. Within God's counter-narrative, Jesus offers a parable of a shepherd who leaves the ninety-nine righteous sheep behind to go in search of a lost, strayed sheep merely because the one was lost, strayed, alone, and in need.

Any tight community, including a church, will experience the issues raised by these terse and brilliant parables.

When I was still in seminary, at my request my bishop appointed me to be the pastor to a small, dying, inner-city, Anglo church in an economically poor, increasingly Hispanic neighborhood. At first we had about twenty persons in our Sunday worship service, on a good Sunday. We didn't have a child to light the altar candles. The Sunday-school building, which had 15 rooms, was unused except for one meeting room and the kitchen. The congregation was dwindling because the members were dying, and because the Anglo members were afraid to invite their Hispanic neighbors to join. And they did not want to make any changes to their worship, their space, and their church life to attract new members from their neighborhood. The church was about to be the fourth United Methodist Church on the north side of the city to close. The faithful members of the church had every good memory of the past, and almost nothing good to say about the present. Most had worked in nearby packing plants or for an aircraft manufacturer. In the good old days, their neighborhood was almost completely Anglo and working class. Then their children grew up and moved away from the neighborhood as quickly as they could. The members became older and older and lost their vitality and health. They were spending more and more time in the hospital and dreaded moving into a nursing home. Inflation outstripped their fixed incomes. Their houses were aging along with them. Then poor Hispanics moved into the neighborhood and eventually took it over. The majority of the new neighbors were undocumented and spoke little English. Most of these newcomers were hard-working and family oriented, and took the best care that they could of their residences. But there were also some really violent gangs, drugs, burglaries, and even robberies, teen pregnancies, latchkey children, poverty, and, perhaps the most bothersome to the members, loud Tejano music blaring from homes and cars late into the night. When our old Anglo members came into the church, they wanted to step back into the safe and familiar past.

The children of these poor, Hispanic families were so much in need of hope, direction, and encouragement. If the church could serve the children, we could attract the parents as well. The children were being reared in a culture that was foreign to their parents, so their parents were ill-equipped to help their children find their way through all the temptations of the new and strange culture. But attracting our new neighbors to "our" church would require more than inviting their children into our church facilities. It would require our having bilingual worship and adjusting how we did everything to make the new members feel welcome and valued. It would require our not treating our new members as if they had been lost.

There was an elementary school across the street from the church. We started after-school and Saturday boys and girls clubs, tutoring, counseling and mentoring. Eventually, we attracted more than 150 elementary-aged children into our building every week, with all their noise and energy. We eventually attracted their parents and made our worship bilingual.

Many of our old, faithful members considered these Hispanic adults and children to be lost because they were different in so many cultural ways. Some of the members were resentful that I was spending so much time with "them" and not enough time with the long-time faithful members helping them to relive their pasts and to cope with their mortality. A few left their church of so many years when we began to speak Spanish in our worship. Some accused me of stealing their church. Some tried to get the bishop to reassign me. Many did not rejoice when we were able to bring in new sheep.

A church I served years later as an associate pastor was large and rich. Its thousands of members were almost completely Anglo, and the overwhelming majority was prosperous and comfortable. The church membership contributed a fortune to clergy and staff salaries, maintenance, upgrade and acquisition of property, exciting worship experiences, and creative programs for the mostly privileged teens and children of the membership.

The church was located downtown in my city of more than 700,000 in population. Most of its members traveled miles to attend. Homeless men and women were among the church's immediate neighbors. The church owned and operated a mission building to serve the downtown homeless and poor. But the mission was located on the farthest edge of the church property two blocks away from the main church. Most of the congregation was proud of its ministries to the downtown homeless and poor, although the relative percentage of the church overall budget allocated to these was remarkably small. And while the church was generally supportive of this "outreach" to the homeless, there was some resistance to "in-reach" to them. Ministry by the church "to" the homeless was good. Ministry by the church "with" the homeless was a problem for some. When some members and clergy organized a worship service and breakfast that was attended by 80 to 120 downtown homeless early on Sunday mornings in the main building of the church, there was some fear of "them" that had to be addressed.

This was the single hour in the weekly life of the church that looked, to me at least, like my vision of the kingdom of God. It was the church's lone integrated hour—racially, ethnically, and economically. It was the sole hour in which everyone felt welcome. But the presence in the main church building of our unsheltered neighbors, who were often dirty and smelly, and who needed the use of the church bathrooms to clean and relieve themselves, made a number of our members and staff uncomfortable and even afraid. And when it was discovered that a very few registered sex offenders ("RSOs") were attending, the Sunday morning worship and breakfast for all of the homeless in the main church building was at risk of termination. Some parents and staff objected to having "RSOs" in the same building with our children, youth, and adults. To refer to the parable, it was good with most of the ninety-nine sheep for a few shepherds to go out from the flock's home pasture to seek and save the lost. But it was not good to bring these particular lost back to the home pasture of the ninety-nine. In fairness, there were many in the congregation who rejoiced when we brought them "home," but there were many who did not.

I am not the least bit critical in any way of anybody who wants to protect vulnerable children. It is a fact that I have spent most of my legal and ministerial career trying to protect abused children. I have personally dealt hundreds of times over the years with the results of violent abuse of children, including sexual abuse. But fear will always defeat mercy. The dominant narrative defeats mercy by inspiring and justifying fear. Jesus spent most of his ministry with "sinners." Sin comes in all shapes and sizes. Some of it is familiar and shared by those on the "inside." Some of it is foreign, unsettling, and even dangerous. Many insiders fear that all sin by the poor is dangerous. Regardless, fear can direct us completely away from Jesus' Way of mercy if we allow it to do so.

The Sunday morning worship and breakfast for our homeless in our main church building was preserved. Additional precautions were put in place by dedicated and faithful people. Hopefully some fears were assuaged. Fears are real, even if some might consider them unfounded and un-Christian. It's generally not helpful to grade someone else's fear. And

everyone should be on the side of protecting children. But there are prudent and faithful ways of protecting children while welcoming the lost.

According to this parable, Jesus still calls us to search for, rescue,
and bring home the lost whether we fear them or not, and whether our
fear is justified or not. We can offer so many prudent and fearful exceptions to this call that the teaching is negated, and we are soon following
a way other than Jesus' Way. Following the dominant narrative sanctions
almost all fears and negates almost all mercy. Surely Jesus didn't include
felons and registered sex offenders in the people we should seek, rescue
and bring home! Surely he didn't mean the mentally ill! Or the dirty and
smelly! Surely he didn't mean people who will foul our restrooms! We
can raise objections until we are only welcoming people just like us. We
can and do raise these objections until we are like the Pharisees depicted
in the Gospels. We can raise these objections until we are living totally
by the dominant narrative and not at all by Jesus' counter-narrative. But
surely we are called to err on the side of following Jesus' teachings. How
to err on the side of protection of the vulnerable *and* to err on the side of
following Jesus' teachings? How many sides are there?

A major impediment to living out of God's counter-narrative is the
fear of the "other" that is stoked by the apologists and beneficiaries of
the dominant narrative. In this instance, as in most, the fear grew out
of a lack of familiarity with the unsheltered as individuals. Within the
dominant narrative, they are the losers in the *agón*. As losers they are responsible for their homelessness. It is just that they are in the plight they
are due. Because they lost, they are not due what they do not have. The
toll that homelessness has taken upon them makes them undeserving of
inclusion in our communities.

For two years, I served as chairperson of the Mayor's Advisory
Commission on Homelessness, appointed by the mayor and city council.
During my tenure the commission wrote an ambitious ten year plan to
end chronic homelessness here. I spent a lot of time among the homeless.
I studied and listened and learned why individuals become homeless,
and why they remain homeless. And I was blessed because they became
Romero and Isaiah and Sarah and Maria to me, no longer "them."

People are homeless because of poverty. They can't afford to come
up with a security deposit and pay monthly rent. About 50 percent of
the homeless have jobs, but these don't pay enough to get them out of
their plight. And people become and remain homeless because they are
all alone with no one to shelter them. They stay homeless because of low

wages, the lack of the necessary job skills to make enough income to obtain their own roof, the lack of available subsidized housing, the continuing lack of family support, untreated mental illness, physical disability, addiction, flight from family violence, a felony record, being a registered sex offender, and because they compile a long misdemeanor record for criminal trespass while they are homeless. And they stay homeless just because they are homeless.

If a homeless person remains homeless for six months, the chances fall significantly that he or she will ever get out of the trap. The person fails to find a roof, falls into despair, and quits trying. Homelessness is like quicksand. If you fall in and struggle, it feels as if you are sinking deeper and deeper. So you just give up. Homelessness itself keeps the homeless from finding work that pays enough to get them out of homelessness. If you are homeless, you probably lack an address to put on a job application. You probably lack the clothing and hygiene to obtain a decent-paying job. You lack a place to leave all the possessions you have to carry on your back while you go on an interview or while you work. If a prospective employer discovers you are homeless, the employer will lose interest unless he is looking to hire the homeless to take advantage of them. You likely have a lack of personal transportation, so showing up on time for any appointment or starting time is more than a challenge. You likely can't access treatment for your mental illness, or accommodation for your physical disability. Or you are a teenager who was kicked out of your mother's house by your mother's new boyfriend. Or you are a woman fleeing from family violence, and you have no job history and no employment skills because your abuser kept you utterly dependent upon him. Or you are a long-term employee who was seriously injured away on the job, lost your job when you didn't recover quickly enough, and cannot find new work because of your age and your lingering impairment.

Our homeless friends tell me that the worst aspect of their lives is not exposure to the cold, heat, wet and wind. It's not their markedly decreased life expectancy. It's not your own smell and dirt. It's not the dangers of being on the street. It's not the trouble finding a place to wash and defecate. The worst is that other people who aren't homeless won't even look you in the face. People are suspicious of you just because you are homeless, as if homelessness is your only defining characteristic. I'd say that the homeless are treated like stray dogs except that many more people will act mercifully to a stray dog than to a homeless person.

The most intractable of all reasons for long-term homelessness is a felony record. It really doesn't matter if your conviction was for theft or for aggravated armed assault. It doesn't matter if your conviction is from thirty plus years ago when you were 18 and stupid, when you were a different person than you are now. By virtue of your felony record, you are likely to be ineligible for public housing. Employers offering work paying a living wage just will not hire you. People serve their time, are paroled, and are expected to start over, repentant and rehabilitated. But we are a fearful and therefore unforgiving culture, and we give no such individual another chance. We are encouraged by the dominant narrative that divides everyone into "us" and "them" to lump all felons together, no matter their individual stories. They are the worst and most undeserving of the losers of the contest. So we "err on the side of safety." They are "they," and we are "we."

The most hopelessly lost of all homeless are people branded forever as "registered sex offenders." I am inviting criticism here by speaking up for RSOs, but someone needs to affirm their humanity. Many RSOs in most states are required to register for life. They are required to keep local law enforcement and their neighbors informed of their designation and where they are living at all times. And they are required to stay at all times a considerable distance away from any location where children are generally located, *even if their crime did not involve a child*. Their particular offense is generally not considered. A forty-five-year-old man who had sex with his sixteen-year-old girlfriend *when he was nineteen* will often be placed under the same restrictions as a man who has been a serial sexual abuser of little boys. All of them, no matter the details, might as well have "RSO" tattooed in scarlet letters on their foreheads. The entire RSO system assumes that these men and women are incapable of repentance and change, and that they have forfeited whatever mercy they may have formerly received, no matter how much counseling and proven repentance they have shown, no matter how long ago their conviction was, and no matter the specifics of the actions that led to the conviction. They are permanently "lost." Being designated a "registered sex offender" is like the sign over the inner circle of hell in Dante's *Inferno*: "Abandon all hope, ye who enter." If a church has children in attendance, in many states and under many laws, an RSO cannot go in or near. A very small percentage of the homeless are RSOs. But a much higher percentage of RSOs are homeless. Because they are RSOs they cannot find housing and cannot find work paying much more than minimum wage. And partly because there are a few RSOs among the homeless, all homeless are feared and shunned.

I have helped put men in prison for rape for decades. In the Methodist Justice Ministry, we frequently try to protect and help adult and child victims of sexual assault. I suspect that I am as familiar as any non-victim can be with the toll of this conduct. But the complete shunning of registered sex offenders by churches, regardless of what precautions might be taken, is, I am convinced, utterly against the counter-narrative of Jesus.

In this parable Jesus teaches that we are called to seek and bring back the strayed even before they repent. This issue of welcoming the lost into our church home would be less challenging if we could first require them to present fruits of their repentance. But we are taught to seek, find, and bring back the strayed to our home in order to *then* move them to repentance and new life. The sequence is critical.

This is important as well to my clients' response when the abusers of their children and themselves say they are sorry and ask for forgiveness. What of mercy to the abuser by the abused? What of the call of the abused to be merciful? Must the abused woman gather her abused children in her arms and run down the road as the prodigal abuser approaches? Must the abused sheep be merciful by welcoming the abusive sheep back "home" whenever the abuser is found and brought back by the shepherd? Is that what the mercy of Jesus requires?

I hope not. Mercy is due to the victims of the abuser, and mercy is due to the abuser. That mercy takes different forms at different times. Part of the mercy to the abuser is an accountability that is intended to persuade the abuser of his wrongdoing, and to face him with the hurt and harm he has caused. By his abuse, the abuser has been merciless to the woman and the children, but also to his true self. He has allowed himself to become a terror and a monster to those he should have been nurturing and protecting. In order for him to repent and be born anew, he must see and appreciate his own abusiveness. To bring the abuser to this repentance and reform would be the greatest of mercies to him, for it would also make him merciful instead of merciless. And the mercy of protection to the abused woman and children will be much different than the mercy of restorative accountability to the abuser.

Surely the lost and strayed of the parable of the sheep include the mentally ill, the felon, the registered sex offender, the homeless and the abuser. The dominant narrative says have no mercy for these lost. They are due no mercy. They deserve their suffering and shunning. The first, last, and only priority is protecting myself and my family. Within the church, most say to err on the side of safety for the vulnerable. Sadly, fewer voices say to err on the side of following the Way of Jesus.

But why settle for erring at all? Poor children, the mentally ill, the felons, the registered sex offenders, the homeless and even the abusers are all vulnerable in their own way. All are "lost" for various reasons. Some are lost because of what they have done and failed to do. Some are lost because we excluded them. All are beloved and cherished by God. Jesus would have us be merciful to all, as he was and still is. Can we in the churches not find ways to protect children while still seeking, finding, ministering to, and welcoming these "lost"? Can we in the church avoid the pernicious prejudice against all individuals in these groups, the blanket and often irrational inclusion of all in the category of predators? These are the most difficult of challenges, and in dealing with them, often the best we can do is sin bravely. But too often we do not see the need to seek and welcome the strayed and excluded at all. Instead we live by the dominant narrative that tells us to fear and forget them.

**

The Parable of the Unforgiving Servant

21 Then Peter came and said to him, "Lord, if another member of the church sins against me, how often should I forgive? As many as seven times?" 22 Jesus said to him, "Not seven times, but, I tell you, seventy-seven times.

23 "For this reason the kingdom of heaven may be compared to a king who wished to settle accounts with his slaves. 24 When he began the reckoning, one who owed him ten thousand talents was brought to him; 25 and, as he could not pay, his lord ordered him to be sold, together with his wife and children and all his possessions, and payment to be made. 26 So the slave fell on his knees before him, saying, 'Have patience with me, and I will pay you everything.' 27 And out of pity for him, the lord of that slave released him and forgave him the debt. 28 But that same slave, as he went out, came upon one of his fellow-slaves who owed him a hundred denarii; and seizing him by the throat, he said, 'Pay what you owe.' 29 Then his fellow-slave fell down and pleaded with him, 'Have patience with me, and I will pay

you.' ³⁰ But he refused; then he went and threw him into prison until he should pay the debt. ³¹ When his fellow slaves saw what had happened, they were greatly distressed, and they went and reported to their lord all that had taken place. ³² Then his lord summoned him and said to him, 'You wicked slave! I forgave you all that debt because you pleaded with me. ³³ Should you not have had mercy on your fellow slave, as I had mercy on you?' ³⁴ And in anger his lord handed him over to be tortured until he should pay his entire debt. (Matt 18:21–34)

Within the dominant narrative, there is no relationship between justice and mercy. In Jesus' counter-narrative, illustrated again in this parable, mercy and justice are interrelated and interdependent. Receipt of mercy creates a just duty to be merciful.

A "talent" was a weight of gold, silver, or copper. Ten thousand talents would be more than two hundred metric tons of gold or silver. One talent was equivalent to about six thousand *denarii* in weight, equivalent to about six hundred day's pay. So the first slave's debt was about sixty million *denarii* and sixty thousand days of work—truly impossible to repay.

Many may question why the king would ever have loaned him so much or allowed him to accrue that much debt. Regardless, the debt was so huge that it could not be repaid in one hundred sixty years, more than twice an entire lifetime. Within the dominant narrative, the king was due to be paid. The slave was due to be punished because he could not pay what was due to the king. He was most certainly not due the startling mercy of having his debt wiped clean.

Under the dominant narrative of Jesus' time and certainly of our time, the conduct of the forgiven slave in refusing to forgive the much lesser debt of the second was shrewd and just. It was just good business. The forgiven slave was due whatever profit he could make as a competitive business person. That he had received such a windfall of forgiveness did not change his relationship or duties with his own debtors. In Jesus' time, perhaps the hearers of this parable would have associated the slaves with tax farmers. Tax farmers were often slaves. Under this understanding, the trusted slave who owed the huge debt could have won a contract to collect taxes for an entire Roman province, explaining the huge amount. This would have required him to agree to pay the ten thousand talents to the king who entrusted him. The slave's ability to pay back his debt and to make a profit would have come from collecting more in taxes than he was required to pay the king. So he in turn would have contracted with his own slaves or servants to collect taxes from portions of the province, and the profits of these subordinates and their ability to pay back the first slave would also have come from collecting more than they had each agreed to pay.

Within this dominant narrative of Jesus' time, the king's forgiveness of the first slave's huge debt would have been most unexpected, imprudent and certainly undue. What the king was due by legal contract was to be paid in full. If the first slave did not pay back the amount due, he was himself due the legal consequences of the time, which within the world of the parable was to be sold off into a much less comfortable position. But when the king inexplicably, unjustly, and mercifully forgave the first slave's debt, still within the dominant narrative, the first slave's demand of full payment from his subordinate slaves would have been in keeping with the usual way of doing business regardless of the king's shocking mercy. Just because the king had done something unwise and unjust did not mean that the first slave should be as unwise and unjust.

Within our own dominant narrative, suppose the first slave was the head of a corporation that owed a bank a huge amount of principal and interest on a loan. Suppose that the loan had been used to manufacture goods for sale. The principal and interest of the loan came due, and the head of the manufacturing business begged the bank not to demand and enforce payment. For whatever amazing and astonishing reason, the bank did not merely extend the deadline for payment, but instead wiped the entire debt off the books. This was totally unjust. The bank was due being paid back the full principal with the agreed interest, and the manufacturing business was due being held accountable for failure to abide by the contract. Now suppose also that the manufacturing business was owed money from other businesses that had received consignment of manufactured goods and which were then sold. So the retail sales businesses now owed the price of the goods to the manufacturer. Within our dominant narrative, it would just be good business for the manufacturer still to demand the money that was justly due, even though its own debt had been unjustly and mercilessly forgiven.

But within the counter-narrative of this parable, the mercy of the bank would have created a just obligation on the manufacturer to be as merciful to the other businesses. The failure of the manufacturer to extend that same mercy to the other business would have caused the bank to reinstate the debts.

Or suppose that a government in the developing world had incurred a huge debt to the World Bank in order to provide basic governmental services to its citizens through purchase of needed electrical, water purification, and medical equipment from suppliers in the developing world. Suppose the developing-world government expected to be able to raise the funds to pay back the debt by taxing its people. And suppose that the government was not able to raise that money because its people remained impoverished, and because the leaders of the government siphoned off a chunk of the government's income through corruption. Then suppose that the World Bank forgave the debt completely, with mixed motives of mercy and the economic viability of the businesses selling to the government. Within the dominant narrative of the corrupt governmental leaders, there would have been nothing unexpected or even wrong about their continuing to demand the citizens pay their taxes and to seize their assets if they failed. Within that narrative, there would be nothing unjust for these leaders to enrich themselves through the corruption that is standard operating procedure within that dominant narrative. But under Jesus' counter-narrative, the mercy given by the World Bank creates a just duty of the third-world government and leaders to forgive the tax debt of its people and of its third-world suppliers.

Or suppose that a married man is a serial adulterer, and that he is constantly on the prowl for one-night conquests of other women. Suppose that his repeated infidelities are exposed, that his wife sues him for divorce, and that she is about to be awarded a very disproportionate share of the considerable community property because of the husband's misconduct. Then suppose that the husband begs for forgiveness and reconciliation. The wife relents and gives the man another chance, partly because she still loves him, but mostly for the sake of their four children. The divorce suit is dismissed. A year later, the husband learns that his wife had a brief sexual relationship with another man when the husband was engaged in his serial conquests. The wife asks for forgiveness but the husband refuses. The husband uses this to return to his predatory ways. He tells her that if she sues for divorce again and tries to obtain more than half of the community property, he will expose her infidelity and embarrass her paramour. The forgiveness she extended him for many, many more infidelities has no effect upon him. Within the dominant narrative as he has received it, he is merely pursuing what he is due by looking out for himself. Within the dominant narrative he lives by, the more sexual conquests, the more successful and happy the man. But within the counter-narrative of Jesus, the forgiveness of the wife creates a just duty for the husband to be forgiving and merciful as well, and not to seek advantage.

The above examples hopefully serve to illustrate just how very counter the counter-narrative of this parable is to the dominant narratives of Jesus' and our own time. This parable is about the relationship between God's mercy and God's justice within the counter-narrative of the kingdom of God. It is about the paradoxical relationship within God's counter-narrative between what is not due and what is due. It is about what just obligations are created by free and undue gifts of what are not due. This parable as much as any other shows that God's mercy and God's justice are so interrelated and interdependent as to be totally intertwined.

The lesson is that the second slave was due mercy from the first slave because the first slave had received mercy that he had not been due from the king. The merciful injustice from the king to the first slave—the debt forgiveness that the first slave was not due—created a just obligation for the first slave toward the second slave. The first slave was obligated in justice to pass on the mercy that the first slave had not been due but that the second slave was due because of the undue mercy of the king. The first slave was obligated to pay back his double debt to the king—for what he had received from the king that had spawned the debt and for his mercifully being forgiven that debt—by being merciful to the other slaves. Verse 33 is key: "Should you not have been as merciful to the second slave as I was merciful to you?" Was it not necessary for the first slave to be as merciful as the king was merciful to him? "Should" and "necessary" are words of due and just obligation created by undue gift.

If the king in this parable is a representative of God, then God is revealed as infinitely and unjustly merciful—unless and until the recipient of God's unjust mercy is in turn merciless to another in need. Then God responds to this mercilessness with the hard justice of mercilessness.

We live as if we are due God's forgiveness, as if we are owed forgiveness simply by saying we are sorry or even if we do not apologize. We live as if God's gift of undue mercy to us is compelled and inevitable because of God's thoroughly merciful nature. We live as if God's mercies—the gift of life itself, the gift of the capacity for self-love, for neighbor-love, and for love of God, the gift of forgiveness, and the gift of capacity for continuing, renewed, or transformed relationship—are assured and so somehow due to us because of God's nature and regardless of our occasional appreciation and response. We live as if God would be somehow unjust *to God's own self* not to be merciful to us, and that God would never be unjust in this way no matter how merciless we are toward others. We live as if the mercies we receive are not the free, astonishing, undue mercies of the sovereign of all creation. And we live as if the only just obligation created upon us by God's undue mercies is for us to personally receive and enjoy them, with nothing due from us in return to God, to God's creation, or to God's other children. We live as if our passing on the mercy we have received from God is merely optional. In short, we live by the dominant narrative.

The free, undue mercy of God creates a just obligation on us to mimic God's mercy without calculation of who and who is not due this mercy. We cannot pay our debt to God directly for the undue mercies we receive from God. So we are due to pay off that debt with the same mercy God has freely lavished upon us, by lavishing our mercies upon our brothers and sisters regardless of whether we judge that our brothers and sisters are due our mercy. The only question will be the form that these mercies will take.

This truth about God's justice and mercy, and the creation of an obligation that is due by the gift of what is not due, is as paradoxical as most of the truths of God revealed in Scripture. You can only gain your life by losing it. You become the greatest by becoming the least. The greatest power is in powerlessness. Receipt of free and unjust mercy creates a just obligation to be merciful.

According to the dominant narrative, the first slave was completely within his prerogative by demanding payment from the second slave, payment that the first slave was indeed due. But that right was upended by the king's mercy to the first slave, which is part of a radical counter-narrative. The king's mercy—this counter-narrative—reversed the right of the first slave to receive payment for what he was due to an obligation of the first slave to be merciful by forgiving the debt. The king's mercy changed everything. "You received without payment; give without payment" (Matt 10:8).

It is like our lives. We were not due being created. We were certainly not due being created into this magnificent planet Earth. When God granted us life, we received a completely undue mercy and an utterly free gift. But having received this undue mercy, mercy is due from us to others.

Is verse 34 an unflattering portrait of God? "He handed him over to be tortured until he paid his entire debt." Given that the amount of the debt was so great that the first slave could never pay it, the torture would go on and on with no hope.

But I do not believe that the point of this parable was to teach us about the nature of God. The main point was and is to inspire us to be justly merciful and mercifully just, and to teach us to respond to God's undue mercy by becoming justly merciful ourselves.

Is it truly so inconsistent with the nature of God revealed to us in and by Jesus that God holds us accountable for being merciless? Or that God is merciful to every fault and sin *except* mercilessness? Being held accountable for mercilessness can be a kind of mercy. If I am moved to be merciful by a promise or threat of accountability, I have received a true mercy. Being provided an incentive to be merciful is a true mercy, because we all are due both mercy and to be made merciful. And the greatest mercy is to be made merciful. It is in being merciful that we find true meaning, honor, and satisfaction. It is in receiving and rendering mercy that we find our true selves, our true happiness, and a true, just relation with God and our neighbors.

In this parable, assuming that the king stands for God, God tried to inspire mercy by being amazingly forgiving to the first slave. Then, God tried to inspire mercy by holding the first slave accountable for his failure to be justly merciful. Most of all, God tries to inspire mercy by teaching this parable through Jesus.

So is this parable in conflict with the unlimited forgiveness taught by Jesus in verses 21–22, because the king places limits upon his own forgiveness? Does God place limits upon forgiveness even though we are commanded to have no such limits?

Some are bothered by this picture of God. But assuming that Jesus meant this parable to reveal truths about God, has the world become increasingly merciless because God either is delaying until some later date the accountability we are due for our mercilessness, or because God is so one-dimensionally merciful that an accounting is never rendered? I fear that most comfortable American churchians believe in a God who is only merciful and never justly holds them accountable for their conduct, even though the dominant narrative under which we live dictates that they themselves should always be just and rarely merciful.

There are two major reasons I would give for this prevailing belief that God is only merciful. One is avarice coupled with fear. The lives we live here in comfortable, fortress America, within our dominant narrative, are deeply in conflict with the counter-narrative of Jesus. We resist evildoers to the hilt. We do not turn the other cheek. We do not love our enemies; we obliterate them and theirs. We are supremely anxious about our possessions and about tomorrow. We give to the poor only begrudgingly if at all. We spend almost all of our money and resources on ourselves. We don't eat with sinners, which is to say people who do not accept and triumph in the dominant narrative. We try to put as much distance as we can between ourselves and outsiders. We never search for the lost sheep. We live as if our value and happiness lie only in accumulating the most stuff, the most enduringly youthful appearance and the most transient pleasures. We live as if we are due whatever we can get and others are not due whatever they cannot. So we desire that God will never hold us accountable. And we fear that God will.

The second reason that we comfortable American churchians believe that God is only merciful and not just is that we see no clear signs that God holds us or others accountable when we are merciless. The prophet Zephaniah wrote:

> I will search Jerusalem with lamps, and I will punish the people who rest complacently on their dregs, those who say in their hearts, "The LORD will not do good, nor will he do harm." (Zeph 1:12)

Zephaniah was writing about those who believed that God is neither merciful nor just because God is just not involved at all in creation. I think it is easy for middle and upper class American churchians to believe that God is merciful because our lives are generally so blessed. And because our lives are generally so easy, it is also easy to believe that God is mercifully behind our ease and comfort. It is no challenge to believe that God is merciful when we are able to satisfy every material and transient desire flung upon us by the media of the dominant narrative. It is much more of a challenge for my impoverished clients to believe that God is merciful.

As for God's justice, we read in every newspaper stories about evil, terror, hate crimes, refugees fleeing oppression, violence against innocent "collaterals," child abuse, sexual exploitation, drug selling and addiction, cheating, fraudulent business practices, narcissistic accumulation of wealth, and endless self-promotion. The thriving of those who are merciless has always been hard to square with a just God. So we see in many of Jesus' teachings, including this parable, a persistent hope and plea that

God will hold the merciless accountable *very soon*, and that God's justice will be merciful and protective towards the innocent.

In the Hebrew Scriptures are many stories of God's holding persons and nations accountable for evildoing. The flood wiped out almost all of the human species because: "The LORD saw that the wickedness of humankind was great in the earth, and that every inclination of the thoughts of their hearts was only evil continually" (Gen 6:5). God "justly" destroyed the cities and inhabitants of Sodom and Gomora for their sins, even as Abraham pled with God for mercy (Gen 18:20–33; 19:24–26). Many innocents in Egypt were killed by divine power because Pharaoh enslaved and oppressed the Hebrews and defied YHWH (Exod 7–12). God caused David's innocent child with Bathsheba to die because David caused Uriah's death (2 Sam 12:14–18). God empowered Elijah to slaughter the prophets of Baal for their worship of a false god (1 Kgs 18:20–40). To me, these stories are not so much testaments to the nature and actions of God as reflections of the human hope that God will intervene soon in human history by holding evildoers accountable for their mercilessness. But there is in these stories a witness that such intervention by God can bring a risk of mercilessness toward the innocent who are caught in the accountability—divine collateral damages. So even these expressions of hope for God's immediate justice also express reservation centering on a desire for God's mercy.

The prophets proclaimed that after patient delay YHWH brought about the just defeat of the political and religious leaders of Israel and Judah through the Assyrian invasion and the later exile into Babylon because of their worship of other gods and their oppression of the widow, the orphan, and the stranger. And the prophets proclaimed that the day of the LORD was coming when there would be a harsher reckoning against the merciless.

All of these prophetic words can be heard as hopes that God's justice for mercilessness is powerful and imminent. No one could be certain that actual events were brought about by God's due punishment. But the hope was there.

By the time the gospels were written, the hope for the reckoning of God's due justice on the merciless had been pushed into the future. This reckoning would occur at the death of the individual, or at the end of history with the Last Judgment. In our time, the hope of comfortable churchians is that there will be no judgment. Or that we will be judged by whether we were just and occasionally merciful under the dominant narrative of our time, not under the counter-narrative of Jesus.

Is God so merciful that God will never render unto us the accountability we are due for our merciless indifference? Is there an unalterable conflict between God's justice and God's mercy, just as there is between the justice and mercy of the dominant narrative?

Does human conduct count for so little in God's eyes that God will never hold us accountable for our mercilessness? What if such accountability would serve to make us and others more merciful? We live as if we will never have to pay a debt to God for being indifferently unmerciful, as if there will never be any accountability for our mercilessness. Is God's nature this one dimensional? Is God such a bad father? Or does God's merciful nature include a will that we be made merciful? Does God's nature also include the mercy and justice to hold us accountable when we fail to render to others the mercy we have been rendered, in order to make us and others merciful? This parable, as so many in Matthew's Gospel, says there will be accountability. If we heed this teaching, and it inspires and leads us to be more merciful, we have not only received but have accepted a great mercy.

Are God's ethical standards identical to ours? Or are we called to mirror God's mercy but not God's judgment? Perhaps.

Is there a tension between mercy and accountability? Is there any tension between mercy and accountability carried out in a way to be merciful to the victim and to the wrongdoer? What shape should that merciful accountability take, circumstance to circumstance?

✶✶

The Parable of the Merciful and Just Landowner

1 "For the kingdom of heaven is like a landowner who went out early in the morning to hire laborers for his vineyard. 2 After agreeing with the laborers for the usual daily wage, he sent them into his vineyard. 3 When he went out about nine o'clock, he saw others standing idle in the marketplace; 4 and he said to them, 'You also go into the vineyard, and I will pay you whatever is right.' So they went. 5 When he went out again about noon and about three o'clock, he did the same. 6 And about five o'clock he went out and found others standing around; and he said to them, 'Why are you standing here idle all day?' 7 They said to

him, 'Because no one has hired us.' He said to them, 'You also go into the vineyard.' 8 When evening came, the owner of the vineyard said to his manager, 'Call the laborers and give them their pay, beginning with the last and then going to the first.' 9 When those hired about five o'clock came, each of them received the usual daily wage. 10 Now when the first came, they thought they would receive more; but each of them also received the usual daily wage. 11 And when they received it, they grumbled against the landowner, 12 saying, 'These last worked only one hour, and you have made them equal to us who have borne the burden of the day and the scorching heat.' 13 But he replied to one of them, 'Friend, I am doing you no wrong; did you not agree with me for the usual daily wage? 14 Take what belongs to you and go; I choose to give to this last the same as I give to you. 15 Am I not allowed to do what I choose with what belongs to me? Or are you envious because I am generous?'" (Matt 20:1–15)

The setting of this parable would have been well known to Jesus' listeners. The grapes of the owner of a vineyard were ripe and ready for harvest. Grapes must be picked when they reach their peak, or much of the value of the harvest will be lost. The more laborers the vineyard owner hires, the more likely that the grapes will be harvested on time; the fewer he hires, the less likely the grapes will be harvested at their peak. But the more laborers he hires, the less will be his profit. So the owner goes at first light on the morning of harvest to the marketplace in the local village where day laborers congregate to be hired. He hires a limited number of these men to see if these can bring in the harvest in time without more help. With these men, the owner enters into a legal contract that they will be due a *denarius,* the customary wage for a day's work, in exchange for a full workday of harvesting.

As the day progressed and the harvest advanced, the landowner saw that he needed more laborers to bring all the grapes in that day. So he went again to the market place at 9 a.m., and again at noon, and at 3 p.m. and even at 5 p.m. to hire progressively more laborers. The contract he entered in with these laborers was that if they would work the remainder of the day (and how much time each would work would depend upon when each of them was hired), they would be due what the owner deemed to be "right." The Greek word the NRSV translates as "right" is *dikaion.* But the translation into English as "just" is more precise to this situation, because this is indeed a contract of sorts regulating what the laborers will be due for their work. I admit that within American jurisprudence the critical term of the contract with the later hired workers at verse 4 ("I will pay you whatever is just") is vague and unenforceable because it gives the vineyard owner all the discretion to decide the amount of pay. But the setting is not modern America, and this contract term illustrates the unequal bargaining power of the owner and the workers. More to the point, this vagueness is part of the genius of the parable, setting the stage for an apparent tension between competing versions of justice and mercy.

Until the shocking end of the parable in which the landowner violates the dominant narrative of Jesus' time by the amounts he pays the workers, the relationship between the landowner and the laborers, as well as among the laborers, is competitors within an *agón*. The workers were selling their labor for as high a wage as they can each extract, and the landowner is offering as low a wage as he can for their work. The laborers see this as a zero sum contest; the more some other group of laborers is paid, the less my group will be paid. There is only so much in wages that can be paid. There was no hint that this was a transaction between members of a covenantal community. And there was no hint of any covenantal relationship among the laborers. They were competitors against one another, each competing to be hired as soon as he could to be "due" more pay for more work. So until the surprising and upsetting end of the parable, when the landowner openly declares what he will pay to each worker, this parable was all about justice—what each worker was "due"—under the dominant narrative of that time.

At the end of the workday, the landowner directs his manager to line up the workers so each could be paid in the presence of the other laborers. This in itself may have been shocking to the hearers. I have worked in private law firms in which it was a violation of firm rules for one employee to disclose to other employees what a specific employee was being paid. This rule was to reduce complaints, to limit demands to give raises to equalize pay among equals, and to reinforce the power and prerogatives of the owners of the firm.

Even more surprising, the owner has the workers who worked the least number of hours be paid first, so the ones who had "borne the burden of the day and the scorching heat" longer witnessed how much the other workers were paid. If the owner had reversed the order, presumably the workers who had worked the longest and received the *denarius* that they had agreed to as their daily wage would have been gone and not seen the shocking mercy of the owner to the other workers. The owner was intentionally causing controversy to teach a lesson about mercy.

Consider human nature. The laborers who were paid first had only worked a few hours. Shockingly, they received a *denarius*—a full day's pay under the dominant narrative of the time. The workers who had worked the longest and were at the end of the line were likely figuring, "We worked at least five times longer than those late-comers. They received one *denarius*. So we are each due five *denarii!*" But they were also paid only one, as was every worker no matter at what hour he started his day's work. Within the dominant *agón*, this was unjust. What was the criterion which the full day workers were using to determine what they were due? The respective lengths of their hard work. So they complained to the landowner that what he was doing was unjust. He replied, at verse 13, that he was doing these workers no *adikeo*. The NRSV translates this into English as "wrong." In this context and true to the actual Greek, a much better translation is "injustice." Friend," the landlord tells them, "I am doing you no injustice." I paid you what I agreed to pay you. Why do you complain because I am "generous" or "kind," which could as easily be translated "merciful?"

The landowner was using a different criterion than the first workers were using, and a different criterion than the one used in the dominant narrative of Jesus' time. Based upon verses 6–7, you could argue that the criterion that the landowner used to determine what all the workers were due was the length of their willingness and availability to work hard. It was not their fault that they were hired so late in the day, because they had been present and willing from the first light. But I am convinced that the end of the parable would be identical without these verses. A key to this is the landowner's referring to all his workers as "friends." This is not a throwaway word. Rather than seeing the workers merely as competitors in an *agón* for the stuff of the competitive market place, their wages as costs of doing business, and their labor as nothing more than the means to his making a profit, he saw them as fellow members of a covenantal community, as "friends."

What was the criterion that the landowner used to determine what the laborers were due? *Their need.* Each of the workers and their families needed a full day's pay, no matter how long they were allowed to work. What they were each due was mercy. What they were each due was to be treated as friends.

What was the point of the landowner's causing the workers who worked the longest to witness that the others who worked a shorter time were receiving what they needed also? The point was so these workers would learn to be merciful. As well as receiving mercy, they were each due to be made merciful.

This parable is another one that teaches that God's justice and mercy are fused. What we are all due is mercy and to be made merciful. What could be more different from the dominant narrative of our time than the way the vineyard owner paid and interacted with the laborers?

**

The Parable of the Sheep and Goats

31 "When the Son of Man comes in his glory, and all the angels with him, then he will sit on the throne of his glory. 32 All the nations will be gathered before him, and he will separate people one from another as a shepherd separates the sheep from the goats, 33 and he will put the sheep at his right hand and the goats at the left. 34 Then the king will say to those at his right hand, 'Come, you that are blessed by my Father, inherit the kingdom prepared for you from the foundation of the world; 35 for I was hungry and you gave me food, I was thirsty and you gave me something to drink, I was a stranger and you welcomed me, 36 I was naked and you gave me clothing, I was sick and you took care of me, I was in prison and you visited me.' 37 Then the righteous will answer him, 'Lord, when was it that we saw you hungry and gave you food, or thirsty and gave you something to drink? 38 And when was it that we saw you a stranger and welcomed you, or naked and gave you clothing? 39 And when was it that we saw you sick or in prison and visited you?' 40 And the king will answer them, 'Truly I tell you, just as you did it to one of the least of these who are members of my family, you did it to me.' 41 Then he will say to those at his left hand, 'You that are accursed, depart from me into the eternal fire prepared for the devil and his angels; 42 for I was hungry and you gave me no food, I was thirsty and you gave me nothing to drink, 43 I was a stranger and you did not welcome me, naked and you did not give me clothing, sick and in prison and you did not visit me.' 44 Then they also will answer, 'Lord, when was it that we saw you hungry or thirsty or a stranger or naked or sick or in prison, and did not take care of you?' 45 Then he will answer them, 'Truly I tell you, just as you did not do it to one of the least of these, you did not do it to me.' 46 And these will go away into

eternal punishment, but the righteous into eternal life." (Matt
25:31–46)

I left discussion of this parable to the last, because it is like a closing argument in the trial between the competing narratives.

At the outset let me note that the NRSV translates the two uses of
the Greek word *dikaioi* at verses 37 and 46 as "righteous." In my humble
opinion, the much better translation is "just."

This parable strongly reflects Matthew's emphasis upon a Christian's call and duty to serve the kingdom through merciful conduct. The
hearing of the word of the kingdom was a gift, but with it came a duty.
One became due rescue at the final judgment by being merciful without
making judgments about who was and was not due mercy by any other
criterion than need. We will not be due mercy at the final judgment if we
have not lived as if all in need were justly due our mercy. We will not be
due mercy if we have not been merciful to all in need, whether we judged
them to be due our mercy or not.

In my discussion of the parable of the rich man and Lazarus, I described this as a double standard, one for God and one for God's children.
We are to render mercy to everyone in need regardless of whether we
judge them deserving. But, at our deaths, God is merciless to those of us
who were not merciful during our lives to everyone in need, even though
we will be at our neediest when we die. But perhaps this is not a double
standard. Perhaps there are two different standards—one before and a
different one at the judgment. During life before the coming, I am called
and obligated not to live as if only some people are due my mercy. If I
limit those to whom I am merciful before my death, at the judgment I
will be judged on the basis by which I had lived—that only some are due
mercy. If I lived mercifully before the coming—if I lived as if all were due
mercy—I will receive mercy at my judgement, whatever else my faithfulness or failures of faith or orthodoxy were. If I did not live mercifully to
the needy—if I lived as if the needy must deserve mercy by some other
criterion than their need to receive it from me—then I will be treated the
way I had treated the needy. Then I will be in need at my judgment, but
I will not be due mercy and will not receive it. This is very much like the
messages of the parable of the unforgiving servant, and of the rich man
and Lazarus.

Note that the goats were not punished for what they did but for
what they did not do. There is no hint that they had cheated, stolen, or

oppressed. There is no hint that they had cause the needy to be in need. They had just not been merciful. They had been indifferent. This is also like the rich man in the parable of the rich man and Lazarus.

Within the counter-narrative of this parable, the parable of the Good Samaritan and the parable of the rich man and Lazarus, we never have the right to judge who is due our mercy based upon their relationship to us or their conduct. To the extent that Matthew witnesses that Jesus taught that God withholds mercy at the judgment when it is not due to the merciless, it is only God who may and can do this. This is also like the parable of the wheat and tares (Matt 13:24–30). The requirement to be merciful to the needy mentions nothing of their ethnicity, religious choices, nationality, race, behavior, personal responsibility for their need, poor choices, virtue, laziness, or whether they would respond as we wish to our mercy. Mercy is due solely because of their need.

As I state above, whether to be merciful is never an issue in the counter-kingdom of Jesus. How to be merciful is always the only issue. How to balance the merciful needs of the needy we encounter is the issue. And these "hows" are not to be decided by the dominant narrative.

Within this parable, which is Jesus' last teaching in Matthew's Gospel and therefore his closing argument in his trial of earthly life, orthodox belief, faith in Jesus and his atoning death, confessing and asking for forgiveness, contributing to the church building fund, regularly attending worship and receiving the sacraments, and avoiding violation of all ten commandments play no part in getting you into the sheep flock at the final judgment. All that matters was whether you used whatever talents and capabilities you had received, and the fruits of those talents and abilities, to be merciful to those in need. Nothing else matters.

Consider how different not just the history of the church but also all of human history would have been if this "Parable of the Last Judgment" had been *the* primary criteria for the Christian way.

Heretics would never have been tortured and burned at the stake for wrong belief. To the extent that torture and burning could ever be justified within the counter-narrative, which it cannot, the criteria for torture would have been whether the candidates for punishment had failed to be merciful to the needy. But of course that would mean that the merciless were themselves in need of mercy and of being made merciful, not torture and death. So any torturers and the stake-burners would be exposed to the same punishment for their mercilessness in torturing and burning.

If *the* dedicated and singular focus and purpose of the church through the Christian centuries had been the mercy to the needy described by Jesus in this parable, would there have been a need for a Reformation? Or the post-Reformation wars of religion? Would there have been the fateful split between the Western and Eastern Church? Would the Crusades have occurred? Or the conquest and murder of the First Nations in the Western Hemisphere by European "Christians" in the name of conversion to the "true" religion?

Would Black slavery have been introduced and maintained in the Americas by European and American "Christians," using the most ridiculous and terrible justifications from Scripture? Would the murderous Jewish pogroms have occurred, justified in the name of Christ? Or the Holocaust?

Or would the barriers between the rich and the poor in the "Christian" United States be growing? And would the comfortable be so blind to the suffering of the poor? Would the crime and addiction rates, the rates of infant mortality, and numbers of children who live food-insecure be as high?

Would churches continue to accumulate so much material wealth? Would senior ministers of large churches be making hundreds of thousands of dollars in salary in communities in which so many children are suffering? Would churches have been able to condition their parishioners that the most valued and valuable giving is to increase and improve the church property? Would the church be declining in America and Europe because it has become just another institution controlled by the dominant narrative?

Would the dominant narrative be so dominant?

Or, if *the* dedicated and singular focus and purpose of the church through the Christian centuries had been the deep and generous mercy to the needy described by Jesus in this parable of the sheep and the goats, would millions of Christians have experienced the greater and deeper satisfactions of mercifulness—greater and deeper by far than the transient satisfactions of buying a luxury car, or spending a fortune upgrading your home bathrooms, or taking an expensive cruise, or even having the new church chapel named after you?

Earlier in this work, I raised the issue of whether mercifulness motivated by avoidance of hell would prove genuinely merciful and effective. Notice that verse 37 of this parable indicates that the "just" were not merciful to make themselves due a reward. There was no hint of self-centered motivation in their mercy. They were merciful only because of their empathy at the need of the recipients, and the joy it brought them to alleviate suffering. The just in the parable were not merciful because the hungry, thirsty, alien, naked, and ill were judged by the just to have been innocent of their plight and therefore deserving of mercy. The just did not even know that Jesus was with and in the recipients. So despite the proclamation of terrible judgment for those who were merciless in their earthly lives, this fear had played no motive for the mercy of the merciful. They were merciful only because of the need of the recipients, their empathy with the needy, their love of mercy, and the joy they experienced in being merciful. In this sense, they were like God (Luke 6:36). God is not merciful because of a fear of punishment or hope for reward. Who can punish or reward God? God is merciful because of the need of the recipients, God's love of mercy, God's merciful nature, and God's joy in mercy.

Recall the colloquy between Jesus and the "lawyer" that led to Jesus' telling of the parable of the good Samaritan (Luke 10:25–29). The lawyer was trying to reduce the types and numbers of the "neighbor" whom he was required by Torah to love as himself. As I recount above, the debate between rabbinical schools in Jesus' time was that only Jews, or only righteous Jews who followed Torah rigorously, were "neighbors" deserving of our love. Jesus exploded any limitation on our duty of mercy. One of the great scandals of Jesus' ministry was that he was merciful through his teaching, presence, feeding, table fellowship, touch, and healing to everyone without limitation.

In the same way and under the same urge, Christians through the centuries have tried to limit the needy who are due mercy from Christians under this parable of Jesus. Some have said that this parable was the product of the early church and not of Jesus, and that the "least of these" whom Christians were called to love were only members of the persecuted, early Christian community. Some argue that these "least" to whom we are called now to be merciful are limited to members of our church.

There is no basis for these limitations. The parable does not state or support any limitation upon whom we Christians are due to be merciful. It says just the opposite. The motivation behind seeking to limit the people to whom our mercy is due is the same as the motivation behind the questioning of Jesus by the lawyer in Luke 10. It is the same motivation by which we, under the influence of the dominant narrative, limit those to whom we are called by Jesus to be merciful—to ourselves, our families, or maybe, sometimes, our close friends.

How can these limitations on our obligation of mercy be sustained or even asserted when the Jesus who told us this parable of the sheep and the goats and the parable of the good Samaritan also taught us:

> You have heard that it was said "You shall love your neighbor and hate your enemy." But I say to you love your enemies and pray for those who persecute you, so that you may be children of your Father in heaven; for he makes his sun rise on the evil and on the good, and sends rain on the righteous and on the unrighteous . . . (Matt 5:43–45)

> You have heard that it was said "An eye for an eye and a tooth for a tooth." But I say to you do not resist the evildoer . . . Give to everyone who begs from you. (Matt 5:38–9, 42)

> But love your enemies, do good, and lend, expecting nothing in return. Your reward will be great, and you will be children of the Most High; for he is kind to the ungrateful and the wicked. Be merciful, just as your Father is merciful. (Luke 6:35–36)

Jesus explicitly commands us to be merciful to our enemies and persecutors, to those we would judge to be evil, and to the unrighteous.

Given the setting of the parable of the sheep and the goats, it may be argued that only disciples and followers of Jesus are obligated and due to be merciful to all in need. But "all the nations" were gathered before the Son of Man at the beginning of the parable (25:32). The Judgment described in Matthew 25:31–46 would come after the Great Commission of Jesus to his disciples in Matthew 28:

> Now the eleven disciples went to Galilee, to the mountain to which Jesus had directed them. When they saw him, they worshipped him; but some doubted. And Jesus came and said to them, "All authority in heaven and on earth has been given to me. Go therefore and make disciples of all nations, baptizing them in the name of the Father and of the Son and of the Holy Spirit, and teaching them to obey everything that I have commanded you. And remember, I am with you always, to the end of the age." (Matt 28:16–20)

So Jesus' description of his second coming in Matthew 25 contemplated that in the interim between his resurrection and his return, "all nations" would have been made disciples by baptism and by "teaching them to obey everything that [Jesus] . . . commanded you." At the Judgment of Matthew 25, all these disciples of all nations were judged based upon whether they had followed Jesus' commandments of merciful conduct. But given that these disciples in all the nations would have encountered many in need in their nations who were not followers of Jesus, there is no basis for limiting those to whom Christians were and are commanded to be merciful. Part of what Jesus is saying in this parable is that every person of every nation is called and obligated to be merciful, because all peoples and nations have the needy and suffering in their midst.

This parable is indeed the fitting final argument of the trial of Jesus' life. It is the ultimate collapse of God's justice and God's mercy into one truth and way. It is an answer to those who see justice as a matter of reciprocity from within the dominant narrative. In this reciprocal view, acting justly requires treating the other as they have treated you and yours. If someone does something for you, then the justice of the dominant narrative requires you to do the same for them as well. If one is merciful to you, you are due to be merciful to them. The other side of this argument is that the other is not due mercy from you if they have never been merciful to you. Under this system of calculation, the only time I am motivated to be merciful to you is when I am looking to set up a reciprocal obligation of mercy from you to me. This is one form of justice within the dominant narrative.

The very last statement Jesus makes to his disciples before his resurrection, is, "and remember, I am with you always, to the end of the age" (Matt 28:20). But where and how is he always with us until the Judgment? He tells us in Matthew 25:40, 45: "Truly I tell you, just as you did it to the least of these my brothers, you did it to me . . . Truly I tell you, just as you did not do it to the least of these, you did not do it to me." Until the end of the age, Jesus is with us in the hungry, the thirsty, the stranger, the naked, the sick, and the imprisoned. All of these are not just Jesus' brothers and sisters. They are Jesus himself. As a matter of just reciprocity, to whom is mercy due from us more than to the eternal and divine Word who became flesh, who emptied himself of divinity to become our slave, who suffered our human frailties and fears, who made himself brother to the homeless, the sick, and the shunned, who taught and showed us mercy above all, who fed us and healed us, who showed us the nature of the Father and of the Way, who was tortured and killed for our sake by the tools of the dominant narrative, who defeated that narrative and death itself, and who is with us still? What is Jesus due from me and from you as a matter of justice? "Mercy is due me," is Jesus' answer. "Mercy to all in need, in whom I live." What mercy is Jesus not due from you and me?

Verse 45 sums up all this. These *dikaioi*—the just—receive eternal life. How were they just? Why did they receive eternal mercy? Because they were merciful. No more, no less.

CHAPTER 8

If There Is No Mercy, There Is No Justice

CAN WE READ IN these parables that Jesus tells us that he would die for our sins so that we need not be merciful and just according to God's counter-narrative? Where in these parables does Jesus tell us that we would be responding faithfully to his central message at Mark 1:15—"The time is fulfilled and the kingdom of God has come near; repent and believe in the good news"—merely by believing the right doctrine about his divinity and crucifixion, and by being "good" by the standards of justice and mercy of the *agón* of the dominant narrative? Or merely by being good churchians who tithe and attend worship regularly?

"Why do you call me 'Lord, Lord,' and not do what I tell you?" Jesus asks us at Luke 6:46.

Under the dominant narrative, justice and mercy have no connection. Indeed, they are in conflict. Mercy undercuts the so-called justice of the dominant narrative. The justice of the dominant narrative is without mercy, and the mercy taught by the dominant narrative is rare and weak. To follow the title of this book, in the world created by the dominant narrative, there is no mercy, and there is no true justice. Under this narrative, we are each due whatever we can get, and not due what we can and do not. Mercy is only occasional and optional; otherwise it would undermine the efficiency of the system of the dominant *agón* to produce more things and more transient pleasures. This dominant narrative would reduce all children of God to soulless and heartless competitors in a contest for these things and transient pleasures that do not satisfy. Produced by this narrative, the competition is unjust and merciless, preordaining millions of children and adults to be losers of the contest by their accidents of birth, and declaring that this random injustice is only just. This narrative appeals primarily to human predation, fear and suspicion. The narrative lives in our bellies and not in our hearts. The narrative declares that our fears and our appetites are what make us human. It devalues and discourages the moral qualities that reflect the image of God within us—empathy, compassion, sacrifice, mercy and justice. It does not truly value discipline and hard work. It only values successful acquisition by any means, for it confines to poverty those who are disciplined and hard working at jobs that do not pay enough to acquire basic necessities. It celebrates the self-obsessed merciless as heroes and examples, and the sacrificing merciful as losers to be pitied for their confusion about what is meaningful, successful, and satisfying. Within this dominant narrative, the individual is everything, and the community is nothing other than the arena for the merciless competition.

As I have tried to demonstrate in this book and harkening to the title, under the counter-narrative of God, if there is no mercy, there is no justice. The counter-narrative of God, witnessed and refined in the parables of Jesus, declares that all children of God are due mercy and to be made merciful. This is God's justice. This mercy can and will take as many forms as there are situations. Christians are to sin bravely and prayerfully when we assess what form our mercy is to take. Most times, our mercy will take the form of utter and unconditional generosity to reflect the utter and unconditional mercy bestowed every second by God upon us all. Sometimes, our mercy will be in the form of conditions imposed before the gift is given for the sake of the dignity and transformation of the recipient. Sometimes our mercy will be free and unconditional forgiveness. Sometimes that mercy will be accompanied with accountability. But always, the truth of God's justice and mercy calls us to be just and merciful to everyone whom God puts in our path. This truth forbids us making judgments about who is and who is not due our mercy. The only judgments we are called to make are how we are to be merciful in any given circumstance and to prayerfully try to strike a balance among what may be competing needs for mercy of all involved.

Consider the lives that are produced by these two deeply opposed narratives.

Under the dominant narrative, we work only to acquire as much stuff and pleasure as we can. We think about stuff and pleasure almost constantly. Our play is another form of this pursuit. We use the blessings of our inherited social position, intelligence, and bodily capabilities only to increase our own acquisitions and the shallow honor associated with those. We rear our children to do the same. We spend all our waking moments in this acquisition or consumption, worrying that we do not have enough of what will never truly satisfy us, when we already have far more than we need and far more than is good for our souls. We are conditioned by the dominant narrative to vote only our self-interest. Our self-interests are only to acquire all the things and pleasures we can, and to gain an advantage over our competitors. The dominant narrative teaches us that we should only rarely be merciful, and that we should be suspicious and condemning of people in need, even of children in need. The life necessarily growing out of this narrative is unsatisfying. As much as we gorge ourselves on it, the fruit of this tree is dry, tasteless, juiceless and unfulfilling. As soon as we acquire one thing or one pleasure, we only want more and more. The dominant narrative conditions us to be like spoiled children on Christmas morning, tearing open the wrappings on present after present, feeling dissatisfied when there are no more to unwrap, and never enjoying any of them. Fear, violence, acrimony, drug and alcohol addiction are on the rise. We lock our doors and hide from our neighbors. The works of the dominant narrative are "enmities, strife, jealousy, anger, quarrels, dissensions, factions, [and] envy" (Gal 5:19–21).

Within the counter-narrative of Jesus, we work to serve. We choose careers of service, or we use the money we make in highly paying jobs first to provide for the necessities for ourselves and our families and the rest in mercy to those who are in need. We choose to live more modestly, choosing smaller homes and less expensive cars, and eschewing shallow pleasure and impulse buying, in order to increase what we can give. Most of all, we give of ourselves, opening ourselves to *see, feel,* and *share* the lives of all of our brothers and sisters, and all of the children within the covenantal community. We worry about other people's children. We learn to open ourselves and to take pleasure in the wider moments of love and sacrifice, and in the new relationships and visions that grow out of these. We teach our children to see and feel the lives—the struggles, the nobilities, the hard work, the sacrifices, the hopelessness, and the perseverance—of those born into need. We stop judging the poor for acting as the comfortable do routinely. For those of us who must work at low paying jobs, and who have no excess beyond the basic needs of the family, we serve with our encouragement, our understanding, our presence and our sharing. Out of this grows a community, not an *agón.* The fruit of the counter-narrative of Jesus is "love, joy, peace, patience, kindness, generosity, faithfulness, gentleness and self-control" (Gal 5:22–23).

The vision of life within the counter-narrative of Jesus does not come from the ivory tower of the closed study of a pastor to a comfortable, insulated synagogue or church, or a priest in a temple, or an elitist expert on Torah. This vision comes from a carpenter's son and an itinerant rabbi who lived the life of the outcast, sick, and homeless, and who personally witnessed and experienced the oppression of the dominant narrative of his time. That dominant narrative tried to kill him and his counter-narrative.

Not many will choose and still fewer will be able to live out this life within Jesus' counter-narrative of justice and mercy. But the small successes of those who try will be the salt of the earth and the light of the world (Matt 5:13–16). Those who do will be the mustard seed and the leaven in the loaf of the world and definitely of American society (Matt 13:31–33). Those of us who are called and enabled by God and the spirit of the risen Christ to live this life, as imperfectly as we are able, will help God keep this counter-narrative of Jesus alive.

It will seem strange to some that I conclude this chapter with an excerpt of an address to Christian clergy by a non-believer. But these words have moved me deeply since I first read them when I was in university. Albert Camus gave this address at the Dominican Monastery of Latour-Maubourg in 1948. In it, he implored Christians to be true to the life and teachings of Jesus. In conclusion, he said:

> We are faced with evil . . . Perhaps we cannot prevent this world from being a world in which children are tortured. But we can reduce the number of tortured children. And if you don't help us, who else in the world will help us do this? . . . I can only speak of what I know. And what I know—which sometimes creates a deep longing in me—is that if Christians made up their minds to it, millions of voices—millions I say—throughout the world would be added to the handful of isolated individuals, who, without any sort of affiliation, today intercede almost everywhere for children and for men.[1]

I believe that the source of much of the evil that causes childrens' suffering that I have encountered through the U.S. Attorney's Office in DC, inner-city ministry, and the Methodist Justice Ministry is the dominant narrative of this American culture. And I believe that we aspiring

1. Albert Camus, *Resistance, Rebellion and Death*, trans. Justin O'Brien (New York: Modern Library, 1960) 55–56.

Christians are called in and through the counter-narrative of Jesus, first and last of all, to intercede everywhere for suffering children, women, and men, for a suffering creation, and for our suffering God.

In the first sentence of chapter 1 of this book, I wrote: "Anyone who doesn't recognize that life is unjust and merciless is a fool." I realize that such a statement begs the question of how an omnipotent, just, and merciful God could allow the random, merciless injustice of life to continue, particularly to children. I have no answer to this question beyond the life and teachings of the One whom we Christians believe was and is the Son of God. It is clear from this life and teachings that God does not will such random, merciless injustice to continue. And it is clear from Jesus' life and teachings that a response of God to this merciless injustice is the creation of a community of God's merciful justice and just mercy. And herein lies the greatest difference between the dominant narrative of America and God's counter-narrative.The dominant narrative embraces life as an unjust arena and a contest for things and pleasures that it inspires. It claims that the resulting consequence of the contest—merciless injustice—is beneficial and just. The counter-narrative of God and Jesus proclaims that the merciless injustices of human life and of the dominant narrative are evils that need to be transformed and from which we all need to be saved.

CHAPTER 9

A *Midrash* on Mark 4 and 5

THE MASTER'S HOUSE WAS surrounded by suffering people. They had discovered him just as the sun was rising on his house in Capernaum beside the sea. Then people ran to get their sick and crippled and possessed and came back and pressed upon the walls of the house, pleading with him to come out and heal the ones they loved. Many of the people had been camped outside the town, waiting for him to arrive. When he came to Capernaum in the dead of night, he drew his cloak over his face and walked quietly through the sleeping crowd, slipping through to his house. Slowly, we who were with him did the same, by ones and twos and threes. In that way he was able to get a few hours of peace. But then they discovered he was there when a man who had seen the Master before and who had brought his blind sister from Gennesaret caught a glimpse of him through a window that was briefly opened. The man cried, "Jesus, have mercy on my sister. Have mercy on her." And the crush was on. The gathered crowd pressed so hard that we feared that the walls of the house would cave in. While we were inside, we could hear dozens of voices pleading for him to come out. The voices tumbled and broke over one another. The Master sat on the floor, leaning his back against a wall, his eyes closed. But soon he could feel the wall shuddering from the weight of people pushing against the outside. He stood and put on his cloak and walked to the door.

When he said the word, we surrounded him in a circle and pushed out through the door, shoving our way through the people down the narrow streets between the mud-baked houses. Our goal was to make it to the bank of the sea, to a boat, so the Master could get in and push out away from the crowds. To speak to them and perhaps to decide which ones of them to try to heal. So desperate they were that people were grabbing at him and us, almost pulling our garments off of us, scratching our skin and tearing our tunics. And some would fall in our path to plead with him to stop and touch them. Their strength seemed doubled by their desperation and hope. There were the blind and crippled, and pallid men carried on pallets. There were men and women with twisted limbs. There were men and women whose entire bodies were covered by their robes. Only their hands reached out from under the cloth to grasp at him and at us. These were probably lepers. Usually, people would draw back from any contact with a leper. But these people were so desperate that they were heedless of the uncleanness in their midst. And all around us, from every throat, rose the cry, "Master, have mercy on me, have mercy on me," or "have mercy upon my child, or my friend, or my wife, or my grandmother!"

When his ministry had first started, he might never have made it to the sea at all. He would have stayed right there for the entire day in the midst of the crush. He would have tried to heal and give a word of hope for every person there. It wasn't just the numbers of people. The number never went down. People who had been touched by him would not leave his presence. And more people came and came. It was the time that every person demanded and the time that he would spend with each person. He couldn't heal everyone who pleaded for his mercy. I never, ever saw him able to heal a person with a twisted limb from an old, bad broken bone. But when he touched people with fever, or blind or deaf people, or the unconscious, or the lepers, or the possessed, and they did not heal, he would not let himself give up. He would stay with them, trying, until they moved away from him or others in the crowd pulled them away from him.

Failing to heal a child was the hardest on him. You could see the energy draining out of him. You could see the pain and disappointment of any unhealed person pouring into him, but particularly of a child. We tried to protect him. We tried to be a buffer to keep the press off of him. He was a small man, wiry but light. He needed protecting. But he was heedless and unappreciative of our efforts. His focus was on the eyes of everyone there. I wondered how this much mercy could survive. He made no distinction between who might deserve his mercy and who might not. He made no distinction between whom he might be able to heal and whom he probably would not.

As his ministry went on, it seemed to us that his first goal became giving words of hope instead of healing. It tortured him when he could not actually heal. He had learned that he could not heal all whom he wanted to heal. It was clear to us that he wanted to heal everyone—regardless of whether or not they were just and righteous, whether or not they observed Torah and were clean, regardless of whether or not they were sinners, and regardless of whether or not they were even Jewish. He wanted to heal everyone. The pain of everyone invaded him. And who came near to him, who had heard of him and could seek him out, seemed so random. But he was always capable of speaking words of hope, of healing with his teachings the fears and the despair of even the people whose bodies he could not heal—especially the people whose bodies and minds he could not heal. I once heard him say that he could only heal so many people in the time given to him, and that there were so many who needed healing whom he would never even see. But, he said, his words could live forever and touch so many more. And, he said, sometimes his words were more powerful than his healings. But to me it seemed that he could express so much more of God by whom and how he healed than by what came out of his mouth.

That day he was intent upon making it to the boat to teach. We were pushing so hard to get him there that a woman and her child were trampled, and the Master himself fell next to them. In the chaos, I could not see through my brothers to where the Master was on the ground. I tried to keep people from pressing in on us from all around and from pushing people on top of him. But suddenly there was a cry of triumph from a woman's lips. "He has healed him. He has healed him! The Master has healed him! My child can see! My child can see for the first time!" And Andrew, my brother, raised the child, perhaps four years old, above his head with his arms extended above the crowd. The child was blinking his eyes, as if he was seeing light for the first time and was in great pain. And the woman cried, "The Lord has had mercy. The Lord has had mercy on my child." And women all around us became to chant the high pitched alleluia, "lululululululu." And the press of people became even stronger, and people began to fall toward us. We began to lurch and sway and push through the crowd to the Sea. Then he was in the boat, the bottom of his tunic sopping wet, and I had jumped in with him. Others of us jumped in. We pushed off and out into the water above a man's head. Some in the crowd tried to swim out to the boat. We fended them off with oars until the Master told us to stop. One old man started to drown, and the Master himself jumped into the water and pulled his face up above the surface. Others swam from shore to the man and swam him back to shore. And a ring of us made a kind of human fence to keep others from swimming to the boat. The Master had clambered back into the boat and sat in the front, facing the crowd on the shore with his head down and his eyes closed until they quieted.

Then he began to teach them in parables, parables that all of us who had been with him from the beginning had heard many times before. And as he taught there was murmuring among the crowd because many did not understand, and because more wanted healing not words. After he had finished speaking, he sat silently and motionless for a very long time in the bow of the boat. Those of us who were with him in the boat saw that his eyes were closed and his lips were moving as if in a secret conversation. We knew then that he was in conversation with *Abba*. And we knew better than to interrupt him. Then he was asleep, folded up like a ball in the bow, his cloak covering him, overcome by exhaustion from the suffering he had absorbed from the crowd. Slowly, the people in the crowd on the bank sat down where they were to wait.

The day began to cool. The wind began to freshen. The sun was in its last quarter of the day. It was long past the midday meal. The Master slept a long time. He had been losing weight over the last months and had en-ergy only in bursts before he would need to pray and sleep. I sometimes feared that his exposure to so much suffering and illness every single day was going to kill him. He gave so much of his own food away that he was not taking enough in to keep his weight up. Those of us with him in the boat had also eaten nothing all day. Some of us were quietly discussing whether to swim and wade to shore to get some bread and fish to eat. Two other boats were alongside our boat. One of us swam to the other boats to see what food they had on board. On the shore, dozens and dozens of people still sat, like sheep waiting for the shepherd to come back and lead them to pasture. It seemed that, as usual, we were going to have to put out into the water and sail for a distance to find a place where we could sleep undisturbed by the suffering.

One of the other boats contained enough bread to feed all of us a little. We shared that as the Master continued to sleep. The daylight faded and it became cold. The wind picked up, blowing onshore from the south. This was the time of day when we had once sailed into the sea to fish all night. The boats began to bob and rock.

As the wind picked up and the darkness deepened, a faint wailing reached us from the southeast. The night came on, and the cry grew a bit stronger. The Master stirred. He sat up and asked for water. He drank it down and washed his face and hands. Then he turned and gazed to the southeast, across the wide Sea, listening to the sound for a long, quiet time. He turned and looked at me. "Simon, take me there." He pointed through the dark toward that other distant shore. "Master, I will take you anywhere you desire. But where is it exactly that you want to go?" I was afraid of the answer.

"There," he said, pointing again. "To the man who wails."

"You don't want to go there, "I said.

"Yes. I do. And I shall. " He paused. "That man needs me. And all of you need to go with me."

"Master. I know that sound. All of us who fished this sea before we joined you know that sound. That is the cry of a possessed man. He has a demon. He lives in the caves where the dead are laid before their bones are gathered, before their bodies have rotted. And he lives with pigs. He is a gentile. He lives near a Roman cohort. The Roman cohort had bound him with shackles and chains in the caves to keep him away. But his demon is so strong that he rips the chains and shackles off. He is hopeless. He is beyond mercy. He is not even human."

The Master listened patiently to me, as if he already knew everything I was telling him but let me speak anyway.

"Master, I love you and I know you want to heal him. But please trust me. I have seen him. He is dangerous. No words or touch will calm him. Not even yours. He is seven times unclean."

"Simon, only *Abba* knows who can be healed, and who cannot. And when they can and cannot."

"It is not that, Master. It's just. . .It's just that there are so many here who deserve your healing so much more than he does, and who need it as much. There is a chance you can heal some of these. Why him and not these? There are so many left here to be healed. Why take us all the way over there? If you touch him, so many people who need your healing will shy away from you because you will make yourself unclean. Why risk so much for him?"

"Is that really why you object, Simon?"

"Yes. And . . . I am afraid. For you. For all of us."

"Then do not come." He called out to the rest of us in the boat. "Who will take me to that man?"

The brothers looked at one another. Are we really going to do this? Then those few who were sailors began to stir, readying the sail and clearing the lines. The others tried to stay out of the way.

I felt ashamed. I crawled back to the helm. The sail up, we made way to the southeast. To the land of the Gerasenes.

The distance to sail was many miles. It would take more than the entire night to sail against the wind to the other side. That was if the wind did not die, or a sudden storm did not blow up, or the wind did not change course. Then . . . who knew. All three of the boats had shallow drafts, very tender to the waves and the wind. The boats were overloaded with us. Many of us had once made our living on that sea by fishing all night. That is how we had heard that possessed man's wails before. When the wind was from the east generally and we were fishing in the northern part of the sea, all night long we could hear his cries of torment coming from the east.

We were accustomed to the pitching of the boat, to the need to suddenly shift our own weights to keep from capsizing. But most of us were not fishermen. And when the wind picked up, we just had to ride it out. Some of our company became ill. All were afraid of drowning. Cries from inside our boat matched the wailing of the man from the Gerasenes. The Master called out, "Just trust. *Abba* did not bring us this far to die tonight."

The wind lessened but still blew. We had been blown out into the center of the sea. As the hours past and we were maneuvering against the wind by shifting our weight, those who were not fishermen began to complain again. A storm blew up . . . in the boat. The fishermen among us were answering the questions of the others about the man we were sailing to save. Arguments sprang up. "This is dangerous. Why does this possessed, unclean gentile deserve to be saved and we to die?" Some admonished those who complained. "Do you follow the Master or not? Do you follow him only when it is to your own advantage? He has taught us to have mercy on those in need. We are doing that." "But why to him and not to us?" they asked.

On the second watch, we finally arrived at the land of the Gerasenes. We were exhausted, wet and cold. There was vomit washing around the bottom of the boat. The Master was crouching in the bow as the boat came closer to shore, peering up into the cliff above the spit of sand. The boat slid onto sandy bottom and crunched to a rest. The other two boats slid along either side. All of us in the boats also peered up the cliff to catch first sight of the possessed man. I had only seen him at a great distance. I imagined a modern Goliath with eyes like a goat, and horns and snout like a hog, wanting to attack and devour us.

Then a man ran out from behind a rock on the shore. He had been crouching there, waiting for us to make land. He was small, almost as small as the Master. He was emaciated. He was filthy. His feet and hands were covered in dried mud. He clothes were rags. His manhood was exposed through a tear. His face was gashed and furrowed down either cheek, and dried blood was caked in the wounds. One ear was torn and hanging partly down. A manacle was around one ankle, with a few links of chain dragging behind. His wrists were swollen and terribly bruised. At first, I drew back, my heart pounding. On his face was the same fear and desperation of the people who had sought the Master's healing in Galilee the day before.

He ran toward the Master in the bow of my boat, screaming out and blabbing words that ran together. I was so scared that it was hard to make out what he was saying at the time. But when we all spoke later, we put together that the man said something like, "What have you to do with me, Jesus, Son of the Most High God? I adjure you by God, do not torment me. Oh please. Do not torment me!"

Before I could try to stop him, the Master jumped down from the boat and walked toward the man! I felt this desire to jump down and protect him, but was nailed to my spot in the boat by my fear. The Master was the only one to get out of the boat.

As the Master approached him, the man fell down, his face buried in the sand and dirt of the shore, weeping. "Do not torment me. Do not torment me," he whimpered. The Master kneeled down next to him. He put his face down next to the man's face, speaking to him in a low voice I could not make out. The man suddenly rolled over and spit in the Master's face, yelling "Leave me alone. Get away from me." But all of us in the boat remained frozen in the boats in fear. The Master stayed kneeling near to the man, motionless, like a shepherd who was trying not to startle a lamb, a shepherd patiently waiting for a lamb to come to take food from his hand. He did not even wipe the man's spittle from his face. We heard him ask his name. We heard the man say in a different voice that he had an unclean spirit, that the Master should get away. We heard the Master say in a calm, firm voice, "Then come out of him, you unclean spirit. Do you not know that this is a child of God, a child of our *Abba*?" And the Master grasped the man by the face, his hands on either side. "Come out of him, you unclean spirit. For this man is not unclean. You are." The man tried to pull back. But the Master held him firmly by his face. The man's eyes widened. Then tears welled up in his eyes and rolled down his face. He lunged forward and wrapped his arms around the Master's body, crying. The Master sat backward awkwardly, his knees forward and his legs under him. The man crawled so his knees were bent and beside the Master's legs. The Master cradled him against his chest, rocking him. He began stroking the man's filthy hair. Many minutes passed. We could hear the Master singing to him softly.

We sat in the boats watching, transfixed, but still too afraid to get out. None of us had ever seen anything like this. Most never wanted to see anything like it ever again.

People who lived in the nearest village made their way down the cliff. Some swineherds were also there from the region. They had no idea who the Master was. They probably thought we were just more Hebrew fisherman who'd had boat problems. But when they saw who it was that the Master was cradling, they were afraid. They drew back as if they expected the man to kill the Master at any moment. They were talking frantically among themselves.

The Master stood. He called out to them, "There is no longer any reason to be afraid of this man. He is your brother. He is no longer possessed. He needs your welcome. He needs your mercy." The local people drew back, disbelieving. They were still afraid of the man and afraid of the Master for the power of what he seemed to have done. And they were disbelieving of that power.

The man knew that he would never be accepted by the people. "Please take me with you," he said to the Master. "Please take me with you. I am not welcome here." All those in our boats who heard this drew back. One of us said aloud, "I am not riding back with him. He will kill us when we are in the middle of the sea." Some said, "He will make us unclean."

The Master looked at us in the boat. He turned back to the man with sadness. "You must stay here. These are your people. You must be the one to tell them all that *Abba* has done for you."

The man began to weep again. "You are going to leave me alone again? You came all this way and touched me and saved me, and now you are going to leave me? I have no family or friends. No one will ever touch me. Please let me come with you." The Master walked back to the boats and gazed at us for a long time. Some of us drew back in shame, all in fear, and some in anger and resentment. "How can he ask us to take this man into our boat? He is unclean. A gentile sinner. Why does he care for him more than he cares for us? What has this man done to deserve this? What have we done wrong? We have left family and our comfortable lives for him. Is this the thanks we get?"

The Master walked back to the man. "I am sorry. I am very sorry. I do not have the power. I could heal you. *But I cannot yet heal them.* You must stay here and proclaim what *Abba* has done for you among the ten cities of the gentiles. *Abba* will be with you."

"And what if the demons come back to me? I am afraid. Please, Jesus. Please."

"Your demons are gone. They have been sent . . . into the swine in this place. Do not be afraid."

"But I am all alone."

Then the Master said something to the man that has tormented me since. *"You are no more alone than am I."* And he embraced the man again and clambered back into the boat. None of us had ever seen anything so strange and fearful, or, as I have thought about it, so wonderful. It was beyond our capacity to appreciate that day.

It felt to me that he would not look at us all the way back to Capernaum. And when we arrived back, some who had followed him fell away. They were the ones who murmured on the way back, "Do you mean that the only reason he took us all that way in all that danger was for *that* man?"

We arrived back at Capernaum at the end of the day. All of us were exhausted. I had wanted to wait to put to shore in the dark, away from any village, so the Master and all of us could sleep undisturbed. But he insisted that we sail straight to his home. "Some are waiting there for me" was all that he said.

There were indeed still some people there with their sick and crippled waiting for him to come home. As he leaped from the boat and waded into the shore, the crowd pushed in around him, begging for mercy.

Suddenly Jairus, a village elder and the leader of the worship gathering in Capernaum, appeared in the crowd. His presence there startled us. He had always made it a point to avoid being contaminated by such a crowd of unclean.

Jairus and many of the elders of Capernaum were openly hostile to the Master because they thought that he made a bad example for the people. They accused him of teaching the unclean and the sinners that love of every neighbor in need was more important than observing the Torah purity code and Sabbath observance. The elders were right about that. Jairus was one of those who believed that the LORD would rescue the people from the boot of the Romans when all Jews observed all of Torah for one full day. Jairus was one of those who believed that the people of God must remain pure and separate from the rest of humanity. The Master was always touching the unclean and then spreading the impurity around. The Master was always sharing table with sinners. The Master claimed the power to forgive independent of the temple, forgiving without even requiring the sinner to purify him or herself according to Torah. The Master's power of healing and the power of his words to pierce the heart were so great and undeniable that Jairus said that he must have a demon. Jairus felt that these gifts gave the Master that much more power to lead people down the wrong path.

But there Jairus was, waiting for the Master, standing with the unclean.

The Master stood face to face with Jairus, waiting. All he said to Jairus was, "Peace be with you, brother." The people around the Master were pulling at his cloak and calling for his mercy. But the Master stood silently before the elder. Jairus finally spoke. "I know, Teacher, that I have not been supportive . . . or even respectful of you. I know that I have condemned you to the people, and told them to stay away from you and your followers, and refused to share a meal with you. I know that I have kept you from preaching anymore in the gathering."

The Master still stood silently, gazing into Jairus's face intently, giving him the time to make his own words.

"If I were not desperate, I would not be here. I know that I do not deserve your mercy." And then Jairus began to weep. The Master put his arm around the elder's shoulder and led him through the crowd to a drying stand for fish. Those of us with him surrounded the two of them, giving them some space to talk. The Master raised his hand and looked out at the crowd. They quieted!

"What is it, brother?" asked the Master. "What do you need from me? Do not be afraid to ask."

"Teacher, it is my little daughter. She is ill, on the brink of death. She cannot keep any food or even water down. It has been so for many days. She is so weak she cannot even roll over on her pallet. The doctors can do nothing. Her mother is beside herself. She insisted that I come find you. When I refused, when I said that you would not come after the way I had treated you, when I said that you had a demon, my wife berated me that I loved Torah and my own righteousness more than I love my daughter.

She accused me of having so much love for my own dignity that I would not abase myself to you and ask for your help. She shamed me. So here I am." He kneeled. "I am asking you for your mercy."

"But I am unclean," said the Master. "I have just been with a gentile. Possessed by demons. Who lives with swine. And in the caves of the dead. And near Roman soldiers. Who has never been purified. Who has transgressed every teaching of Torah. Will you bring that into your own home?"

"I am here in the midst of the unclean, asking for mercy from one who does not believe that anyone is unclean," said Jairus. "My world is being turned upside down by my love for my daughter." He began to weep again. "Master, will you come to my home and try to work your mercy on her, wherever that mercy comes from?"

"Yes, brother. Right now."

The Master and Jairus walked single file through the crowd, Jairus leading, almost at a trot. It was necessary for them to make their way through a narrow, winding space between buildings. Those of us with him jumped ahead and led the way.

Suddenly, the Master came to a halt. Jairus was pushing on when he realized that the Master was no longer with him. He turned back. "Master, my daughter is dying. We must hurry." He walked back and took hold of his cloak, frantically.

"Wait, brother. Someone touched my cloak."

Jairus said, exasperated, "Of course someone touched your cloak. Look about you. We are surrounded by people."

The Master pushed backward through the people until he came upon a woman on the edge of the crowd, covered by her cloak and cowering, lying with her face down to the dirt of the path through the buildings.

The Master knelt beside her. "Daughter, did you touch me."

Jairus screamed at the Master. "Jesus, come with me now! That woman is a whore. Her mother was a whore, and her father put her mother away with a bill of divorce. This woman gave herself to tax gatherers and Roman soldiers for money. So the LORD cursed her with an unquenchable flow of blood. It was the LORD's just punishment. She deserves her suffering. She does not deserve your mercy. Do not call her 'daughter.' She is daughter to no one. She is a stray dog. My little daughter is innocent. She does not deserve to die before she has truly lived. Come now before it is too late. I am begging you, come NOW!" He grabbed the Master under his arm and yanked at him.

The Master turned to him. "Peace, brother. This woman is as much our daughter as your own daughter is. I will come in good time. It will not be too late. It is this daughter's time now. Your daughter's time is about to come. Do not fear, but only believe."

The Master turned back to the trembling, fearful woman. Jairus screamed out a loud, guttural groan. "Cursed be you! You are of the devil! You purposely delay with this whore so my daughter will die. Do you not know who is deserving and who is not?" And he kicked the cowering woman as she had been kicked many times before.

The Master turned toward Jairus, took a step and stood face to face to him. "Jairus, you will never kick anyone again. Do you hear me? Never again. If you feel the need again to degrade some poor outcast with a kick, then you will kick me instead. I ask you again. Do you hear me?"

Jairus' face turned deep red, and his eyes filled with tears. I could not tell if it was from shame or anger.

The Master turned back to the woman. "Daughter, why did you touch me?"

"I am sorry. Please forgive me, Master. I thought that if I just touched the hem of your robe, that your healing angel would enter me and heal me. I have been waiting here, trying not to be ordered away just for the chance that you would walk by."

"Why did you not call out to me like the others do, asking me to heal you?"

"Why would you? I am a sinner. I am unclean. I have been bleeding for a dozen years. The leader is right. I am cursed by God."

"Daughter, no one is cursed by God. Only men curse. Then they claim God's sanction. Have you no family to care for you?"

"None, Master. They have pushed me out."

"How long have you been abandoned by your family?"

"Since my father divorced my mother, since he charged that she had been with another man and publicly shamed her."

"Who was the other man?"

"I never knew him."

"And your father and his family?

"They will not see me."

"Did something start your bleeding?

"I was pregnant. While I was pregnant and hungry, only a few weeks from my time, I went into a village to beg for food. A man called me a sinner and kicked me in the belly. I started bleeding. My little girl was born dead." She began to weep. "I have been bleeding since then."

"How have you survived?

"As the leader said to you. And singing and begging. And stealing."

"Daughter, there is another who is your father, your *Abba*. He will never reject you. To *Abba*, you are not unclean. Those who are merciless to you are the ones who are unclean." Jesus said this so that the Leader would hear.

The Master knelt down beside the woman. He took the hem of his robe and dipped it in water I had run for and brought forward. He wiped her tears from her face. Then he cleaned her face of its grime, slowly and thoroughly until her face shined and the grime was replaced by her tears. As he was doing so, he was whispering to someone, too softly for even the woman to hear. And he gently placed the tips of his finger on her belly. It was one of the gentlest and most tender acts of mercy I have ever witnessed. Then he stood. As he did, he took that hand of the woman and helped her up.

"Daughter, you are healed. Your blood flow has stopped. Your own trust has made you well."

She looked up into his face with her eyes wide and trembling. She looked down at her body, still for a moment.

"Can this be true?"

"Daughter, mercy is always true. Hear me now. Mercy is always true. Now I want you to do one thing for me."

"Anything, Master."

"I want you to come with me. I want you to join in our *shalom*."

"O Master. You want *me* to follow you? I will follow you wherever you lead me. I will go wherever you tell me to go."

The Master turned and looked directly into my eyes.

"I am sure you will, my daughter."

Others in the crowd started crying out and grabbing at him.

"Have mercy on me, Lord!"

"Have mercy upon my father!"

"Have mercy on my mother!"

"No . . . on my wife."

"No . . . on my husband."

The Master looked through the crowd and saw Jairus at the end of the street, waiting at the edge of the village, his head bowed against a wall, standing with a group of people.

"Come with me now, daughter."

The woman followed him. As he approached Jairus, a servant from Jairus' house said resentfully, "Why trouble the teacher any further. Your daughter has died while he was touching that whore."

"Do not fear," said the Master to Jairus. "Trust *Abba*. Lead me to your house."

He turned to the crowd. "I am asking you, out of respect for a child who is in need, wait for me here. Do not follow me up that hill." Then he turned to me. "Simon, only you, James and John will come with me. I do not want to frighten his daughter."

Then he took the hand of the woman. "And you, daughter. Come with us."

Jairus spoke up, as if from a trance. "My wife will not let her come into my house. She will make everyone unclean."

"Jairus. Jairus, please look at me. If your daughter is dead as your servant says, then your house is already unclean. But your child is not dead, only sleeping. And this new child of mine . . . she is no longer dead, but awake again after a long sleep forced upon her by the mercilessness of men. And she was never unclean in the eyes of *Abba*. Only *Abba*'s eyes count."

The healed woman's eyes grew wide.

As we walked up the hill away from the village and the sea, we could hear the sound of loud weeping and wailing. As we came closer to the leader's house, we saw a commotion. Jairus' wife was covering her face and arms in dirt, and tearing at her face with her fingernails. Young women around her, probably servants, were trying to subdue her.

The wife looked up and saw the Master. "It took you so long to come!?" To Jairus she said, "It took you so long to bring him!? And you see yourself as so important. You cannot bring a charlatan to the bedside of your only daughter until after she has died."

The Master said again. "Daughter, your daughter is not dead but only sleeping." The male servants who were with Jairus laughed derisively. "This man is a fool," one said.

The Master took Jairus, his wife, the woman who had been bleeding, and us into the house. As he entered, he said as always, "*Abba*'s peace be upon this house."

We walked to the daughter's bedroom. Jairus led the way.

The little girl lay unmoving on a pallet in the far corner. She was pallid and thin. Her eyes were closed. She did not appear to be breathing.

The Master took the hand of the healed woman and led her to the pallet. He sat her on the packed dirt floor beside the child and beckoned Jairus and his wife to sit there as well. Then he turned to the healed woman. "You said that you sing while you beg. Do you know any children's songs?"

"I know a song for a child with troubled sleep."

"Then sing it to this daughter. And sing it to the daughter you lost."

The woman's voice was at first so soft that we could not hear. But as she gained confidence, her voice sounded clear, sweet and pure, with so much pain and still so much hope. I could feel the peace and the presence of *Abba* in the room. I believed at the time and I believe now that it was the most beautiful song ever sung.

When the woman finished, the Master told all of us to stand as he remained kneeling on the floor. He took the little girl's hand in his. He said, "*Talitha cum*. Little girl, wake up. Get up now."

The little girl's eyes fluttered and opened. She looked at her father and mother standing over her. She looked at the woman. She looked at me, John, and James standing back. Then she turned her face to the Master. "How long have I been asleep?"

"Just the right amount of time," he said. And he helped her stand up. He led her to her mother's and her father's arms, and the three of them held one another. We could see on the child's face that she was confused why her parents had been crying.

After a time, the wife bowed deeply before the Master. She tried to fall down and kiss the hem of his robe, but he pulled her up. The wife went to the woman who had been bleeding and who had sung her daughter back to life and she thanked and embraced her.

Jairus asked the Master to stay the night in their home. The Master thanked him but said that he had promised to return that day to others in the village.

Jairus walked us all to the edge of the hill overlooking the village and the sea.

"Master," said the Leader, choking and searching for words. "Forgive me for the way I treated you. And her. I will never kick, or be disrespectful to anyone, ever again."

Jairus and the Master embraced.

"Master, I have a confession."

"What is it, brother?"

"I admit . . . . that I . . . felt that my family and I somehow deserved mercy, that we were due the LORD's mercy more than others, because of the way that I have tried to obey Torah. That the LORD somehow owed that to me as a matter of his justice and righteousness. Somehow I thought that my daughter deserved his mercy because of my righteousness. But then I saw how merciful you were to that woman. How you delayed coming to my house to save my daughter to save that sinner. At first I was angry with you. How can you have power from the LORD, as opposed to from Satan, if you were touching and healing such an unclean woman? But you were so kind. And you had the power to heal both of them, my daughter and that woman. And that woman was so sweet, her song was so sweet and heart rending, and she was so kind to my daughter. Surely such mercy must come from the LORD. I had never allowed myself to be around such a sinner before. It's as if I am seeing now where I did not before. Before today . . . I thought that those who deserved mercy received it from the LORD, and those who did not did not receive it. But I saw you heal the woman and then my daughter . . . So many children die. So many women are cast out. Why do some receive mercy and so many do not? When is the LORD merciful?"

"When the time comes," said the Master.

"When what time comes?"

"When the time comes that *Abba*'s mercy is born in all his children."

"So it is entirely up to us?"

"No. But we must live as if it is."

"Then how do we decide who receives the LORD's mercy from our hands. Who can be due such mercy?"

"No one," said the Master. "And so . . . everyone."

www.ingramcontent.com/pod-product-compliance
Lightning Source LLC
Chambersburg PA
CBHW030945150426
42814CB00023B/71